MIRRORED REFLECTIONS

For my daughter

MIRRORED REFLECTIONS

a memoir

Kitty La Perriere

International Psychoanalytic Books (IPBooks)
New York • www.IPBooks.net

International Psychoanalytic Books (IPBooks),
Queens, NY
Online at: www.IPBooks.net

Copyright © 2019 by Kitty La Perriere

All rights reserved. No part of this book may be used or reproduced in any manner whatsoever including Internet usage, without written permission of the author.

Cover artwork by Author
Interior book design by Maureen Cutajar, gopublished.com

ISBN: 978-1-949093-45-2

Contents

Author's Note vii

BEGINNINGS
   Miroslav 3
   Disruption 25
   The Story of Geigei 47
   Initiation 67
   My Father's Rescue 73
   Good-Bye, Czechoslovakia 77
   Geneva 93

GETTING STARTED IN AMERICA
   A Not-So-Soft Landing 129
   Becoming a College Student 139
   First Marriage 155
   Yale: A Road Not Seen 167
   Uncharted Territories 179

LIFE IN NEW YORK
   Profession: Family Therapist 203
   Private Lives 225
   Life's Desserts 255
   In the Land of the Old 299

Author's Note

Looking back over such a long life opens a terrain defined by the length of this perspective. As if to prepare me for the time when diminished vision will be joined by error-pocked hearing, scenes of great detail rush in and lead me to a reliance on my inner world, in order to maintain connection to ongoing life. Clearly remembered cameo scenarios alternate with stretches of total blankness, as if I had moved out of myself and lived those years as someone else. Notwithstanding the unreliability of specific details, broader themes stand out. Given my profession as a psychologist and psychotherapist, there is an almost irresistible tendency to discern connections between past and present, sometimes venturing to posit cause and effect. How do I keep from making conclusions postulated by this or that developmental theory and stay, so to speak, with my raw data?

We pay lip service to the universally accepted trope that early experiences matter. In their unfolding, they shape the substrata of everything life superimposes on us. The persistence of this fundamental truth minimizes, or even wipes out, our optimistic insistence that we can reinvent ourselves multiple times, all within the course of a lifetime.

There are two basic emotional lodes in my life. I am fundamentally optimistic about people's potential, about possible solutions to seemingly intractable problems, about people's kindness and flexibility (despite the horrific historic times I have lived through and live in again), and, in my innermost self, I find the quality of basic human evil to be alien. Yet what I encounter inside myself, overlaid upon what I think of as my basic temperament, is a murky layer of unease, alienation, a sense that I belong nowhere, forever seeking my community and never finding one, of depression and isolation.

At no time am I unaware of having lost my home, as well as a large part of my family, to the Holocaust. I am not, precisely speaking, a Holocaust survivor. I spent those perilous years in safe Switzerland. Only my father's incarceration in French concentration camps labels me as a child of Holocaust survivors, a label that is only partially descriptive. I personally was shaped by the catastrophe that befell my world during much of my childhood and adolescence. I only learned over many years the details of how and where members of my family and friends were murdered. None of those horrible experiences did I suffer firsthand.

In my family, these events were hardly mentioned. If so, the facts were given out as information, almost in passing. There were comments made about the postcards that arrived from Buchenwald with diminishing numbers of signatures. This, of course, was interpreted as an indication of who was still alive and who had died since the last card was sent. Later, there were the entries in the books kept in the camps that gave dates of death, and listed fictitious causes, such as pneumonia. At another time, survivors told me the story of my cousin Annemarie. Wearing her prettiest sweater, she arrived on a truck in Terezin, but wasn't allowed to disembark before the truck departed. Instead, the Wehrmacht deposited her in a brothel, where it was reported she lasted less than three months.

As I learned these details, they seamlessly found their place within the murk of my pain. When other people speak of childhood, their grandparents, aunts, uncles, and cousins, my own first thoughts are of the horrible deaths my family members experienced. In unearthing long-ago memories, I found myself rushing eagerly to my pre-catastrophic world, before it was annihilated by the events unleashed by Hitler, and to the world of ambiguity I inhabited in my next decade, which was in a place of privilege and safety compared to almost all other Jews in Europe at that time. Simultaneously, I lived as an unwelcome and marginalized refugee, akin to an undocumented alien with an aggressive and clamping-down immigration agency in action.

The *paradise* that was my Moravian childhood became that only in retrospect. At the time, there were sufficient family and political problems that created their own shaping influences, a preparation for feeling marginal, outside the mainstream of community, and solitary as I searched for my path. I fell into exceptionalism, rather than group identity. Often I took pride in these feelings. I managed to find a way forward toward success. But frequently any temporary allegiances and loyalties that were formed would later turn into sources of betrayal, when it became obvious I really did not belong to the groups and people with whom I had formed alliances.

The path I followed was more typically male than female. Work, not marriage, was at its center. Although I had more in common with men than with women, it did not accord me any reliable membership or status inside the male world. My interest patterns alienated me from women for many years. This remained so until the larger world of women caught up with me. The time finally came when finding a husband, having babies, and trading recipes were no longer a woman's defining preoccupations.

At the end of my first decade of life, my existence underwent a dramatic shift. My first years were lived within my family, in my home country where I belonged and felt appreciated and loved. My young self had incorporated aspects of Czech, German, and

Jewish identities, sometimes all vying for attention, but which, during that period, were not at war with each other. Until that point, I would likely have proceeded to become a patriotic Czech woman. When I was 10, that entire world disappeared, like Atlantis sinking into the sea. I had left on vacation, never to return. The abrupt disappearance of friends, family, and language went hand in hand with a slow disappearance of culture, meanings, sense of self. I was no longer that cute little girl to whom people were drawn.

I forgot what I had lost, and constructed a new self, one that was bereft but inwardly rebellious, with the self-esteem–protecting behavior of an outsider. I feared and hated Switzerland. Yet I loved it too. I complained about the fit of my shoes rather than being grateful to have shoes at all. I became an adolescent in Switzerland and was fortunate to attend good schools. I loved life in the way an unfolding life demands to be loved. Fear lurked around the edges; I could be expelled for any minor infraction. Switzerland was surrounded by Germany, and Germany meant my death. This dread usually stayed in the background but would start to lift as reports of the beginnings of Germany's defeat came in daily from the war's fronts.

Around the time the battle of Stalingrad turned in favor of the Allied forces, I began to remember a bit of Czech, and soon thereafter memories of Miroslav reappeared. I recalled primarily childish ideas of sexual mysteries mixed in with more reasonable sexual information: basic things such as where children came from and how animals and people had sex. I had forgotten all of that, along with my Czech language and the details of my former life. It is only in retrospect, and from the distance of age, that my life in Miroslav has acquired such Edenic tones. A most profound experience happened during a reunion for my then-partner, Al, which brought together his extended family and friends in an effort to heal his metastatic lung cancer. While he was bathed in the love and care that came toward him from everyone present, I suddenly had a vivid image of the Miroslav garden and all the people who had made up my world. I was overcome with the enormity of the losses that I had suffered, and broke into sobs. Joan Speck, one of the therapists in attendance, comforted me, saying, "Now is not the time." I quickly withdrew into myself, reinforcing the barriers between my inner reality and the world in which I lived.

During the course of writing this memoir, my love flowed to the people of Miroslav who did not survive the Holocaust. I wanted to set down a portrait of the little town as it was before disaster struck and wiped it out: a small word monument to its people as I remembered them, the Jews who perished in the camps, the Czechs who starved during the war, and even the Germans who were killed in the war and those expelled afterward. The whole memoir drew me into its flow more by the people and places I remember and love than by a desire to build a monument to myself for my professional successes.

At various times in my life, the early wounds of dislocation were at different removes from my daily self. While I was a student and trying to make a life, they were acknowledged in a matter-of-fact manner, as a given and not dwelled upon. When I lived in St. Louis and was married to Art, they receded into the background. I was trying to reconcile Art's working-class lifestyle with my own professional status.

As I became older and the immersion into a New York Jewish environment called forth more of my core identity, the early injuries loomed larger. This coincided with the time when, quite naturally, one begins to look back. People celebrate grandchildren, seek out their high school friends on the web, and generally return to thoughts of their origins. The burden of my loss increases when such a return reveals only past desolation. In the writing and revisiting of my life at this late stage, I hope to heal lingering grief and affirm my belief that humanity may indeed have a future.

Kitty La Perriere
November 2018
New York

Beginnings

Miroslav

As my mother told the story: It was the 22nd of November 1927, and after she and my father finished eating their supper, she cajoled him into taking a stroll in the garden of the maternity clinic where she was awaiting her time. I was born at half past midnight. This made me a Scorpio in Brno, Czechoslovakia, the place of my birth, and a Sagittarius in the New World, where I have lived most of my life. Gently touching her arm, the smiling doctor reassured my mother, "You have a beautiful, chubby baby girl!" And she did feel relieved.

My brother, her first child, was born nine years earlier after a punishing labor, the umbilical cord wrapped around his neck. He emerged long and scrawny, and became a poor eater and a dreamy, difficult child and remained so well into his teens. Thus, he captured Mother's worry, attention, and care, and, finally, secured her special love. Nevertheless, she had been eager to have more children.

Many years later, when my brother or I presented problems, my father would tease, "And she always wanted a dozen!" Ultimately, our family consisted of only my brother and me. My arrival was preceded by at least two miscarriages. In contrast to the previous pregnancies, which had been difficult, the one preparing me for the world had been easy, ending in an uneventful, speedy delivery with a labor of only two hours. My father was ill at ease around events of female physiology and had been tense and worried.

During my brother's birth he became faint and nauseous, drawing the nurse's attention away from my mother's labor to tend to his emergency. The happy normality of my arrival pleased him. I suspect he fell in love with me then and there.

By contrast, my mother's feelings ran differently. She looked at me, heaved a sigh of relief, and said in some inchoate fashion, "She'll be all right. She won't need me all that much." Within the first months, and then during my childhood, her initial and unformed notion solidified. Many years later she told me, "I was not so preoccupied with you. I knew that you would have to live with *them*, and I should not interfere too much." I remember the mother of my childhood as a somewhat remote, elegant, and awe-inspiring figure.

The *them* my mother had relinquished me to were not only my father's extended family, in whose midst we were living, but also our small town of Miroslav, where we returned after the two weeks' postpartum hospital stay. *Them* also encompassed all of Czechoslovakia, where my mother had moved following her marriage.

When the spirit moved her, Mother could be impetuously affectionate. This was a welcome, if puzzling, counterpoint to her usually poised manner, which conveyed beauty and elegance. She tried to ensure that I conducted myself as a lady, with impeccable table manners, and wore fashionable made-to-order clothing. She worried about my appearance, my thick ankles and wrists. She even delayed my horseback riding lessons for fear that I might become bow-legged. For my mother, it mattered greatly that I become a socially polished and acceptable young woman. These goals constituted the largest part of her guidance to me. Generally, she kept me at arm's length. When I was overcome by a desire to be physically close and touched her, she would ward off my hands, saying, "Not my face, not my face!"

I remember a confusing bit of teaching when one day my mother said, "Darling, you have to be careful. A kiss is the beginning of all evil." Whereupon she bent down and kissed me. I watched with love and fascination as she sat in front of her kidney-shaped mirrored makeup table with a bench that was actually a bidet. She carefully tended to her face, applying the almond rosewater my father prepared for her, and then engaging in a disciplined and routine facial massage, tapping and smoothing and checking her face. While she was doing that, she said, "Kitty, what is outside doesn't count; it is only inner beauty that really matters." Very early on, I recognized that outer beauty was her domain. I was a lost cause in her eyes.

Miroslav's modest population of only about 5,000 people did not prevent its inhabitants from enjoying a proud and affectionate allegiance to its long history. Many years later in my life, I found among my parents' belongings a booklet printed in 1912 celebrating the 1,000th anniversary of Miroslav's founding. Whether it actually documented historical facts or a rather grandiose myth born out of civic pride, the booklet traced the historic roots of the little town far back to the beginnings of the Austro-Hungarian Empire. Leafing through its pages, what impressed me most was a list of the prominent citizens of 1912.

This list included the names of German, Czech, and Jewish families intermixed alphabetically. It was a stunning reminder of a time when the community peacefully embraced its diverse cultural groups. As part of the Austro-Hungarian Empire, it had survived the many waves of Europe's fortunes, and had maintained its presence in southern Moravia as a small marketplace and agricultural center. Miroslav's glory declined under the Communist government when it was, as I discovered, left off the road grid and omitted from the map.

My father brought his wife and two-week-old daughter to a house situated at the lower end of the village center: a broad cobbled square at the upper end of which stood the Rathaus, or City Hall. Around us were a variety of small shops that facilitated daily life: a greengrocer, owned by the family Grünbaum; a baker; a dairy; a candy shop, acquired by my second caretaker Marenka Svobodova (after she married and left me); a café Bader. Closer to our end was the butcher, Zwieb; the volunteer fire department; and a photo shop, owned by Mr. Tichy. The square thinned into a street that wended its way up a small hill, past the German grade school and, set back a bit, the German high school. The tower of the Catholic church could be seen from a distance, surrounded by the village. The street was called Church Street. Our house was number 4.

It was a two-story house with a pleasing façade, French windows, and a decorative railing along the roofline. A small bridge in the front crossed a hollow that ran along the square and could well have been the remnant of an open sewer, but only overflow rainwater ever dampened it in my childhood. The path that crossed the bridge led to a large gate and passageway that divided the lower story of the house into halves: the left side held two or three administrative offices, and the right side contained several labs, where my father's older brother, Kurt, plied his trade as a nutritional chemist. Aromas of flowers and fruit often permeated the air, welcoming you into the mood of the season.

In spring and summer, horse-drawn wagons would cross the bridge and pass into the inner courtyard. The wagons were laden with mountains of fruit, mostly strawberries and sour cherries, which were deposited on long wooden tables that had been set up in preparation. Benches accommodated seasonal workers who washed and stemmed and pitted the fruit for processing. There might have been as many as 60 workers or more, all women. I loved to find a place on a bench and work along with them. I felt proud of my labors and accomplishments. I can still picture the wooden sieves with net inserts we used to rinse the strawberries three to four times in running water.

In high season, the courtyard became part of the manufacturing plant, surrounded by the ancillary buildings required in the manufacturing process. The factory converted the fruit into etheric oils and esters, components for the food and perfume industry. There was a large boiler housed in its own barn, also a carpenter's shop and a barrel maker's shop. In between these structures was a penned space that held our two big watchdogs: a German shepherd, Bella, and her brown son, Harry, who resembled a hound dog. He was the only puppy in a litter of 12 who had not been born with his mother's black coat, and he was the only one we had kept. Even as a young child, I noticed that along with the different fur color, he had a wholly different personality: He was a friendly, relaxed, and playful oaf of a dog. And he was big and comfortable enough for me to lean against and even try to ride.

At the back of the yard stood another gate that opened into a deep cellar, where the products were kept cool before shipment. During the German occupation of World War II, the cellar was taken over by the Gestapo and used as a prison. A set of steps led upward toward a terraced garden; on the other end stood Kurt's house. Our own apartment, and that of my father's parents, occupied the second floor of the main house.

I felt intensely at home among the buildings and with the workers of our small factory. I often watched them at work, and made friends with some of their children, although I had no intention of entering the family business later on in my life. Perhaps there was a tacit assumption that it would become my brother's legacy. I was quite certain from childhood that I would grow up to become the minister of public health for Czechoslovakia. Nevertheless, my father was very pleased with my interest in his work. It cemented our good and warm relationship. I think he rather enjoyed my being a tomboy. From his rare business trips, he always brought back practical, easy-to-wear, easy-to-wash dresses. These contrasted dramatically with the highly constructed dresses my mother had made for me. Those dresses required great care in how they were worn, as well as careful attention to how I moved while wearing them.

My father often took me when he visited the farmers whose fields yielded the strawberries we processed. Early on, we made these trips by horse and carriage. I had a wonderful sense of surveying the countryside and the growing rows of strawberries and enjoyed talking with the farmers who spoke to my father. Occasionally in the evening, my father and I would go for a short walk along a stream bordered by willow trees, which led to a forest where it was often possible to hear nightingales singing. These are some of the images that come to mind when I think of the deep happiness and contentment I experienced in this paradise of childhood.

Next to my grandparents' property was a good-sized private park. It was enclosed by a tall iron fence and dense shrubbery, which shielded a modest castle, rather mysteriously rumored to be owned by a minor member of the Austrian nobility, rarely present and unknown. The thick perimeter of bushes permitted only glimpses of its grey stone walls with tiny windows and fierce turrets. A sense of unease and vague danger accompanied this evidence of the foreign intrusion.

An underground tunnel led from the castle's cellar past that of a farmhouse owned by friends of my grandparents, and it was reputed to have played its part during a siege laid by the forces of the king of Sweden to the encampment of the Austrian army. Somewhere along the line, one of my father's ancestors was honored by the emperor with a ring and given a title for the help and succor offered his soldiers—food, drink, and care of the wounded. My father was in possession of this ring. It found its way to my brother's pelf, and, after my brother's death, to me; it is still in my possession.

A few minutes' walk straight out our front door and up a small incline stood the new Czech schoolhouse; it was friendly and inviting with clean, modern lines and large windows. This is where I went to school, while my brother was still attending the German school. The rifts in the life of Miroslav, of the whole republic, and of Europe had not yet emerged.

The family business was inherited from my grandmother's uncle, for whom my grandfather had worked as an accountant. My great-great uncle was a man of imagination and vision. He had used as the company's logo *"mein Feld die Welt"* ("My field, the world"), and traveled widely, including to China, among other places. And it was in China that he was inspired to bring back the idea of a terraced garden. Our house was flanked on one side by a strip of land abutting the castle, on the other by a sloping orchard. Into our parcel that lay between these sloping hills, our China-traveling ancestor had blasted a series of stepwise terraces, each measuring six to eight feet tall and of various depths.

Each level had its own ambience and function. The lowest one, part of the inner courtyard, held a small gazebo, a bed of peonies and hydrangeas, and, as an afterthought, a large rhubarb plant. It was a shady, inviting gathering place outside my grandmother's kitchen. The next level comprised a square of lawn on which to play, partially shaded by a giant lilac bush. One series of steps higher up led to a small copse with an assortment of deciduous trees; walnut, chestnut, maple and one pine. A seating area, with table and chairs, illuminated by lights, was set against a raised stretch of a rose and tulip garden, with a back wall of espalier apricot and pear trees. Another flight of stairs took one to a vineyard, as well as a vegetable garden, and then to a berry patch of raspberries, red and white currants, and gooseberries. The border of the berry patch was a lilac hedge beyond which lay a pebbled yard from which one entered my Uncle Kurt and Aunt Frieda's elegantly decorated one-story house.

Their living room was furnished with Bauhaus furniture, and in their bedroom were matching pillow covers, a quilted duvet, and black-flowered chintz window treatments. Next to the dining room was a smoking room, with humidors for cigars and pipe tobacco, as well as a few bottles of liqueurs. For me, this house was even more forbidding than my parents' living quarters. Indeed, my Aunt Frieda forbade my entrance, suggesting I beg for a cookie or carrot from the backyard by the kitchen window. She also referred to me as a "*mezaroch*," a name used to designate the nomadic gypsies who visited our village a few times a year.

Facing Church Street was number 6, a tiny house snuggled up against ours. In that house lived two spinster sisters, whose brother, also a traveler, had covered their tamped earth floors with sumptuous Chinese carpets. From his travels, he filled their plain rooms with ivories, silks, and china.

In contrast to my great-great uncle, my father limited his travels to studies at the Handelshochschule in St. Gallen, Switzerland, School of Economics and Commerce, where he met my mother a couple of years before World War I. She was a 16-year-old beauty and fell in love with the dashing foreigner. He kissed her at a university fraternity dance, and she sighed, "Oh, we are engaged." And so they were. With the outbreak of World War I, my father served in the Austro-Hungarian Imperial Army as a mounted cavalry officer and spent much of the next four years in the trenches. He emerged from the war with stomach ulcers and in frail health. My mother had waited for him, and in April 1918, six months before World War I ended, she agreed to meet him in Vienna, where they were married in a military wedding. Even then, she had been fearless and focused on what she wanted and remained so for her entire life.

While World War I convulsed and reconfigured Europe, Switzerland, as usual, had remained neutral. My mother had finished her studies and started working as an executive assistant to the director of Saurer, a heavy equipment company. After the end of the war, my father joined her in Switzerland and entered his father-in-law's textile business. He lacked a talent for business and possessed little affinity for lace and embroidery. Luckily, his business association with his father-in-law came to an end a few years before the worldwide Great Depression of 1929, which sank the textile business. My grandfather's merchandise, bought and loaded on ships in China, arrived in Europe worthless.

My father had decided it would be best if they returned to his family home. My parents, with my then three-year-old brother, moved back to Miroslav, which was now in the newly constructed state of Czechoslovakia. Father joined the family business run by his father and his older brother. My mother was by then weary of the six-hour commute to the Saurer offices. She agreed to follow her husband into the gentle and gracious countryside of southern Moravia, living in the same house as his parents. She held romantic notions about her future. She was very much in love, and also hoped to develop a full intellectual and active working life in her new home.

Putting these plans into action proved impossible. In preparation for living in the newly founded republic, my mother studied Czech, while my father's family, with its cultural roots in Vienna, spoke German. The arrival of a foreign bride caused quite a stir in Miroslav. My mother's arrival particularly upset one family, whose daughter believed she had been destined to marry my father. Most importantly, village life, while genteel and warm to insiders, was petty, gossipy, and unwelcoming to a newcomer. Over the 16 years my mother lived in Miroslav, she was never fully accepted. She found no entry to working with my father in the family business, and certainly no occasion or opportunity to look for intellectual or creative activities elsewhere. The women in the family, as well as those in the community, retained a suspicion of her.

Wounded feelings caused her to withdraw emotionally. Mother strove to maintain a cultured and intellectual atmosphere within her own home. She read a great deal, and both my parents were actively aware of political and world events. Sometimes they hosted visiting celebrities, writers, or politicians who swung by Miroslav on lecture tours. Mother cultivated her elegance, and while many considered her haughty and aloof, she enjoyed the occasional innocent flirtations with gallant men. She had no women friends.

My father was comfortable, easygoing, a flirt, and a charmer, full of fun and the love of life. My mother was jealous of his easy intimacy with old women friends and the occasional flirtations that may or may not have represented a just cause for concern. He felt confined, and perhaps a bit frightened, by her grasping attachment. He had occasional bursts of temper, which usually intimidated her. He could puncture her pretensions with an edgy sarcasm that was deeply injurious.

When things became particularly difficult between them, their squabbles, with accompanying verbal recriminations, could be heard outside the house. At a desperate point, my father, with his mother's and the family doctor's help, considered sending my mother to a sanitarium for recovery from *nervousness*. Understandably my mother feared he was trying to institutionalize her in order to get rid of her. She fiercely fought the attempt to send her to Graefenberg, where the clinic was located, and won.

When I was in the first grade, Mother and I ran away from home. We lived for a few weeks in an apartment at the *Americka Domovina* (American home) in Brno. We both got the flu. I was ill first. When I recovered, my mother developed a fever. I had learned how to take care of a sick person by watching Mother take care of me. I felt proud and grown up as I took my turn at bringing her water to drink and putting cold compresses on her forehead. Soon after this, my father arrived and took us back home.

When fighting would break out between my parents, my grandmother and my Aunt Hilda, my father's unmarried younger sister (who lived on the same floor) came to get me to protect me from the turmoil. I can hear my grandfather's stern voice declaring, "A child belongs with her parents." He would then pressure his wife and daughter to return me across the hall, back into the battle zone. I suspect it was mostly his own peace of mind that he desired. "Get that kid out of here. That's what Hans gets for marrying that fancy woman." During the day, my grandfather went to work. That is to say he went downstairs into his office, where he spent his mornings and afternoons.

I liked to hang out with my grandmother. She was a tiny roundish woman: her head was a small ball atop the bigger ball that was her body. She and my grandfather lived simply. Their bedroom was also their living room. There was always a saturating and comfortable aroma of good food surrounding my grandmother. Often she prepared her special strudel. I can envision the dough being stretched on a white tablecloth that covered the entire kitchen table before she filled it with nuts and apples and raisins. Grandmother plied me with snacks and encouraged her husband to eat. Grandfather ate his breakfast at a small table, which stood at the foot of their bed. His morning meal was bread and rolls, which he dunked into milk coffee, to which he added butter by the spoonful. Grandfather was a mostly silent man. I don't recall him laughing, or even engaging in much friendly banter or conversation. Grandmother fussed over him with the movements of a pecking chicken. I deeply loved their daughter, my Aunt Hilda. She sang and played the piano. I loved sitting with her in her room. She slept in what was originally the living room. Once I was asked whom, of all the people in the world, I loved the very best. When I answered that it was Aunt Hilda, everyone was shocked.

Occasionally I was teased at school about my parents' fighting. We occupied a somewhat elevated position in the social hierarchy of Miroslav; the other kids were probably pleased to have something on me. My father was a ranking member of village society, having lived there his entire life. My mother would always remain the aloof foreigner. In retrospect, I realize that my brother joined Mother in the position of *outsider*. This was reflected in his difficulty of learning to speak Czech well. On the other hand, I was a village kid, and Czech was my first language.

My mother's personal history was consonant with her tendency to keep our attachment at a distance. She had had a somewhat remote relationship with her own mother while growing up. My mother had the emotional resources to deal with her mother's lack of love for her daughters. If she was hurt by the absence of maternal warmth, she never showed it. Mother did not engage in attempts to win her mother's affection or attention; later in life she turned to her husband and son to buttress her. Her relationship with her mother contained a certain formality, and there was grudging respect across a friendly distance. There was an absence of expressed warmth, even anger. They were not lovingly close, especially when compared to my mother's besotted devotion to my brother. In my mind, it was love that almost exceeded the usual Jewish preference for a male child.

When I was small I adored my mother. I looked up to her admiringly from my lowly position, but Mother seemed utterly unattainable. After breakfast, she would summon me for my French lesson and I would sit at her feet as she reclined regally, dressed in an orange and black silk kimono decorated with dragons and chrysanthemums. We practiced simple sentences and sang a song or two: *Frère Jacque*, or *Il Etait un Petit Navire*. At the end of the lesson, she would rather abruptly stand up and disappear. There wasn't a good-bye ritual. I was left feeling both excited and shortchanged. At that point, my nanny would come to collect me and our day would begin. It is unsurprising to me now that my mother felt distant from me. She was primarily interested in the world of men. Her own father adored her. And Mother was intensely in love with her husband. Her remoteness from me also made sense, given her outsider position within the Miroslav community.

To a small child, she seemed a semi-regal presence, belonging to a different social class than I did. I played and ran around, got dirty, and felt barred from access to her elegant living space. She could not then foresee that neither she nor I would live with *them* for very long. But during that time I became friends with village kids and tried to hide that I was better off than they were. For the first six months of my life, in conformity with local customs, a professional baby nurse had cared for me. After that, Marenka arrived. She was my very own caretaker, who stayed with me until I was about four years old. She would come in the morning, get me out of bed, dress and feed me, spend much of the day with me, prepare my food, and take care of my clothes.

Often she would put me to bed at night. Through Marenka, Czech would become my first language. It was the language of early and deep emotion, the language of basic identity, the language whose imagery structured the world for me. To this day, it is my language of basic arithmetic. As we took long walks together, Marenka taught me folk songs and told me fairy tales. She was a tender, affectionate, and loving girl. She must have been in her mid-twenties when she came to us and then left us, when, as almost an old maid in our culture, she found a husband. Marenka and her husband opened the candy store on the square across from our house, where, for as long as I lived in Miroslav, I could go for some affection and a little sweet. I loved Marenka fervently, and she loved me. Many years later I met her daughter, who looked me over and then made some slightly sour comment about meeting the girl her mother had loved all her life.

Edith replaced Marenka. She was also a farm girl. Edith was considerably less tender and sweet, but she was active, and lots of fun to be around. Perhaps it was her no-nonsense, somewhat rough demeanor that encouraged me to become the tomboy I really was. I looked up to my elegant mother, uncomfortable and ill at ease as if I were a servant in a rich house. I acquired no genteel manners. I spent my time running with the other children. We hung out on farms and in the woods. We observed the love life of animals and of single people that took place outdoors. Occasionally, we experimented with each other, discovering the mysterious regions of our bodies.

I started school early, at the age of five and a half. Impatient to get going, I had to pass an acceptance interview to determine if I was mature enough for first grade. The school principal interviewed me. I answered a decorous "yes" to innumerable questions, until my eagerness broke through and I expelled a long string of "Yes! Yes! Yes! Yes!" to the question of whether I wanted to be in school. Luckily the standards of appropriate behavior were not stuffy, and I started my official public life by entering first grade in September 1933. It was an ominous year in the history of us all.

There is a photograph of a young girl, seven or perhaps eight years old, wearing a mid-thigh length dress with an unbuttoned cardigan, light brown hair parted on the side and loosely contained in a large barrette that looks like it might slide down her silken hair at any moment. She has a light, friendly smile as she leans casually and comfortably against the open glass door, ankles crossed, hands lightly folded behind her back. The door is the entrance to my Czech school, and since the place is deserted, it must have been taken on a Sunday.

Mirrored Reflections

This photograph of me was taken by the youngest and most recently arrived of the eight men who constituted the permanent labor force in my family's small factory. While the other men were family men, middle-aged, conservative, divided between Czech and German, Zlotchenko had come from the East, spoke Slovak, had radical political ideas, and was probably Jewish. He was enjoying his new camera and perhaps intended to present a little gift, this snapshot of me, to his boss, my father.

It is evident in the picture that I was at ease with the photographer, as well as with the location he had chosen. The school and the local population naturally and imperceptibly had become my community of reference, in many ways more so than my family. At school I learned to love our new republic, a state whose relatively recent birth still seemed to be in everyone's constant awareness. Its newly minted existence represented the fulfillment of a longing for autonomy and freedom for a people that had been ruled by the Austro-Hungarian Empire for centuries, and whose history contained a number of popular uprisings or peasant rebellions against an essentially feudal yoke.

Czechoslovakia was created as part of the Treaty of Versailles in 1918. The Austro-Hungarian Empire was dismantled and carved into a series of nation states, most of them representing multiethnic compromises that carried the seeds for later troubles from their very inception. I was a fervent patriot. When we learned the song directed at TG Masaryk, the Republic's first president, I sang the words passionately: *"Taticku stary nas at se nam zachovas dokud ty jsi mezi name dotoud bude dobre s name taticku stary nas."* ("Our dear old father, be preserved for us. As long as you are among us, we will be safe.") Indeed, after Masaryk's death in 1934, political clouds darkened, and foreboding signs of peril appeared.

In school I was encouraged to join the Sokol (later known for its Fascist leanings), a youth athletic organization, and was proud to march on national holidays wearing its beige uniform banded in red. My tangible love of Czechoslovakia was shared by its Jewish community; as I discovered as an adult, that love grew out of an explicit, active awareness that the state Masaryk helped birth was one of the first to give full rights of citizenship and full protection of the law to its Jewish population. As the joke went: Who is a Czechoslovak? Only a Jew. The others are either Czechs or Slovaks. Perhaps it was this history that allowed the Jews of Miroslav to continue the peaceful coexistence that had prevailed under the Austro-Hungarian Empire, and to live in confidence and on friendly terms with both German and Czech neighbors.

A regional exhibit of agricultural products was a big event in 1935, in which Czechs, Germans, and Jews participated. In retrospect, it expressed the tensions that would mar the peaceful picture and signal the beginning of the end. The German population had begun to strut around in ethnic German clothing, men in boots and brown shirts, women in dirndl dresses and white knee socks knitted in a braided pattern. And yet, in a second photograph, sits the same girl, eight years old, wearing a white embroidered blouse, a dirndl skirt with black velvet embroidered suspenders, and the infamous white knee socks. I am sitting in front of a large cutout of a cow next to the German mayor of the village, showing off how I drink a glass of milk as he smiles at me.

What had my parents been thinking? Was dressing me up in enemy costume a futile gesture to delay the inevitable? This deceptively peaceful scene occurred during the same time that the large German minority in the Sudetenland, the border areas between Czechoslovakia, Germany, and Austria, had begun their aggressive political agitation. My firm identity as a member of Czech youth helped me face up to the fear and terror that would befall me when the men of the German national socialist party, organized by Henlein, started marching through the village streets in their brown shirts and heavy boots, hands raised high in the Hitler salute. I would run home and hide, holding my hands over my ears to drown out their thundering, threatening slogan-shouting and their Nazi songs. "*Heim ins Reich*" became their cry—"*Home into the German Reich!*" Thus began my lifelong apprehension of crowds. Even when there is a happy occasion, such as the Fourth of July in the United States, these fears linger: I worry any crowd might turn ugly and possibly become violent.

For the first five or six years of my life, I had had little awareness that the ethnic groupings of Miroslav (about 500 Jews who constituted 10 percent of the population, with the remaining 90 percent pretty evenly divided between Czechs and Germans) contained serious political tensions. I think I was more aware of social class issues. My family was well off in a modest sort of way but were definitely considered "rich" by the farmers and working people, Czech, German, and Jewish alike. I identified mainly with the Czech village children, and as such was aware that there was rivalry and some bad blood, but mostly avoidance of contact between the pupils in the Czech school and those in the German school.

At the time my parents decided to enroll me in the Czech school, it was their vote for Prague and against Vienna, reflecting my mother's determination to make herself into a true Czech citizen. When my brother's education had begun, some nine years earlier, he entered the German grade school, in conformity with the German-speaking tradition of my father's family. My parents transferred him into a Czech high school halfway through his studies, but the basis for a cultural divide within our family had been laid: me, the ardent Czech patriot whose first language was Czech, and my brother, who had to struggle with Czech and dreamed of studying German philology.

By 1937, when I was 10 years old, the threat of war hung heavy over our lives. In school, we began to learn Morse code and first aid, and we learned to recognize the insignia of the fighter planes of various nations; we were going to have an active and helpful role to play if the republic was attacked; we were going to carry messages and tend to the wounded. In school, we were reading stories of heroic children who helped the partisans during the Russian revolution. I heard the stories of long trains riding through endless snow-covered landscapes with happy warriors singing songs and heating their tea over a fire that burned in each carriage. I had my own Red Cross first aid kit assembled in a khaki-colored canvas bag. For good measure, my mother had our dressmaker run me up a military-style three-piece khaki outfit with a Red Cross armband.

While we children prepared for what we saw as our soon-to-arrive hour of glory and heroism, the adults in the community began to admit that the political situation was close to catastrophic. Of course, people varied in their ability to recognize this, and even more in their ability to mobilize themselves into some kind of action. The world climate was ominous, but no awareness of the dangers hinted at the magnitude of what would come. The most likely cataclysm believed, or perhaps even hoped for, was a war against Germany: Czechoslovakia with her Western allies against Germany.

That view may have shielded Jews from the immediate recognition that whatever befell the world, something more specific and horrific would befall the Jews. News from Germany and Austria contained frightening events of anti-Semitic and political repressions and murders. The news was worse every day. It became imperative to ready young people to immigrate to Palestine. I started taking classes in modern Hebrew, and I joined a Zionist youth group that trained us in physical fitness and intellectual competence. I felt bloated with self-importance when, at the age of ten years old, I was asked to report on the management of water resources in Palestine and assembled the background material and presented my findings to an attentive audience.

I now belonged to a second youth organization, the Zionist Makkabi Hazair. On national holidays, we children would assemble to march with their group. Where did I belong? Would I wear the beige and red outfit of the Sokol or the blue and white uniform of the Makkabi? I chose Sokol. My attachment to my Czech identity went deep. Its roots included my mother's embrace of her new homeland when she married my father and my grandparents' unwavering loyalty to the state, even though they spoke only German. Whenever a question arose about possible emigration, the whole family closed ranks solidly against the idea. My grandfather spoke of our duty to Czechoslovakia. He ordered our foreign bank deposits back home to be put at the disposal of the state. Ultimately, only my mother maintained a wider view. At the critical moment, she prevailed and got her immediate family, her husband and two children, into greater safety.

As for me, I had no thoughts of leaving. I was firmly grounded in my village, and in my school from the very first day I entered. Every year at school's end we would take a class picture, lined up on the steps behind the school. My second-grade photograph captured who I was at the time, before the devastating political reality fundamentally disrupted me. In the photo, I am standing in the right end of the first row, leaning my head toward the teacher, whose hand rests on my right shoulder. When that photograph was taken, I had been intensely aware of her taking her position next to me and of where she placed her hand. An electric current pulsed through me, running from my shoulder down to my toes and electrifying every relevant point along the way. What was going on?

I had developed a huge crush on my second-grade teacher. Her name was Helena, and she was the first woman whom I was able to see as an individual, rather than as someone's wife or mother. She wore her hair cut short, her clothes unfussy and sporty, and she moved light and fast. She lived with her husband and three-year-old daughter, Iva, in an apartment, the first self-contained apartment I had ever seen, in a complex built next to the school for the teachers and officials who came from out of town. Since I loved school and was a good student, I made friends with Helena. I would visit her house to play with her daughter. I was infatuated with the simplicity and airiness of where she lived. I became a teacher's pet.

While I was quick and smart, my artistic talents had always been sadly deficient. We did a great deal of artwork in class, and I tried my best, but the results were lacking. One day, Helena asked us to draw our family, and for some reason I thought she had looked directly at me and singled me out with her instructions, which made me try harder, and I succeeded even less than usual. I looked with dismay at my pitiful stick figures, nudging my neighbor whose picture looked colorful and cheerful. Helena, who had been going from desk to desk, inspecting our artistic output, noticed the commotion. She briefly looked in my direction, a short reprimanding glance, I thought, but continued her path, made a suggestion here, gave encouragement there. When she finally reached my desk, she stopped, paused, and bent down. I felt very embarrassed, fidgeted, not knowing what to do when she sighed, gave a small laugh, pushed me to make me move over, and then, with quick resolve, said, "Let me." She bent down and slipped into the small two-pupil desk that I shared with a classmate.

These were small desks, with a bench attached to the desktop, which lifted. We were expected to be quiet when we sat in them, arms folded behind our back at the elbows. Helena squeezed in, pushing me over with her hips and, taking the crayon out of my hand, set about to upgrade my handiwork. Excited and thrilled, I whispered loudly to my desk neighbor, "Look, she is doing the whole thing for me!" Helena stopped for a second, looked at me, and corrected my perception. "No," she said. "I'm just putting clothes on your naked people."

I felt warm and excited by her nearness. How I loved being touched by her. I was thrilled to be in her class, watching her, listening to her, trying to do well to impress her. Helena was my teacher again in the fourth grade. In the meantime, she had given birth to a second daughter, Eva. I was a regular guest as well as babysitter at their house. It was hard for me to reconcile our relationship with the fact that, by 1937 and 1938, the Czechs, too, had become increasingly anti-Semitic. I did not want to believe it. There were rumors that her husband, a high school teacher, had spoken out against some Jewish students, and she herself had taken a political stand against Jews. I must have shrugged it off. In 1947 I visited Helena; her girls welcomed me and asked about Switzerland. Helena wept and hugged me. I felt like I was visiting long lost family.

Disruption

March 1938. We were listening to the radio when we heard that the German army had invaded Austria. We feared for the safety of family and friends in Vienna. Feelings of anxiety and foreboding were mixed with desperate dreams of heroically protecting our beloved homeland.

I wore my Red Cross outfit and carried my first aid bag as my friends and I played war games. We hid behind rocks and crawled on our bellies through the grass, pretending to be soldiers hiding from enemy artillery. We shared our fantasies of resisting a German invasion. We were expressing a feeling that briefly and intensely pervaded the Czech adult world in those months, to arm ourselves to defend our country.

At the same time, seemingly disconnected to our anticipation of a glorious and desperate defensive war, I wanted to skip our usual summer trip to Switzerland. I started to pester my mother about permitting me to go to a Maccabi-run summer camp in the High Tatra Mountains in Slovakia. Presumably, my reason was to prepare for the possibility of immigration to Palestine. My parents quickly quashed that idea with the logic that at only 10 years old, I was too young to go to camp by myself. And so we set off on our annual summer journey to St. Gallen, Switzerland.

The trip that July was different from the ones we had undertaken every year before. Our route always took us from Miroslav to Vienna and from there, via Salzburg and Innsbruck, through the long, mysterious Arlberg Tunnel, finally crossing the Swiss border at Buchs/Sargans. Every segment of that trip was familiar to me. I knew the mountains by name. When we would finally cross the Rhine River, my excitement about visiting with my grandmother neared its peak.

This trip provided none of these familiar and joyful emotional markers. The route had changed because of the Anschluss (the annexation of Austria by Germany). It was no longer considered safe to travel through Austria, with a stopover in Vienna, as we had done in the past. Instead, our journey traversed Germany via Munich. I cannot explain why this was considered safer. Perhaps Germany seemed in less of an uproar than the recently occupied Austria. I regretted missing the opera, a treat associated with an overnight stay in Vienna, as well as our visits to the elegant gardens of Salzburg and their playful water works.

We set out from Miroslav to Prague for a two-day stay. That weekend in Prague was my first visit to the beloved Zlata Praha (Golden Prague). I was unprepared for the splendor of Prague, and the time we spent there was touched with the unreality of a dream. I experienced something like a first date, and that further enhanced the dreamlike quality. The 14-year-old son of family friends agreed to show me around town. With a sense of heightened excitement and a rapidly beating heart, I tasted the first delights of romance that my 10-year-old girlfriends and I had fantasized about in our private talks. Just by walking next to a "him" on the street, not even holding hands, I quickly added ephemeral adolescent feelings to my inner source book. Alone in my hotel room that evening, I lingered by the open window, my insides astir by the adumbrations of future possibilities that afternoon had brought. And, also, I was in a restless and anxious state in anticipation of what may lie ahead of us on this new passage to Switzerland.

The panorama of Prague lived up to its fairy-tale aura: lights and roofs and bridges and church spires mysteriously and temptingly aglitter. I drank, ate, and inhaled the evening's gift, and I started my very first diary, which opened with a full embrace of Zlata Praha. The intense experience of that evening became the embodiment of longing for a lost paradise, a longing that would remain with me during my long years of absence from home, which began at the end of that day's journey.

Though uneventful, the ensuing trip through Germany was somber, hushed, and scary. Passport control and customs manned by swastika-adorned, booted German guards kept us silent, not wanting to draw attention, and hoping the inspections would proceed quickly. Perhaps at that moment the groundwork was laid for the heeding of my father's later admonition: "Don't be seen. Don't be heard. Don't make waves."

We entered Switzerland at Basel with a great sigh of relief. It was a ride of about an hour from Basel to St. Gallen. As we arrived at the St. Gallen railway station, our oppressive mood suddenly lifted. The station was a large, square, weighty building of light grey hewn stone with a wide square clock tower whose large and clearly visible dial helped me track time for many a day in the times that were to follow.

Barely two streets away stood the family's house. The neighborhood was tidy and orderly. Every block consisted of three attached houses, each with a small front garden. In the back there were equally small, and, on the whole, less well-tended utilitarian backyards. These formed an alley, and ours housed a convenient small grocery and vegetable store run by the Andreoli family.

I saw the house as elegant, grand. I defined it as an urban home because our family lived in what was referred to as a first-floor apartment. My Uncle Leo's business was on the ground floor. It consisted of an office with a small sales room and two or three rooms where a few seamstresses sewed undergarments. The bustle of the manufacturing, quite small scale in retrospect, drew my attention and added to my sense that the family home in Switzerland was a special place.

Walking up a flight of stairs, one encountered a small landing with a glass panel door opening onto the central hall of the apartment. To the left was a short hallway leading to the kitchen and bathroom, where an open-flame gas heater provided the hot water. At the kitchen's entrance stood an icebox, which depended on weekly deliveries of blocks of ice. The central hallway also contained a washbasin, equipped with cold water only, and a small mirror. This washbasin was used for handwashing before meals, the common and necessary washing of dirty hands, as well as the ritual washing of hands before prayers were said.

There was a square-shaped den that held a beautiful oak table, which eventually found its way into my brother's possession. The den and its table served as our informal dining room. My grandmother spent much of her free time sitting in a straight chair and reading the Chumash (a printed book form of the Torah, written in Yiddish). There were two separate bedrooms. To the right was a sitting room and, behind that, a formal dining room.

Whenever I arrived in Switzerland, I immediately felt welcome. My grandmother was affectionate, fussed over us, and provided, or prepared, ample food. Uncle Leo enjoyed our visits and liked to have fun. He planned programs and excursions he knew would please us.

Even though our street was outside the medieval nucleus of the old town, it had been constructed in human-sized proportions. Sometimes it felt as if the whole of St. Gallen was my living room, familiar and safe, and often quite cozy. The weather in that part of Switzerland was frequently dismal: rainy, fog-shrouded, and damp. St. Gallen was situated in a valley between two hill chains of modest height. These hill chains were wooded and green, and they provided easy access for excursions, where our imaginary adventures enlivened the relatively mundane everydayness of the landscape. At times I felt confined, almost suffocated by the surrounding hills. Wherever I looked, my glance hit an obstacle.

I loved traveling the 12-kilometer distance to Lake Constance, a large body of water also known as the Swabian Sea. Floating in the water there, I positioned myself so that I could not see any land. I felt unbounded and untrammeled. A different way to reach freedom was to ride in Uncle Leo's car, when he took us "to the mountains" ("*In die Berge*" was the emotional equivalent of going on a pilgrimage). On sunny days the meadows were an incredibly succulent green. Blooms of all kinds abounded, be they fruit trees or planted gardens or the occasional wildflower-strewn meadow. At such times the sky would turn a radiant blue, and, with good luck, a glacier-covered Alp would include itself in the easily visible panorama.

It did look like a Swiss postcard, but it was a postcard that expanded and had the aroma of all the smells of the region, from sweet alpine air to cow dung. While the environs of St. Gallen were often a sad grey and monotonous, the alpine heights were glorious, and made me feel as if I were touching eternal life, even while considering myself religiously an atheist. I had always been a nimble athlete at home in Czechoslovakia, but the stamina required for Swiss trekking came hard to me. Nevertheless, I loved the brisk air, the fragrant alpine meadows with their clear sparkling streams carrying ice-cold water as it melted from the "eternal" glaciers (now mostly gone) and the other summer pleasures we indulged in: picnics and dipping in the nearby Sitter River, where the sharply biting flies seemed to be the size of fat thumbnails.

The radiant weather made the landscape fresh and vivid; the intensely green meadows were filled with flowers; the dark green pine forests were lush and thick. Above all, there was the granite grey of rock and the clean majestic white of the glacier-covered mountaintops. But that kind of weather was a scarce commodity. Often it rained all week, and our activities had to be canceled. Instead of the joys of the outdoors, we moved to the inner land of longing and waiting.

I remember clearly a sudden and unexplained change at the end of that summer. It was an anxious August afternoon when Uncle Leo walked me to school for an entrance interview. The political situation had worsened. The Munich conference of September 1938 was just ahead. The decision had been made that Mother would return home to be with her husband while the "children" (my 18-year-old brother and I) would stay on in St. Gallen with my mother's family. It was probably primarily my mother's decision. It saved my life, but at the time I was very unhappy about it. My longing had found its target: the lost childhood paradise.

I was unaware that anything catastrophic had happened. When my uncle and I took that walk, I didn't fully understand the politics of what was going on. I narrowed my radius of vision to the situation at hand and engaged my uncle in an anxious, urgent review of German orthography. I was desperate to know when you doubled consonants, when it was *das* (it) and when it was *dass* (so that), when it was *wen* (whom) and when it was *wenn* (if). It was as if my life depended on getting this right. Throughout most of my life, that narrowing of focus, turning away from the wider surroundings, has remained a skill as well as a liability. I was admitted to the sixth grade at Vadian elementary school, half a year ahead of grade level, and entered in the middle of sixth grade.

There was a striking and heavy contrast between the atmosphere of my former school and my new one. The bright, sunlit building of my Czech school radiated an active pride of a new state ready to teach its only recently legitimized and elevated language. The classes were small and coeducational. Our teachers were dedicated, lively, and personable. The atmosphere was orderly but also kind and friendly. We sat up straight with our arms folded behind our backs and were expected to sit still and speak only when called upon and to pay attention by looking at the teacher. I loved that school, the building, the teachers, and learning. I was one of the quartet of good students in the class, three girls and one boy. I don't remember any competitiveness among us, we were good school friends.

The red and beige of Sokol merged to give color to my memory, which is the image I held as I started my first school day in St. Gallen. I entered what seemed like a dark classroom—long desks filled with rows of girls dressed in dark clothes, with a serious-faced, dark-suited teacher, solemnly nodding to me and pointing me toward the second row. There was a new language, a new syllabus, a new national history, and my loss of competence as a student. All of these combined to make the first half-year a sad and sobering experience. I had difficulty following the lectures; I did not recognize their content. I was an insecure speller. My classmates were serious-looking and quiet-acting girls. Many had long braids; they wore hand-knitted woolen stockings and sweaters in muted colors. Their skirts ended below the knee. They wore dark aprons, which covered their school outfits. I was told later that the purpose of the aprons was to protect their clothing from wear and tear.

I presented an embarrassing appearance the first time I was called to the front of the class. In contrast to my classmates, my hair was very short, as was my skirt; it reached mid-thigh at best. When I reached up to write on the blackboard, my panties showed just a bit, as I was not wearing stockings, but rather knee socks. Instead of an apron, I wore a navy-blue sweater, which was decorated with multicolored diagonal stripes of fuzzy angora wool. Here I was, a picture of foreign frivolity and Jewish immorality. I was almost 11 years old.

In my school in Miroslav I had felt at home. I belonged there. Feeling fully accepted translated into gratitude and love for the State, and, specifically, for its first president, T.G. Masaryk. He was universally beloved, perhaps as Roosevelt had been. That spirit of optimism, loyalty, and anticipation of a happy future had permeated our school.

Switzerland was very different. The atmosphere was pro-German; Jews were met with a certain suspicion and enmity. This attitude obviously intensified as Europe drew closer to the onset of World War II. My mother, who had grown up in Switzerland, did not remember such anti-Jewish experiences. She had felt included and welcomed as a child and then as a young woman.

At that earlier time in history, my mother was able to make her way in the Swiss community. As an exceedingly charming and beautiful girl, in any gathering, she exhibited early on the social qualities of an adept and agile woman. She was smart, quick, and a sparkling conversationalist. She was also focused, determined, stubborn, and sure of her perceptions. Mother saw only what she wanted to see and could eliminate all unpleasantness from her awareness. Later on, these would turn out to be the very qualities that would contribute significantly to the survival of our family.

As an example, in early 1939, after my father had received an invitation to work in Paris, my mother was successful in receiving an exit visa as well as a permit for a "lift," as the shipment of furniture was referred to. In a situation where Jews were busy avoiding any contact with the occupying Germans, my mother had gone straight to the German commandant to submit her petition. In this manner, she encouraged and made possible their move to France. She did that against the anxious objections of the rest of the family, who were loath to envision the peril that seemed to be awaiting them. It must have been a very difficult time for my parents. In later years, when I would occasionally try to talk to my mother about some of the stress and pain I had experienced in my own life, she would silence me with a wave of her hand and a slightly dismissive "What do *you* know of real pain?"

Back in her homeland, her concern for her children took a backseat. We were in Switzerland, after all, and were safe from the raging war engulfing all of Europe. We were safe from Germany's specific hunt for people like me. I had found shelter in my mother's childhood home. When we think of Switzerland nowadays, we picture watches, cheese, chocolate, and hidden bank accounts. Back then it was the rock of refuge in the stormy, fiery sea that was war-torn Europe leading up to and during World War II. Access to this protected haven was difficult to reach; it was barred to most.

Swiss Jews of means already had left the country, some for Palestine and others for the United States or South America. Those who remained comprised a small, shrunken community that had lost most of its successful members and leaders. The population increased with the arrival of various foreigners, who were classified into a number of categories: First there were Jews and non-Jews, then immigrants who had arrived with valid (albeit gradually expiring) papers. Then there were the refugees who had managed to cross the borders illegally, as well as a variety of ex-combatants and ex-forced laborers.

The foreigners who made it past Switzerland's borders were grateful to have escaped what, for most, would have been certain death. Stories abounded about people who were expelled across the Swiss border into German territory and then immediately shot. News about the horrors committed by the Nazi regime trickled in, vague and rumor-like, lacking in specificity, and probably disbelieved and unaccepted, as they simply were too awful to bear. News from the front was catastrophic: most foreigners' experience combined gratitude with an ever-present basic hum of fear and despair, as any moment might bring mortal danger. Nevertheless, time also constricted into ordinary daily life.

From a distance, in the occasional letters she sent from France, my mother encouraged me to make friends with the children of the affluent families who had been friends in her youth. I learned quickly that those doors were closed to me. On one occasion, following a particularly friendly moment at school, one of my classmates invited me to a party at her house for Saturday afternoon. The following day she sought me out and, with embarrassment, told me that her parents had forbidden her to bring a Jew into their home. That was a rare moment of explicitness, the other children simply never offered invitations or company. These blatant, hostile, and prejudicial incidents were not ubiquitous, but occurred often enough.

Throughout the seven years I attended school in the small, static town of St. Gallen, verbal attacks against me, both as innuendo and more directly, were not infrequent. A teacher of German literature might address me in class with rising passion and anger: "Here you sit, a parasite on the world, while our German brethren are being slaughtered by the Asiatic hordes in Russia." Another teacher might say, in a friendlier tone, "You are all right now, but one can never tell when the Jew will poke out."

In my early school days, I made friends with children from working-class families. The two girls who befriended me had hardly any family at all. Myrta was the only child of a single mother (her father was never mentioned, and there was the impression that he had been in their lives briefly, if at all). Myrta's mother was a seamstress who supported her own aged and infirm mother as well as her daughter. It was Myrta's job to clean house and help with cooking. Once a week, on Saturdays, she scrubbed the wooden plank floors of their two-room apartment on her hands and knees. She was only allowed out to play after the place was spotless. I met her mother and grandmother briefly, but they evinced little interest in me.

My other friend, Edith, was an orphan, who seemed securely loved by her two older brothers. An aunt, who was a deaf-mute, kept house for them. I visited Edith often, and had a little crush on Eugene, the older of her two brothers, who, at 16, was handsome, bathed in an air of adult responsibility. We spent weekends together wandering the hills surrounding St. Gallen. There were no other diversions: no television, no radio available beyond news programs. There were evening movies, which you could only attend if you were over 16 years old. Just as I reached 16, the age was raised to 18.

Although I was fond of my two friends and felt no political animosity coming from them, I was not at ease with them. I think they were personally reserved in a way I had not been used to. Each had a family life that defined them as damaged outsiders; they were ashamed of that and so they tended to keep private. Perhaps my status as a differently damaged child allowed our connection to flourish, at least for a time.

Within a few months, a tragedy befell Edith. Since she was an orphan, she had been assigned a guardian, whom she visited weekly, and of whom she seemed in awe. One week she missed school, and rumors of some mysterious evil doings began to attach themselves to her name. It turned out that her guardian had been molesting her, and a court hearing removed him from his appointment. Edith returned to school, shamed and shunned. When we talked, she confided that she felt the loss of her protector rather than relief at being rescued from her abuser. "He would bathe me and dry me all over and especially between my legs," she told me in a wistful manner, as though she missed him.

My friendships with both Myrta and Edith lasted only a few months. Toward the end of my first Swiss school year, I had caught up a bit with the class work, and my difference in class background asserted itself. While my two friends opted for the two-year program at the vocational finishing school, I turned toward the intellectually challenging path of higher education. My grades, while acceptable, still reflected my foreign culture and unfamiliar language. My teacher was willing to recommend my application to the secondary school, but the pre-university gymnasium was out of the question.

The Talhof (loosely translated as Valley Estate) was a nonacademic finishing school for young ladies. Swiss public schools were academically demanding, and the curriculum core was classic academics, supplemented with art, music, gym, and household skills of cleaning, sewing, and cooking. We spent most of the day in school, from 7 am to 3 or 4 pm. By this time, I had found a marginal place in Swiss teenage society and a central place in the hearts of a few friends. As my German improved, I kept pace comfortably with my classmates. In my second year in Talhof, three of us decided to aim for a transfer from the fourth year of Talhof to the fifth year of the academic gymnasium.

Whatever their anti-Semitic attitudes might have been, the Talhof teachers put together a program and tutored the three of us over three years in daily, private lessons to prepare us for the exam. We clearly had to learn much that was not in the regular syllabus of a girls' finishing school. As the time of the exams arrived, the three of us were well prepared and firmly bonded in friendship. We took written tests in certain subjects. In addition, I was tested orally, separately, and at great length. It turned out that my test performance had surpassed that of my friends. This was very fortunate, because it forced the gymnasium to accept all three of us, despite their reluctance to let in any more girls. They could not very well accept one Jew and fail two Swiss. That's how I arrived at the graduation of the gymnasium at the age of only 17½. I needed personal permission from the Federal Department of Education to graduate before the mandatory age of 18.

During my years at school, many horrific things had happened in the outside world: Czechoslovakia was betrayed by France and England, her Western allies. In Munich in 1938, Chamberlain and Daladier surrendered to Hitler. Czechoslovakia had been peeled like a banana; the fortifications along its very long borders, which stretched from west to east, were ceded to the German Reich, and the country was left amputated and defenseless. Slovakia was lopped off to become an independent Axis-supporting state, and the Eastern tail, Carpatho-Russia, was donated to the Soviet Union.

The catastrophic fate of Central Europe at the time of World War II had begun to reach my native village and my family. The village itself was on the border between the Sudetenland, as the lopped-off elliptical rim was referred to, and the Czech Protectorate, as the German-occupied Bohemia and Moravia were known. Jews and some Czechs had left on foot to get away from the occupying German army. Some ran into trouble at the Protectorate border because they were considered German. Jewishness had not yet become a trump-everything identity in the eyes of the Czechs.

My father's family, including my parents, became refugees, fleeing from Miroslav, which had been ceded to Germany, to Brno, the nearby capital of Moravia. Entry into what would become the Protectorate was first denied them because they were considered German. But in the end, my grandparents made it across, together with the rest of the family. The upheaval was unexpected, the disaster beyond imagination. My grandfather, then 83 years old, lost his mind and died within three weeks. My parents, propelled by my mother's foresight and clarity, helped by the fact that she was a newcomer to Miroslav and hence perhaps less fundamentally rooted to it in her soul, soon escaped to Paris via the exit permit they had obtained and the job there that my father had been offered.

From that point, my parents' fate differed from that of the rest of the family. They were the only ones to survive the war, the others falling victim to the murder of Jews in a number of extermination camps. The first to die was probably my cousin Annemarie, who was shipped to a German Wehrmacht brothel and was reputed to have lasted barely three months. My Uncle Kurt and his wife, Frieda, died in Buchenwald in 1941 and 1942. My grandmother died in Terezin in the early 1940s while my Aunt Hilda was shipped from Terezin to Auschwitz with the very last Czech transport in July 1944 and subsequently gassed.

Of course, I knew none of this at the time. I only knew that the home I had left for a usual summer vacation had become invisible, and no longer manifested in any way. Almost overnight, I forgot how to speak Czech.

I also forgot all the sexual information and misinformation I had begun accumulating from the time I was three, watching animals and through conversations and conjectures with other ill-informed friends. I discovered the odd linkage of the Czech language and early sexual memories, both of which had been repressed in the dark years when German victory seemed likely. After the German army suffered some severe losses, it became possible to foresee their defeat. It was then that I slowly recovered my Czech language, most notably by recalling an earlier memorized long, romantic poem by Karel Hynek Macha, entitled *Maj* (May).

At this same time, all kinds of childish, sexual hypotheses began to reappear, such as: What happens to a sperm when it enters a wife and produces a child as compared to when it enters a non-wife and produces no child and maybe an illness? How does a kiss transport a sperm from the man to the woman? How does adultery lead to a deadly infection for the woman? A woman in the village had developed septicemia, probably from the swimming pool, but also was rumored to have carried on a love affair. The two events became linked in our early sex explorers' minds.

In Paris, my parents had found an apartment and my father went to work for a company that had been his client. Mother wrote admiringly of the owner, Mr. B., and his elegant lifestyle. She was particularly impressed when a white-gloved butler served dinner at their house. They had begun to settle into a modest life. My mother was, for the first time, without any household help. She was cooking and shining my father's shoes. There was a letter or two giving fleeting thoughts about whether my brother and I might be reunited with our parents. Then, in June 1940, the Maginot Line was breached. France surrendered and the German army occupied Paris.

Images of long columns of refugees fleeing toward the south of France became familiar after the war. I don't remember what we, in insular and isolated Switzerland, knew about this. I learned from my mother that Mr. B. sent a car and chauffeur for my parents and they made the trip south in style, ending in Nîmes, where he had another factory and another job for my father. My mother remarked on their good fortune in passing, barely or not at all commenting on the streams of refugees fleeing south on foot that they surely must have passed.

Some time later, when my parents considered seeking a visa to the United States, my mother approached the U.S. consulate in Marseille. Desperate people waited in long lines, apparently extending for blocks, for their turn to see the consul. Many had camped there for days. My mother briefly noticed them and wondered to herself what they were doing there as she walked down the middle of the two lines, straight into the consulate, and got to speak to the consul immediately. It turned out that waiting time for a U.S. visa for people of my parents' places of birth (Moravia for my father and Poland/Lithuania for my mother) was years and years. My mother considered it hopeless, and so did not bother applying.

I can't be sure how true this story of my mother's self-serving blindness is, but it is consistent with the way she always functioned in the world. Unpleasant truths were best unacknowledged and wish often took precedence over some literal reality. Some years later, when I decided to terminate an unwanted and unfeasible pregnancy, my mother lovingly took care of me while I recovered for a few days. That did not stop her from insisting, two years later, that I was still a virgin. My mother's ability to construct reality as best served her infuriated me, and probably pushed me toward a profession where I could find out how things really were. In a sense, my mother had the last laugh, as psychotherapy, my chosen profession, has become the art of creating perceptions that make life possible. When I was unhappy, my mother would say, "Put on a smile, and inner happiness will follow." How dismissed I felt at those times, and how detached and unsympathetic she appeared to me. And yet, according to current research, how right she was.

My mother had been the apple of her father's eye. She was the oldest of three surviving children; my grandmother lost two sons, one in infancy to diphtheria and one after 12 harrowing years of searching for a physician to cure his cystic fibrosis. The family had come from Grodno, a town that was alternately Lithuanian, Russian, or Polish. They were Jewish Orthodox, Litvaks in the Jewish nomenclature, or "black Orthodox" of the cerebral rather than the ecstatic Chassidic bent. My mother asserted her autonomy and independence of spirit when she married my extremely assimilated father.

My grandmother had, in fact, attended a secular gymnasium, and perhaps she had encouraged my mother in her studies. As I reconstruct parts of the history, my grandmother, at 26 years of age, was a little old for a bride of that era. Even in old age, when I knew her, Grandmother was a handsome woman, but she did not carry herself as a loved and cherished wife. I think the marriage to my grandfather may have been beneath her station. In spite of her position as a formidable matriarch within the larger family, Grandmother was unhappy and lonely.

My grandfather may well have had a roving eye. At the very least, he was not particularly devoted to his wife. Instead, he lavished attention on his eldest daughter, my mother. He would take her on vacations; he would select beautiful jewelry and choice fabrics for her dresses; nothing was too good for her. Growing up, my mother took the role of the *bridge child*, a term coined by the family therapist Dr. Judith Landau. She was the child who found herself in the position of helping the family, whose culture had been shaped in the ghetto society of Eastern Europe, to transition into the more open social structure of Switzerland. My mother was only three years old when the family settled in St. Gallen. She acculturated quickly, and with plenty of charm, beauty, and brains, easily won a respectable place in St. Gallen society.

Neither she nor her younger sister, Fanny, ever found a way into their mother's heart. Each escaped the family as young as possible, my mother into an early marriage, my aunt into a job at a girls' boarding school. My grandmother's unconditional love was reserved for her youngest child, my Uncle Leo. He remained devoted to his mother until her death. He was a lifelong bachelor, and he continued to live with his mother until the time came when she lived with him, in the house that he inherited after his father's death.

Uncle Leo became the head of the family. He tried his hand at business but had neither the patience nor interest required to build up the bra manufacturing business, alluringly named Sinabel. The company crept along for as long as his mother and sister Fanny were alive. Immediately following his sister's death, Leo liquidated the business, sold the family house, and cut his ties to St. Gallen. Finally freed from family obligations, he moved to Zurich. There he constructed an agreeable bachelor's life, maintaining low-key involvements with members of his extended family. Although Leo remained a bachelor, he never lacked glamorous girlfriends, all of whom adored him.

He looked after his mother with tenderness and devotion all her life. When the war deposited my brother and me into their house, Leo looked after the two of us. Among the adults in my family, Uncle Leo most consistently behaved as a supportive and loving parent to me. He helped with my homework and was always ready to listen and to offer advice. Uncle Leo's concern was especially sustaining after I became an adult. He was encouraging and loving; he spoiled me. He noted my birthdays with valuable and thoughtful gifts: a gold watch, a gold bracelet, 50 long-stemmed gilded roses for my fiftieth birthday, and a large collection of Hermès scarves.

He also supported his sister, my Aunt Fanny. My grandmother had ordered Fanny home from her position at the boarding school to help in the household once my brother and I were living with them. This had disastrous consequences for Fanny, who had dismissed the idea of being a housewife. She had a brief romance with a man whom her mother declared unsuitable. There were rumors about him and another marriage, either ended by a divorce, thus making him less desirable, or not ended at all, thus making him completely unacceptable. That personal misadventure hit Fanny hard, and only added more unhappiness to an already heavy burden of resentments and grudges. When she was teaching, Fanny had been able to put those corrosive feelings behind her. She brought love to her students, who adored her in return. She became their favorite "Aunt Fanny."

Fanny did have a few close women friends. A particularly dear one was named Claire; she immigrated to America in the late 1930s. Before Claire's departure, she and Fanny traveled to Spain for a vacation. The memory of that trip, of another world and time, brought joy and vitality into Fanny's face. She felt the warmth of the Spanish sun, saw the glow of the orange trees, smelled white jasmine blossoms, tapped her feet to the rhythm of the flamenco, threw her head back, and proudly straightened her shoulders. Her fingers snapped the castanets she had brought home to chilly grey Switzerland as a captive token (*Pfand*) of possible happiness. Sometimes Fanny pretended she was draping a mantilla over her head and shoulders. She would bend her waist backward, and for a moment looked both imperious and seductive as she risked a few dance steps.

Quickly the updraft of her energy ebbed, and she reverted to the low-key, depressed mien in which she dwelled. Once again she returned to the reality of her life, back in the oppressive house she had fled. And now she was saddled with housework and two children who were not hers. Aunt Fanny found herself in a situation of unappreciated, unvalued, and criticized servitude. She was back in her parental home very much against her will. Yet she went all out to try to be a good parent to my brother and me. It was a difficult and often thankless task. By then my brother was 20 years old; he treated her somewhat disrespectfully as a challenging equal.

On the other hand, I was a truly disobedient child. I openly challenged her authority. I yelled, "You're not my mother. I don't have to do anything you tell me to do!" Nevertheless, Fanny and I did a lot of things together. We took a vacation together to St. Moritz, hiking around the Hahnensee, having tea at Pontresina.

She managed to get me into the bar at the Palace Hotel, then and for many subsequent years, the absolute seat of glamour and wealth in the Engadine. Sitting in the bar during the *Dansant* (afternoon tea dance), I became mesmerized by the carryings-on on the dance floor. A beautiful young woman in high heels, wearing a décolleté dress, danced and flirted with a handsome uniformed young officer. I imagined, or perhaps observed, in my 14-year-old mind, that the dance became increasingly passionate. I saw it ending in bed. I was thrilled at this forbidden glimpse, even though my glimpse could well have been the creation of imagination alone.

I did love Fanny. In some ways we were like friends, but I also resented her. As Fanny's mental health deteriorated from depression into what ultimately became bouts of paranoid psychosis, I was ashamed of her. We shared a room, and I became aware of her confusion and loneliness; her need for a friend; her battle with her mother, who treated her like a second-class maid; and her attempts to pull herself together and claim a shred of a life of her own. Increasingly, there were dramatic failures to ward off collapse. She spent days and weeks sorting textiles, lengths of lace and embroidery and cottons left over after my grandfather's business had dissolved. These remnants were stored in an attic room. Fanny would spend entire days folding, packing and repacking, labeling and relabeling, stacking, reorganizing.

At other times she directed her unhappiness at the family: at her mother, who seemed emotionally disengaged from her; her brother, who earned his favorite son status by living with and taking care of his mother; and finally, me, and less so my brother, the two albatrosses the war had tied around her neck, shutting the door to any chance of an escape from the family. She would carry on a loud, long plaint, a liturgy of the wrongs done to her while she had tried so hard to be kind and do the right thing. Her wailings recounted insults, hurts, and injustices; she recited the details to an unnamed audience, or perhaps it was meant for the world at large. Sometimes she wandered from room to room, slamming doors as she went, leaving the lingering sounds of her heartrending, unlovely song, which could last for hours.

Fanny chainsmoked, always holding a lit cigarette in the corner of her mouth. Her cheek, nose, and fingers were by this time stained an indelible tobacco brown. At the end of an agitated episode, utterly exhausted, she would fall into a deep sleep. At those moments, I felt love and tenderness for her; I remembered how much time she had devoted to me when I first arrived in St. Gallen, and the trips we took together.

Shortly after World War II ended, I received my Matura, which was a prerequisite for enrollment in a university. I left my grandmother's household to move to Zurich and enter medical school. My brother moved away also. My father had obtained a working permit to head a lab in a perfume factory in Duebendorf, a small town outside of Zurich, so my parents moved there as well. My mother's family, who had opened their home to us and changed their lives for us, had a quiet life again. But they were also left bereft and isolated.

Fanny had tried to bring some life into the house by mentoring a young refugee girl. I remember meeting her and experiencing mixed feelings of jealousy and relief. Soon after we left, my grandmother died. She was 86. Being an Orthodox Jew, she refused pain medication for an intestinal blockage and suffered in agony for three weeks, screaming in pain. I was not informed of her illness, or of the funeral, until afterward.

Before her marriage, my mother was a Swiss citizen, but she lost that citizenship when she married my father, who was a foreigner. During the time my parents were in France, first in Paris and then in Nîmes, Mother's former citizenship (or perhaps her friendship with some influential Swiss people) allowed her to obtain permission to visit my brother and me in Switzerland for a week, once a year. Our father was not allowed to visit. I have no memory of these visits, other than the anger I felt toward my mother at the time, and then let loose on Aunt Fanny after my mother's departure. I do have a great deal of guilt about the way I treated Aunt Fanny.

I stayed in Switzerland another four years before finding my way to America. Two months after I had reached New York, Aunt Fanny killed herself. With her condition continuing to deteriorate, she had taken an overdose of pills. She timed her suicide so that her brother, with whom she had continued to live after their mother's death, would find her on the morning of his birthday. When he and I spoke about her fate years later, he said there had been no effective medication to help her. The only choice would have been to commit her to an asylum. It had been against his religious belief to imprison her against her will.

I had lived with Aunt Fanny from the age of 11 to almost 18, and truly loved her. I watched her change from a charming, albeit tense and nervous woman, into an increasingly unhappy, symptom-ridden, often out-of-control person. Because I had watched the evolution of mental illness so up close, my later work in a state hospital for schizophrenic patients was less frightening to me. What had happened to Fanny enabled me to establish connections with these patients when other clinicians confronted only walls.

The Story of Geigei

By now the story of Geigei has been in my mind for a long time. It has a beginning, a middle, and an end, but at this point in my life, it lacks a sharp or specific meaning. I do not want the story, or Geigei himself, to become a mere vignette from the distant past. I hope the story's tendrils become visible as they inform the present, as everything in the past adds its hue, wisdom, and implications to every experience that ensues. This, then, is the story of Geigei.

At its simplest, it is the story of a student's infatuation with her teacher, and his response to her. The attraction between an older man and a young girl was an attraction unmindful of rules and boundaries, marked by risk-taking, misuse of authority, power, and charisma. It is about the bliss of being noticed, affirmed, and responded to by someone appreciated as special and as a superior. The nourishing flow of learning and its excitement merges into love, romance, and longing. What kinds of dreams for a future does it seed? More than anything, it is learning about how to love from a disallowed, secret position and then feeling larger than life, exceptional, and yet discounted, all at once.

One day, when I was in my mid-fifties, an airmail envelope arrived at my home. I did not recognize the handwriting, but the envelope's general appearance was familiar, with its cheerful red and blue zebra-striped trim, the upper-right corner covered in stamps, the Swiss stamps that combined iconic landscapes with elegant graphics. Whenever I saw an airmail envelope peeking out from a stack of plain everyday U.S. business-colored mail, a spark of warmth ignited. As I opened this envelope, a photograph, in the formal passport style, fell onto my table. The accompanying note was addressed to me:

Dear Dr. L:
I felt sure that you would like to have the enclosed photograph, taken a few weeks before Dr. S. died in his sleep of a heart attack. As you know, he had heart surgery a couple of years ago, and was living on borrowed time. We were close friends. He would come to my house for dinner, and I did my best to look after him. His last years were spent in serenity and contentment. I found your address among his papers and remembered that you had been dear to him.
With best regards....

I looked at the picture. It was of Geigei. He did not look much different from the way I remembered him at 35, except that his features were more delicate. It was as if an overlay of thin, dusty, veined paper had been placed on the lens of the camera, changing the texture of his face, giving him fine lines, a velvety surface, blurred contours. If I imagined a slightly sharper definition, some plumping up of his face, I could see him just as I had that first time. He was standing in front of our class of 16 girls in ninth grade and the first-year general division of Talhof, the women's high school. He stood ramrod straight, a bit stork-like, long-limbed, his small roundish head propped up by a tightly fitting bow tie. His brown eyes were large, round, and fishlike, his dark hair side-parted and trimmed short like a good altar boy's. He talked to us in a strong but soft and somehow seductive voice. He addressed us as *young women,* accompanying his words with expressive hand gestures.

His hands were his pièce de résistance, his seduction tools, his trance inducers. Large, square, yet delicate, they promised the skill of a surgeon, the resonant touch of a pianist, the evocative power of an orchestra conductor. He posed them in front of himself, in full view. They were the portals through which your glance first passed when you looked into his eyes as he spoke.

We were all expected to sit attentively, with our faces turned toward him. This expectation met no resistance. He sat behind his desk, his elbows propped up as his hands found each other in the middle, just at chin and mouth level. At other times, he paced the room between the rows of our writing desks. He would dictate to us or watch us as we wrote a composition. When he wanted to get a student writer's attention, he would touch her shoulder lightly with the rubber tip of a pencil.

"To touch your shoulder with my hand," he explained, "would be much too arousing for delicate young women like you."

I don't know whether my classmates saw what I saw, heard what I heard, felt what I felt. They were good Swiss girls: solid, well-behaved, and sober. Geigei's promises of enchantment did not seem to resonate with them as they did me. I was a foreigner in Switzerland, an emigrant, and a Jew. I was like a poodle among Swiss mountain dogs, a yellow canary among brown warblers. I was far from home, I was displaced and separated from my parents. It was 1942, and often I was frightened for my life. The German armies were winning the war, winning the world, and holding Switzerland in its tight vise, surrounding it completely. Austria had been annexed in 1938. Italy had relinquished an identity separate from its Axis partners.

I was sad. I felt lost, and dreamed of a future in a faraway land, never to be seen, never to be reached. Yet, perhaps because of such enormous uncertainty in my life, I seemed lighter, more enterprising, more life-seeking than my cautious classmates. I felt they disapproved of me, and that they also were a bit frightened of me; their parents didn't want them becoming too close to me. They were friendly enough. I understood they considered me as belonging to another category of being. They dwelled in the certainty of their world, where they knew the rules and followed them. And on the whole, those rules served them well. As women they would find their places, their husbands, and have their children. They would not find the right to vote, to work if they married, a place in the public world, but they would be sheltered in a family. In that world of women, children, church, and neighbors, they would always be welcome.

For me, there were no such expectations. By the set of rules applied to me, I would soon be dead, or at least no longer very visibly alive. People like me were destined for extermination in the camps. At best, some of us were able to find a marginal escape from the rules.

A few of my classmates bridged the chasm, and we became friends. In life's daily doings and in our talks, we found commonality. Over the years, we have alternately envied and pitied each other, admired what the others could do, and were sad about what we didn't have and glad of what was ours. Despite our vast differences, a few of these friendships have lasted our entire lives.

Among these black clouds of war and tragedy, nevertheless, teenage yearnings asserted themselves. The daily exposure to Geigei's voice; his hands; his wonderful introduction to ancient history, literature and poetry and to his philosophy of life slipped seamlessly into my soul, into my mind, and under my skin. He taught history and German language; he included in our education what one might describe as life science and practical philosophy. He talked to us about our lives, about who we were and who we might become. These were topics not mentioned by anyone else. They were among the unspoken mysteries of the adult world.

At times, when we had worked well, he rewarded us by reading poetry or short stories. I particularly remember one novella by Rudolf Binding, about a woman who, after her husband's death from cholera, dons her husband's cloak and continues his daily walks below the windows of his also-ill lover, waving to her in his characteristic way, thus leading to her recovery. The title of the tearful tale was *Der Opfergang,* or *The Sacrificial Journey.* I haven't read it since my school days, but what remains with me is the wife's generosity in overcoming her jealousy and blending her identity with her husband's. Fractional reoccurrence of this pattern at various times later in my own life creates a ripple of memories.

He explained to us that the name, "Geigei," was his fraternity *vulgo,* or daily name. It was supposed to have derived from a Chinese word for "dreamer," "romantic." He clearly loved being referred to thusly by students and fellow teachers. He awakened my own romantic dreamer and turned dreams into action, albeit timid and weak action. Every two weeks, we were given a composition theme to write about and turn in to him. By that time, I was comfortable expressing myself in German. While to this day the Czech language remains my first access reservoir for certain emotions, German had become my medium for philosophical talk, drama, and debate, as well as the wistful longings of adolescence.

Newly comfortable in the German language, I turned neutral, objective compositions into personal statements. I described how my eyes hurt themselves against the foreshortened view of Switzerland, as compared to the vast plains of my native Czechoslovakia. In delicate, neat, almost printed, red-penciled handwriting came the return *love letter* from Geigei: "Look up to the heavens, dear K., there you will find all the expanse you need." For me, those words were as the first note from a beloved. I stroked them, read them 20 ways and back, interpreted them as the promise of a heaven where we might meet. Although always veiled and indirect, my requests for his participation in my world persisted, and usually received an answer: a few personal, caring, delicate words, in addition to, unfailingly, the top grade in the class. For almost a year, my sub rosa, perhaps one-sided, perhaps shared, love connection with Geigei continued via biweekly homework, daily classes, and my hourly (no, continuous) dreams of him. I had neither the wit nor the inventiveness nor perhaps even the desire to change it, to take it further. I was warmed by what existed and was content in my unfulfilled longing.

The Czechoslovakia of that day, today's Slovakia and Czech Republic, was by no means akin to the western plains. In fact, a return visit some 20 years ago showed me that they were hilly and wooded. About half a mile from my native village, a totally flat, small landscape asserted itself. "Miroslav was built on a drained swamp," a distant cousin explained to me in a voice full of disdain. It was a disdain for the ancient days, for the then-impending collapse of the Communist government, and for my mother's foreign and bourgeois ways. He had been the family hothead and a teenage Communist, who, when imprisoned in a concentration camp, was there as a political prisoner rather than a Jew. He was one of only two people in his immediate family to survive the camps. The other was his then 78-year-old grandmother. My dreams of the freedom of the vast plains of my homeland that I nourished as the closeness and steepness of the Swiss mountains confined and oppressed me had sprung from a small anomaly: an ugly, unwanted swamp.

I spent school hours and homework time with the Swiss students. I seldom visited their homes, and barely knew their parents. They came to my house only on rare occasions and stayed briefly. I did have a best friend, a somewhat unofficial friend. I am tempted to say that I had a best friend on the side. Elly was a few months older than I, but in a class behind me. She was precocious, flirtatious, pretty. She was a Viennese Jew of refugee status, one level below mine. She was also my brother Fred's girlfriend, nine years his junior. In our relationship, I had the status, money, and brains; she had the looks and success with boys.

Often in the morning, she would leave her house early and walk past the school in order to pick me up so we could walk back to school together. At the end of the school day, we often ended up at my house, where my grandmother was usually able to procure enough food to provide healthy, delicious vespers: a jug of milk, perhaps even a bar of chocolate. We would devour it, and then curl up on my bed and talk, talk, talk. One of the problems between us was created by our unequal sophistication in sexual matters. She had an adult boyfriend, my brother, and I had never held hands with a boy, at least not since leaving Czechoslovakia at age 10. Before that time, I had lots of boyfriends starting from when I was about 3. In my childhood village kids hung out together and played all sorts of games, children's and adults' games. In Switzerland, I had reacquired childlike innocence.

My unknowingness, my inexperience in the events between the sexes, was very frustrating to Elly, because it naturally limited my level of participation in our talks. I could listen but could not respond from any personal experience. Furthermore, I had very little romantic interest of my own to add. Perhaps it was this imbalance of knowledge, this inequality of standing in life, that forced me to unpack my Geigei story. Was it fantasy competing with reality, stretching to equal it? I suspect I told her about him after she described some intense experiences with Fred. I must have felt I had to put something on the table to up my ante. "You know, for a year, I have been in love with Geigei, and I believe he likes me too." She perked up, listened carefully, and then became animated. With a look of compassion, she said, "You poor dear, how awful. You must tell him!"

I don't remember what I felt then. I imagine it was a mixture of shock, excitement, and awe at her daring, compared to my timidity. She encouraged me to cross a line between two realms that must not be crossed. I likely looked confused, reluctant, and doubtful: in any event, I was not about to act. I remember clearly that she gave herself a push, sat up, and declared, "I will do it for you." The next day, she sought me out at school, and whispered, "I spoke to Geigei and told him I must talk to him. I will walk him home after school. Go home and wait for me." Walking Geigei home after school was not unusual. It was like going to see the teacher after class. He lived a 15-minute walk up the hill behind the school. His habits were predictable, and he often walked home with this student or that. I don't know why, but I had never offered to walk him home. I may have assumed only girls who lived in his direction, the better part of town, were his accompanying walkers. More likely, though, the thought didn't cross my mind. On that day, when Elly walked Geigei home after school to have a serious talk about what was in the heart of one of his students, I was at home in a fever of excitement, malaise, anxiety, hope, and impatience.

She came in only a little later than I had expected her. Her eyes sparkled, and her cheeks were flushed. Her smile seemed cheerful and friendly and did not warn me of anything. She jumped on the bed next to me, snuggled in, and said happily, reassuringly, "Yes, I told him." And then, as I was still struggling to recognize and order my changed emotions, she added, almost as an afterthought, a naughty, apologetic little snicker. "I told him the whole story, but in the end, I told him I was the one who was in love with him." I don't recall if I grasped the depth of her betrayal. Instantly, I had slipped from being the central character in my story to that of a barely significant bystander. I was now a mere witness, a confidant to a story I suddenly no longer owned.

Was I also a bit pleased to learn that she had cheated, at least emotionally, on her boyfriend, my brother? Perhaps I had been angry with him for appropriating my girlfriend as his lover? Perhaps I felt sorry for both of us, since Elly had hurt us both with one sly act of deception. Perhaps I had all these reactions, but I hardly had a chance to define them.

"I made a date to see him next week, after the city council meeting lets out. You'll have to help me get out of the house. You know my mother doesn't let me go out after dinner unless it's with you!" Without fully realizing it, I was now being moved to a supporting role. I became the facilitator, the shield, the cover story. Did I hate her? Did I feel bitterly betrayed? I don't remember. Breaking off our friendship did not cross my mind. I adjusted to the only available place for me, as the friend of the bride, so to speak. Perhaps this place was familiar to me. In a sense I had already been in that position by being her confidant in her relationship with my brother. We set about planning the event and subsequent ones that occurred almost weekly, in meticulous detail. I had to call for her, wait for her, and deliver her home. What was I to do while she was on her date with Geigei? We decided I would draw in one of our Swiss classmates, a serious, loyal, discreet girl. I came to believe she also harbored a crush on Geigei, but one that was much less articulated than mine.

Cordelia was the eldest of nine children. Her parents, her soft-spoken quiet father and her mother, a long-suffering, child-burdened saint, had been missionaries in India. They continued to live devoutly and modestly, leading a ministry to a small missionary sect.

Cordelia lived in sparse circumstances, helped out at home, and looked at the world with resignation and from somewhat of a distance. Later in life, she became an expert medical lab technician and eventually chief of a federal laboratory. She never married and was adored by and remained devoted to her boss for a lifetime. She helped look after her siblings' many children. She was almost undone once or twice by unhappy, exploitative affairs with sleazy, lightweight men. Cordelia was my devoted, virtuous, earnest, deeply religious friend.

Two or three years after our joint Geigei adventures, Cordelia suffered the ignominy of the revelation of her father's dalliances with parishioners. It led to his public humiliation and dismissal, and the family's move to another town. Barred from all spiritual positions, he tried to support his large family on the meager wages of a printer. Had Cordelia's future always been written on her face? It is unknowable, but I could not have picked a better assistant in my secret and sorrowful task.

Cordelia was a willing ear, a companion who comforted me, and who could share my thrill watching events unfold. She derived satisfaction from the services she rendered. Not unimportantly, she was my alibi, which made the evening getaways possible and plausible in my own family. To my family, Cordelia was serious, reliable, and safe. She dubbed our doings "Novel 35," which was Geigei's age. I believe she drew some vicarious excitement from what we were doing. She never explicitly acknowledged her crush on Geigei, but blushed and breathed hard whenever we spoke of him.

Elly filled us in on some of the details, generalities mostly, as the three of us made our way home after each date. I dropped Elly off at her house and said good night to her mother. Next, Cordelia said good-bye to me at my house. She did not have too far to go to her own home. The next day, Elly would fill me in on the more intimate details of her times with Geigei, which I can no longer remember. I do recall the logistical details of how we got Elly to the assignation, and how Geigei covered his tracks in his life: the late arrivals home after meetings, slipping out of the theatre before the last act. Cordelia and I became familiar with the dark streets of our little town, unlit by street lamps during the general blackout of the war.

Geigei was a colonel in the Swiss army. A few months after he and Elly had begun dating, he was called up for active duty. He left to join his division, promising to write to my friend in care of my address, since her parents did not believe in the privilege of postal privacy. Elly's mother checked all her possessions, as well as any letters she received. Within a few days, a pristine white envelope with his delicate handwriting, so known to me from my compositions for class, arrived at my home, addressed to me. I opened it and read with joy and trembling a note that might have gone as follows:

Dear K:
   The weather is turning cool; the fall colors are brilliant. I miss my teaching and my students. Will you be kind enough to give the enclosed note to your friend?
   Sincerely,
   OS

There would be a second envelope, folded to fit into the first one, with Elly's name printed on it. As we both breathlessly opened the inner, secret compartment, the heart of the matter, we would catch our breath as the most beautiful of all love letters was revealed. It might have gone:

My darling Elly:
   As the moon rose in the sky tonight, my heart extended its wings toward it, hoping it would touch your tender dreams up there. My days are enriched knowing you, etc, etc, etc.

We would read mine, we would read hers, we would get sad, we would get hot, and then we got down to the business at hand, namely, composing the answers. We were, after all, writing to our German teacher. And I was a better student than Elly. So, we did the logical thing and collaborated. First, I would write a cordial, brief note, such as:

Dear Dr. S.,
Thank you for your kind and friendly note. School is good, although we miss you and your replacement is not very good. I gave your note to my friend.
With best regards,
K.

Once this simple task was done, the act of creation followed next. I sat down to write a love letter, which easily flowed out of my heart, but in words Elly might have used. I did not yet know about Cyrano or similar substitute courtships. We thought this was our unique invention. It wasn't even an invention; it just seemed the natural thing to do.

So I would write:

Your sweet words sustain me. I see the moon only through my tears of missing you every waking moment. I fall asleep with your face looking at mine. I awaken to the touch of your hands.

After the love letter was finished, Elly would copy it in her handwriting. I don't believe she ever changed a word.

When our vacation time came, we made plans to go visit Geigei in the field. We knew the 8th division, which he commanded, was stationed somewhere near the old monastery town of Einsiedeln, about 80 kilometers away. Today, the trip is a scant hour by car, but in those days, preparations rivaled an expedition to unknown lands.

First, we had to find an alibi that would stand up to family scrutiny. Second, we needed money. Third, as an emigrant (me) and a refugee (Elly), we did not have permission to travel beyond the city limits. The journey was illegal, illicit, and financed on a shoestring. We wrangled an invitation from my English teacher, a lovely woman whose family had a house in Lucerne with a spare room. This represented a legitimate, if fictitious, destination, as well as a reason why not much money was needed. Neither family would, nor probably could afford to send us on a costly trip, and certainly would not allow us to go without the necessary resources. We had to show a plan that required no resources, so during the weeks preceding the intended trip, I, in my function as money provider to Elly, saved, scrimped, and stole change out of my aunt's pocketbook, finally accumulating a bare minimum.

We had to take the train. On the Swiss railroad in those days, minors under 16 and an accompanying adult could share a cheap ticket. The details of the deal are no longer clear in my memory. I do remember that, although I was three months Elly's junior (she was about to turn 16), I looked older, and was appropriately attired. I traveled as the accompanying adult. The conductor looked us over but gave us no trouble, didn't ask to see any papers, and all passed well. In the late afternoon, we arrived in Einsiedeln. It had a magnificent cobbled square with a monumental, massive monastery in the town center, which appeared to contain half the town on a semicircle. Facing it stood the town's best hotel, the Schwanen, or Swan. It, too, seemed elegant, and, in memory, forms an architecturally intact unit with the square and monastery.

There were no guests in Swiss hotels during the war. There were no tourists, no visitors. The borders of the country were closed. The Schwanen was empty. Only the bar and sidewalk tables were active, where locals might stop by for a drink or a light meal. With an unconscious trust in fate and much nerve, we asked for a room and were given the best front room overlooking the somber, majestic square, with its dark, red stone lending warmth and depth to this lightless night. We had packed two tubes of sweet condensed milk and some crackers to sustain us, since our money had just about covered train fare and the hotel room.

We found ourselves in a strange, grown-up, dark world, far from home. Adventure and unknown dangers hung palpably in the air. The purpose of the trip, to visit my imaginary beloved, surged strongly from the fluid miasma of the evening. I became focused and obsessed with my love for this man in a way that I had not felt, since the day Elly had stolen my place. It was as though the intervening year had not happened. I loved him, he at least liked me, and I had come to see him. Elly, in the meantime, reacted to the situation in her own way. She thought it was fun, an occasion for flirting, and she shortly came upon a group of young officers whom she introduced to me. "The staff of the 8th division," she announced. "Dr. S. is their commander." After unsuccessfully trying to discourage us from visiting such an ancient man, they got word to him that two young ladies had come to see him and were waiting at the Schwanen.

Geigei arrived, walking in his usual measured manner, appearing first in dim silhouette, wearing riding boots, breeches, and a stiff-collared tunic, keeping his small head high. A cigarette for each of us, a carafe of light red wine, and we sat in silence. A walk was suggested up the dark hill to a bench that faced the statue of St. Benedict. It was dark. Our cigarettes glowed. When apartments are small and no cars exist, nature becomes the trysting place of those not lawfully wed to each other.

We walked arm in arm in arm, a slow, friendly amble up the hill, with one of the arms experiencing a disembodied awakening of physicality all on its own. I had never been this close to Geigei, or to any other man. The warmth and pulse of his arm through the barrier of his tunic sleeve was as alive as a naked body. It was my arm that felt his breath, fathomed his odor, and remembered a prior occasion when I had been an unseen observer of his arousal. During a year-end talent show, one of the rich, precocious, upper-class girls had danced a sensuous, steamy seduction to Ravel's Bolero. By happenstance, Geigei stood behind me in the audience, watching intently and breathing in rhythm with the dance, his body heat streamed toward me, packaged in the smell of maleness, cigar, and wine. I did not know him at the time but at 12 I was both seduced and possessed by his rhythm, his breath, and the music.

We sat on the bench, with my arm continuing its silent rapture, while the rest of me sat timid and awkward, wondering what would happen next. How was I to know that a poker of molten metal was being readied to be plunged into my heart, where it caused such total pain that I forgot who I was? Geigei let go of my arm, leaned away from me toward Elly, and kissed her. The next second, I was lying prone on the grass, alone, sobbing, not knowing where I was. I felt lost, adrift, cast off. After what seemed like days, a hand touched my back and Geigei's voice inquired what the matter was—was I ill? His touch brought me back to life. I sat up. He helped me stand. We lit cigarettes all around. I felt embarrassed and relieved, encouraged by Geigei to tell him what was troubling me. Between sobs of pain, I poured out the whole sorry story. He listened, turned to Elly, whose nods confirmed my account, and he quickly regrouped.

Looking me fully in the eye, his voice reassured me. "You know that I have always valued you highly. You are very dear to me. In no way do I want to hurt you, or to come between the two of you and damage your friendship." We walked down the hill, no longer arm in arm in arm. The conversation continued. Geigei tried to smooth things over. I was deliriously happy, but Elly was annoyed. On arriving at our hotel, Geigei bid us an impartial good night.

We returned home the next day. The situation had changed, but the pattern of our letter-writing continued. This was one secret we had not revealed. I wrote now how happy his caring had made me. And for Elly, I composed letters of disappointed love, in the vein of "How could you drop me so quickly just because she opened her mouth?"

What did it do to me to take on one voice, then another? There seemed to be no choice. I simply did the next thing that was required, that flowed out of my bond with Elly, as well as from my infatuation with Geigei. The life of the soul was intense and complex then: full of poetry, Hoelderlin, Rilke, Verlaine, the striving, the reaching, everything to be happened upon through mystery and tentative touch. We had no television, no life scripts observed and rehearsed, no movies that delivered a beginning, middle, and end of destiny within a couple of hours. Adult life was in explicit, unspoken; it was lived with an inner elaboration of response, not choice of action. When Geigei spoke in class, when he read poetry aloud, when he slipped one of his own poems into his selection of famous authors, when in it, he spoke of the loneliness of fall, along with the lines of *Herr, es ist Zeit. Der Sommer war sehr gross. Wer jetzt allein ist werd es lange bleiben*—inside, I answered, "Yes, yes, I am here. You are calling me, and I will soothe your loneliness."

When Geigei came back from active duty, he proposed in a letter that we meet, just the two of us. In the pattern I had come to know so well in myself, I responded with eagerness, happiness, but a heavy heart as well. One night, he instructed me in the steps necessary for a successful rendezvous at the outskirts of the blacked-out town. A small valley ran along the crest of encircling hills: it cradled a road, and within the forest that clothed the hill, a quiet footpath linked the two entries. At precisely 9:30, I was to start walking into the woods from the eastern entrance, while Geigei started from the west.

It wasn't a long valley, so we might have met up in the middle within 10 minutes. I remember starting down the soft, unlit path, made darker by the pine forest that surrounded it. My steps were inaudible; the soil was soft and needle-covered, and an occasional pebble made a small *slurp* against my shoe. The night and the solitude were cradling and alerting me at the same time. The anticipation of meeting my oncoming lover lifted me into an alternate state. My hearing became sharper, I strained to sense his step, and the occasional shadows both exhilarated and frightened me. Finally, I saw a small light glowing way ahead of me. I thought, that is him! A cigarette, an approaching figure. Are there erotic buildups any more intense? We met and we kissed. Nothing further. And then we parted, each returning to our original entry point.

For me, it was a flight of ecstasy, a visit to paradise. And what was it for him? He tried to double track, meet with Elly, then meet with me. He wrote one thing to me, another to her. He never understood that she and I were in it together, in spite of whatever else was occurring between us. So, she read to me the letters he wrote her, and I read to her his letters to me. At one point, he wrote that he had wanted to add "an altar of worship to his cathedral of love." He wrote first to her, then, in the exact same words, to me. Finally, feeling betrayed and disgusted, we confronted him. For the first time, Geigei wrote a letter addressed to both of us. He said that he felt like "a toy ball in our golden hands."

And then it was over.

Elly settled in again more securely with her boyfriend, my brother, Fred. In school, I soon learned that Geigei specialized in this kind of romantic lead-in and lead-on. Every few years, the cast of characters changed. Perhaps he varied the action some, but essentially, it was only this: romanticize, seduce, but never sleep with his students.

As an adult, as soon as my finances permitted, I visited Switzerland to spend some time with my family and friends there. Among the friends I included was Geigei, with whom I had carried on an occasional correspondence. As he wrote in one of his letters, "Once you love, you love forever."

He was particularly happy one summer. Finally, he had found a way out of the unhappy marriage he had been pinned in for years. His wife had been unavailable to him ever since the birth of their only daughter and was in poor health. "I never saw her naked; she kept her clothes on and the light off," he said. She had been averse to divorce, which, in any event, would have resulted in a financially impossible situation. His salary as a high school teacher, even when supplemented by stipends as a university lecturer, barely took them into a thrift-beset middle class. In the years before my visit, salvation arrived, in the person of one of my former classmates. I was surprised when he informed me that he and Lucretia had set up house together, and that they were extremely happy. He helped with her lesson plans, and her father's financial resources permitted a more expanded life. At last, his divorce was accomplished. With a dreamy smile, he said they planned to adopt a baby boy from the south of France. They had hired a woman who was turning the country house in which they lived into a comfortable and well-run home. She cooked, baked, mended, and sewed for them.

After a life spent in a claustrophobic three-room apartment, shackled to an unhappy wife, it was a great relief. Geigei beamed, rejuvenated by new love. More importantly, his life was eased by the comforts of having enough money. I remembered Lucretia; she was a solid and quiet girl, with rust blonde braids. She had a pleasant face, but one that lacked animation. She struggled with her schoolwork. Her father was a well-known veterinarian from a moneyed family. She was certainly not a Geigei fan when we were in school together. Apparently, she caught up with that opportunity later in life. I believe she had been married but hastened to divorce her husband to make a new life with Geigei, who was full of plans for their joint life and how he would help her with her career. I wished him well.

On a later visit, I learned that Geigei was no longer living in St. Gallen. That seemed strange to me, as his teaching position was considered lifelong. He was a member of the city council; his parents owned a historic small bar/restaurant in the old part of town. Inquiries revealed that he was teaching in a boys' school in a nearby state. Further inquiries revealed that his new bride had discovered his dalliances with students. In spite of his happier new circumstances, it was such an ingrained habit that apparently he had been unable to purge the behavior.

Lucretia promptly denounced him to the appropriate authorities. Undoubtedly buttressed by her father's local power, the authorities made short shrift of Geigei. He was stripped of all his positions in school, the army, the university, and the city council. He lost his pension as well. He was transferred to an environment where it was felt he could do no harm: a boys' school. I saw him there in 1975 for the last time. Melanie, then 16, accompanied me. He was very happy to see me. "So, you've come to visit me in my exile," he said. "I see you brought a chaperone." Undeterred and unwavering, he had remained true to his path. "I thought you might have come to complete our connection," he mused.

He told his version of the story, and some of it seemed credible. Shortly after their marriage, his new wife also lost interest in him, and she installed a girlfriend in their home. The situation rapidly deteriorated. In a fit of rage, his wife brought an end to their brief marriage and his long career. He did not seem bitter or frightened by his diminished circumstances. He loved the new students and explained that teaching boys was a different challenge.

He had located another former student, a history teacher in a nearby school. "She lives alone," he said, "and so she doesn't eat right. I go over there for dinner, which encourages her to prepare a meal for the two of us. We have a nice and mutual caretaking friendship."

I was glad he was unbowed. After a life of seducing his women students but staying within the limits of the law, later life seemed to bestow a gift of freedom upon him.

Initiation

As my German improved, I reclaimed my academic proficiency. University studies became a possibility. Two other girls and I approached the Talhof faculty at the beginning of our third year with a plan to transfer to the Kantonsschule from our fourth year into their fifth year. For two years the Talhof faculty tutored us privately. We applied for admission jointly. Girls were largely unwelcome in this school, and I triply so: in addition to being a girl, I was a Jewish refugee and too young to boot. I had good reason to be pleased and proud; I had passed all 13 subjects of the exam, scoring exceptionally well. In addition, I proved my mettle during the extensive oral exams that were added specifically for me. As a result, all three of us got accepted. We had started as study partners and soon developed a deep friendship that lasted all our lives. Finally, I had settled into a path that might eventually lead me to the study of medicine. Ever since childhood I had dreamed of becoming the Minister of Public Health of Czechoslovakia.

By this time my friendship with Elly had weakened, strained by our involvement with Geigei and my move to a new school. Still, the symbiotic marriage-like bond that linked us for more than three years exerted its influence. It was 1943 and I was almost 16.

Incongruous and improbable as it now seems, the shrunken Jewish community decided to hold a formal dance.

The Jewish population consisted primarily of Swiss Jews who did not have the means, or perhaps the will, to emigrate from

Europe to escape impending persecution by a seemingly victorious Germany. And then there were the few refugees who had arrived in Switzerland early enough to become semi-accepted by the local community. Several years earlier, I attended a season of dance classes, arranged for by Aunt Fanny. Fanny was ever trying to turn me into a lady, but I stubbornly remained her eldest sister's tomboyish daughter. Attendance at the formal dance was modest, and included parents, grandparents, and other family members.

One evening, sometime after 10 pm, we heard a commotion at the door. Members of the St. Gallen Repertory Theatre had arrived following their evening performance. Elly excitedly rushed toward me, bursting with the good news. "Finally, something is going on! Now we'll have a little action." The St. Gallen Playhouse was small, but we thought the leading actors and actresses were glamorous. For us, it was as if Hollywood movie stars had stopped by a high school prom.

Whenever Elly was around, I became invisible. She always managed to get first dibs on the eligible males. She herself resembled a Hollywood starlet: she had a small nose framed by high cheekbones, wavy reddish-blonde hair, green eyes, and was long-limbed, high-breasted, and a world-class flirting expert. By contrast, my hair was dark and quite straight, and I was short, full-chested, long-waisted, and painfully aware of my long nose.

Suddenly, tall, blond, and blue-eyed Otto, the matinee idol himself, directed his steps toward where Elly and I were standing. I wanted to sneak away to a seat designated for the wallflowers. Dare I say he looked Aryan? Nordic? In some strange way, he also appeared safe. It was as though for one moment the rules of war were suspended, rules whereby blond people like Otto were supposed to kill dark people like me. Observing Otto as he walked our way, Elly rejoiced. "Look! Here he comes!" Indeed, Otto approached us. In the surprise of surprises, he turned to me and asked, "May I have this dance?" It was a wonderful evening. I felt like the fairy-tale princess at the ball. And true to the last detail of such stories, I left the dance not with the prince but with my aunt and uncle.

Otto courted me for the next three weeks. St. Gallen was a small town; everywhere you turned, you would run into someone you knew. I ran into Otto at the café; I passed him on the street. He smiled at me as we talked. And we arranged our meetings. One day, Otto suggested I have dinner with him at his house, noting that his mother would prepare our meal. I was well past my sixteenth birthday, and ready to say goodbye to childhood innocence. I had flown to cloud nine during the dance and had remained floating there. In my conquest of Otto, I experienced the pleasure of having bested Elly. Hopefully I would soon match her in sexual experiences, in which she seriously preceded me.

As I think back on the vagaries of my life, it is increasingly clear that what I valued most was the knowledge that I deliberately inhabited these decisions, in spite of many ill-informed courses of action and the high prices they often exacted. It was not unlike driving in winter. When the car begins to skid on ice, you must not fight the skid, but instead turn the steering wheel in its direction to regain control. I understood the meaning of accepting a dinner invitation at Otto's apartment. I had chosen a probable sexual engagement. And I was proud of having done it. In my general spirit of rebellion against the norms of a society whose rules did not protect me, I had hoped to lose my virginity before the legal age of consent which was sixteen. While I had missed that goal by some months, with Otto's help I came close enough. Did I also consider the possible outcome of an intimate involvement with a man 13 years older, whose wife would return shortly? The immediacy of my desire for Otto's attention far outweighed any cautionary thoughts. I worried neither about pregnancy nor any consequences nor emotional costs.

I arrived at his apartment. A festive-looking table was set for a tête-à-tête dinner. I'm not sure whether there were flowers or candlelight, but I recall crystal wine glasses and pretty dishes. Otto's mother, a roundish, housewifely woman, greeted me cordially and proceeded to serve our meal. Her presence made the situation simultaneously more acceptable and more puzzling. She stayed to clear the table, and then discreetly disappeared.

Otto and I sat down with another glass of wine. He questioned me about the extent of my experience with physical affection. He appeared pleased when I indicated I was a novice. Then he began to talk softly about the wonderful experience ahead of me. Otto suggested I have another glass of wine, to reduce my fears and allow my inhibitions to diminish. When I relaxed and was just a bit tipsy, he suggested that I lie down. He kissed and stroked me, almost imperceptibly removing my clothes.

I experienced some anxiety that the penetration would be painful. He reassured me, saying he would be gentle. He also explained that I might not experience much pleasure the first time. With more sexual experience, my body would relax, and sexual encounters would produce wonderful feelings. Things went pretty much as he had led me to believe. He was extremely attentive and considerate throughout. At the critical moment, I said, "Stop, stop it hurts," and he squeezed my hand and gave a little push. The deflowering was accomplished. From a physical perspective, I could not have had a better introduction to the sexual experience.

If not completely detached from emotion, this experience was detached from any romantic illusion of a lasting future, which could be considered either a stroke of luck or quite the contrary, as it might well have led me to an excessive lowering of personal barriers in future sexual encounters.

I saw Otto a few more times before his wife returned.

One Saturday afternoon, as I was walking past the café with a girlfriend, Foxy, Otto's fox terrier, suddenly tore out of the café and came running to me. He barked and jumped with recognition and excitement. I looked up and there was Otto, sitting at a table with his wife. His wife carefully observed Foxy's familiar greeting. There was no question she understood the context of Foxy's behavior.

About a year later, standing in the girls' smoking room at school, I overheard a conversation between two students. One related to her friend the story of her involvement with the first man she had ever slept with. It was Otto. I felt diminished.

My Father's Rescue

"Jean Fischer!" the guard yelled into the wagon of the deportation train. It was standing at the last stop before it crossed the demarcation line between Vichy France and Germany, just before the doors of the cattle cars were welded shut for the deportees' final journey east. My father hesitated briefly before answering. At the prior stop, a prisoner had been called out in this same manner, and when he identified himself, he was shot dead, right there by the tracks.

I imagine that my father briefly considered remaining silent, not identifying himself. But he got up, handed the luxurious emergency gear he was carrying (a leather-bound wool blanket, hand-sewn boots, a warm sweater) to the people huddled next to him, and stepped forward. He was prepared to die. My father was not a fighter. He abhorred violence; hardship corroded him. He resigned himself to his fate with great passivity. Above all, he believed deeply in the inviolate rights of legal authority.

I visualize him walking toward the guard, perhaps with fear, but more with an acceptance of whatever was awaiting him. Unlike the prisoner who had exited the wagon before him, my father was not shot. Instead he was returned to the assembly camp from which he had been selected for deportation. Being extracted from the train headed for Auschwitz offered only a brief respite. Within a few days, prisoners would be selected for the next transport; he was at risk of reselection.

It was the Swiss envoy to Vichy who had requested my father's release. My father was removed from the train just before it crossed the border into Germany. The envoy had been a fraternity brother of my father's. My mother had enlisted his help, even though my father was not a Swiss citizen and technically did not fall under his jurisdiction. But the ties of early friendship proved strong.

Nevertheless, the diplomatic steps that were required to secure my father's release from the internment camp were slow and unpredictable. Waiting for the legal next step was perilous. A cousin stepped into the breach and provided an alternate solution. As the owner of a shipping firm, he was able to send a car and driver with enough money to bribe the camp guards. He also provided false papers for my father to get out of the camp and into Switzerland. But what did my father do? He refused to go, insisting he would not participate in any illegal actions. In the midst of the most horrendous illegality of mass extermination, my father could not stop himself from upholding his standard of moral behavior.

Was he just afraid? Did sticking to the letter of the law absolve him of the need for personal action and responsibility? Was he unable to think, to plan, to take any personal risk? Whatever the case, fate intervened. Official channels provided legal exit papers, an entry visa into Switzerland, and a permit for him to remain in St. Gallen.

My father rarely spoke of the events surrounding his rescue. At times, I wondered if he would have preferred not to be a survivor. That was especially true when, after the war, we learned that the entire extended family, which had remained in Czechoslovakia, was murdered in a number of the extermination camps, some very early, and others toward the very end of the war.

Although I was not a witness to any of these events, and wasn't even fully informed of them, they have been etched in my fate in innumerable ways, from my father's admonition of "don't make waves; don't be heard; don't be seen" to his lack of support for my educational dreams, which went way beyond the usual "women don't need to be educated" level. While he wanted me to succeed, to be effective, his dreams for me, because of his experiences, were modest. At most, he thought that if I could become an executive secretary to a successful man, I would be well provided for. He knew that would not take long to achieve. In contrast, my wish to study medicine stretched into a haze-shrouded future. Who knew whether it would ever arrive?

There was a photograph taken a few weeks after my father had arrived in St. Gallen, which I found years later among the few things my sister-in-law had not discarded after my brother's death. In the picture, my father is sitting between his two children. He looks shrunken, ashen, wearing a grey suit, which matched his grey face. In contrast, my brother and I appear robustly healthy. My brother is dark and handsome. I am overflowing with baby fat, a ripe 16-year-old girl. The contrast between our father and his children gives a hint of the struggle we were going through to maintain some semblance of a reunited family.

Good-Bye, Czechoslovakia

On a Labor Day weekend some decades after the war had ended, I found myself visiting my colleague Jane in Walton, New York, and staying in my usual guest room, which faces east. The room has large windows, double triangle ones that fill the upper part of the wall and reach snuggly into the gabled ceiling, allowing the rising sun to flood the room with morning energy before it actually reaches my face directly. I always come alive in this embrace with nature and go back to being the person I was so many years ago, before I settled in New York. Before I became a fast-paced, urban professional on the go, trying to achieve, to amass, to arrive.

Please don't misunderstand. I love New York and the energetic activity that permeates my life when I am there. I have even relinquished my underlying assumption, unspoken and inexplicit, that my cerebral, thoughtful, measured city-self is only for now; that at some point, I might leave the city to find a comfortable, quiet spot in the country, perhaps on a green meadow or by a small brook, with a view of some hills, without much evidence of crowded civilization.

It appears now I will probably stay. I am in the process of realizing that New York really could become home, as much of a home as someone like me; a person shaped by the sudden, harsh and total disappearance of her childhood world, as happened to me during the events leading up to World War II, can have. It amazes me how ubiquitous and close to the surface this particular self-definer dwells, as if it were an essential aspect of every event in my life ever after, whether directly or indirectly, a little or a lot. It is always there, somewhere, ready to call attention to itself.

In 1987, I visited Russia, when it was in the last stages of being the Soviet Union, still somewhat Third Worldish and at loose ends. I noticed no conversation ever failed to include, within the first few sentences, a reference to the losses of "the war," as if World War II had just ended for the Russians. I thought at the time about how overwhelmingly defining that catastrophe of over so many years ago remained. I don't believe it is this way any longer, with the current turmoil of unpredictable events demanding our attention. As important as the events of those years remain in my mind, does that mean I am somewhere else, stagnated, like Russia once was? Would I let go of these old defining events if new ones crashed in over me?

Indeed, it seems true these old events now emerge and assert their significance for me. When I found myself in relatively safe Switzerland during World War II, I forgot how to speak Czech. I also forgot all sexual information and had to be *aufgeklaert* (enlightened) by my embarrassed older brother when I was 13. He tossed me a heavy medical volume on human sexuality by August Forel, and growled, "Read that. It's about time!" I read it, together with Elly. Perhaps that helped shape the bond on sexual knowledge and concerns, between the two of us and my brother. But somehow sexuality became closely linked with my sense of who I was, where I was from, and where I belonged. When the tides of war turned and the dreaded German victory began to seem less likely, my forgotten Czech language slowly reappeared. First came the multiplication tables, and then memorized poetry, a long poem of romantic tragedy about love, betrayal, murder, punishment.

The war ended just as I graduated from the Gymnasium. Recently, Gret, one of my Swiss friends, wrote me about the current political issues regarding the behavior of the Swiss, the banks, as well as citizens, during that war. "I don't remember much of that time," she wrote. "I probably didn't put myself in your place. Kids didn't. But I remember the dress you were wearing when you walked toward me outside of school, happy, smiling, and shouting that the war had ended."

I do not remember that. The end of the war brought with it the acknowledgement of the deaths of almost all of my father's family, as well as the impossibility of ever going back to what had been. The mood was one of elation, confusion, and attempts to find direction. I wanted to study medicine, but there was no money. My father, who was thoroughly broken by the events of the war, could not, at the time, visualize nor support any optimistic long-range plans.

With some assistance from my uncle, and with my mother taking her first paying job in 25 years, I enrolled in medical school. It would take 13 semesters to complete, with the first two essentially devoted to fulfilling pre-med science requirements. For half of the first semester, my mother and I shared a room in a genteel mansion on the Zuerichberg, one of the better sections of town, near the university. When I moved in some of my things, carrying my heavy suitcase on my shoulder as best I could, my mother chided, "A lady does not lift a suitcase to her shoulder." She didn't say, "Don't lift anything too heavy" or "Get help." She was primarily concerned with appearance. I was proud that I was strong enough to do the lifting. This difference in our outlook and style defined the uneasy way we shared our quarters for the few weeks this arrangement lasted. I no longer recall why we had arrived at this plan, nor precisely why it ended.

My mother then returned to my father who had remained with her family in St. Gallen, some 50 miles away. I moved into quarters more appropriate for impecunious students, and went on to survive four semesters, barely. I was without firm resolve, without direction, without plans or visions or dreams. I lacked money to buy books and pay lab fees. I couldn't buy clothes. I barely managed the rent on a furnished room and carefully allocated food. Things became so dire that, at one point, one of my friends introduced me to a man who was supposedly looking for a young lady to become his mistress.

Post-war Zürich was, in contrast to its pre-war sedate and upright climate, a town in ferment and motion, perhaps like a port typically is. But at that time, it wasn't ships that were coming and going, but rather a variety of people from all over Europe who found themselves cast into relatively intact surroundings. Physically undestroyed by the war, the city was amply supplied with food and other necessities, open to the world, and more fully neutral after emerging from the grip and shadow of Nazi Germany. Zürich welcomed a mix of students, artists, war profiteers, children of politically suspect parents from Europe and South America, black marketeers, currency manipulators, and art dealers—a teeming mix of legitimate and not-so-legitimate people. Some were stranded and poor; many others had plenty of money from dubious sources. Two of my medical school colleagues financed their studies through liaisons with older people, one of whom was an American divorcée in her thirties, the other a diva at the local theater. In an attempt to remain "one of the guys" with the generally poorer students, my colleagues joked unkindly about their older "sugar mommies."

"Oh, I just put a pillow over her face, so I don't notice how old she is," one said with a smirk. Still, their example opened a possibility, and so I agreed to meet the man who might become my protector. We met at the Café Gotthard, an upscale businessmen's lounge fastidiously decorated in dark brown leather. He introduced himself as a Hungarian dealing in gold. It was an occupation one referred to in those days as a *schieber*, someone who knew how to circumvent the various commercial and currency restrictions of the era to profitable ends. I was only slightly put off by his illicit business activity. I felt the rules were made to favor those in power, those who drew them up and implemented them. Everyone else had to live as best they could. Strangely, I don't remember the man's name. He was short, slight, and pale, with black hair and eyes. He must have been in his early forties. Not bad looking, but intense, and, to my years, very old! He suggested he would rent me an apartment, give me a generous monthly stipend, enough for me to live on, to buy clothes and books and pay my tuition.

"Don't you want to look pretty? Don't you want to have the things women enjoy? You could concentrate on your studies and not worry!" he cajoled. He would visit me once a week at most, but strongly emphasized fidelity on my part. He outlined a specific and rational agreement. I accompanied him to his hotel room, with a notion that I would consider the proposition from my perspective, not as a rational contract, but how it felt. Even in this unpromising situation, I was looking for a boyfriend! He asked gently and politely if I would lie on the bed. He looked at me, stroked my face, and then pulled down my panties. He made no move to remove his own clothes; I wondered what would happen.

Slowly, he stroked my legs and then brought his mouth to my genitals. I was totally surprised and embarrassed, I thought I would sink through the floor! I had never heard of such a thing! What was this strange man doing? Was I in the clutches of some sort of pervert? He must have sensed my discomfort because he stopped, patted me, and pulled my panties back up. He said he liked me and could grow to love me. By then, I was scared and wanted nothing but out. I told him I had to leave and would think about his proposal, and I never saw him again. Only much later in life—much, much later—did I learn about oral sex.

A few weeks later, I was fortunate to make the acquaintance of the man who would become the first Indian ambassador to Switzerland, after India's independence from Britain in 1947. Dhirupai Bhulabai Desai had come to Zürich for a number of reasons, including to obtain medical help for his wife, Madhuri. They were staying at one of Zürich's good hotels, the Eden au Lac, and he was in search of a German teacher. We came to an easy agreement; I would tutor him in German, and he would teach me Indian history. Since these lessons took place after classes, a meal at the hotel restaurant was usually included.

Today, the Eden is considered to have one of the finest kitchens in Switzerland; it wasn't bad back then either. Dhiru comforted me in my despair about my future and suggested that perhaps I might eventually study medicine in India. Actually, it didn't make much sense for a noncitizen to go through medical studies in Switzerland, since exams were segregated; only Swiss citizens were allowed to take Swiss exams. And you needed to pass those to be eligible for a license to practice. I don't think I thought these things through clearly; they just added up to a fog of no-can-do.

In my first two semesters in medical school, I was busy teaching German, learning Indian history, and eating at the Eden. I also attended lectures, but the absence of means to buy required resources, such as texts and lab materials, distracted me. I am not usually a particularly proud person, but I believe that the impossibility of the situation mostly embarrassed me. I dealt with it by general avoidance and neglect. To this day, I am terrible at planning a project and then making sure I buy all the equipment necessary to carry it out. Somewhere inside me, a voice always urges, "You can do it with less. That one will do. Don't waste. Too expensive."

The third semester brought an influx of American ex-GIs into our medical school. These were men who, for reasons such as age (one, a former navy captain, was 48; another, a veterinarian wanting to upgrade to humans, was 35), were not eligible for American medical schools. Most of the ineligible ones were Jews. American universities had a *numerus clausus*, a quota that allowed only so many Jewish students. God knows why Jews want to study medicine so badly. Well, actually, it is not such a mystery. It was a relatively independent profession that did not require being hired by industries that often had a no-Jews policy, and had also been traditionally open to Jews in Europe, when many other occupations were not.

The arrival of the non–German-speaking Americans opened another area of activity that helped me in many ways: I began to translate the German language workbooks for them and became something of a cultural intermediary. One might think that in doing so I would have caught up on my studies, learned what I translated, and got on with it. Instead, I became interested in America, and also proceeded to fall in love with the aforementioned veterinarian. I had been in love a number of times before, each time a little differently. There was my long romantic attachment to Geigei. I had fallen for a Norwegian medical student and lost him to a girl named Jeanie, who appeared to be a sexy goddess from the American West. (I imagined plains and buffalo and Indians on horseback, having read Karl May. Much later, I learned Jeanie was from West Hartford, Connecticut. My view of America did not have much to do with reality.)

The first Americans I had ever seen were sitting in the living room of a country inn. They were pilots who had been shot down on a mission over Germany and somehow made it to Switzerland, where, owing to their government's solid financial standing, their internment took place in the guestless facilities of the Swiss tourist industry. During one of our frequent walks, my friend and I happened on one of those country inns that had become facilities for

American internees. We peeked through the glass window into the lounge area, where we saw what appeared to us as exotic creatures. They were pale and huge, tall and perhaps also bloated, as their skin color matched their drab uniforms—tan pants and shirts, not militaristic at all. There were three or four of them, sitting in armchairs, feet on the table, eating from a tray of pastries. They seemed bored. They looked unreal. I don't remember hearing any sounds or seeing any animation. But that might have just been me: curious, awestruck, and somewhat scared.

The Americans who came as medical students were, by contrast, quite human, yet they, too, were a bit larger than life. They had been in the war, and most were officers. They had money, the value of the dollar was high, and the GI Bill payments went far, allowing them to live several notches above local students, even those much better off than I was. Some even had cars. While they worked hard, they also played hard. They were free in their movements; their bodies were loose and graceful. Even Jerry, the only enlisted man among them, somewhat overweight and a hard drinker, was in good, relaxed physical shape.

For about a year, I was part of their gang. We hung out together, ate together, sat in classes together. Harris, who had been stationed in the Pacific, was the one on whom I got stuck. A ladies' man, obsessed with sex, he taught me all kinds of things. As I think of him, I find a reluctance to remember. I don't understand, and for sure I don't like, the kind of pain I exposed myself to and tolerated in so many of my dealings with men. Harris made wonderful love to me, taught me to get excited by just his touching my nipples, to pace myself, to delay. In the middle of it all, he would cup his hand in a gesture I since discovered was quite frequently used by those men and rhapsodize about the small Asian women whom he could hold in the palm of his hand. He found what might have passed for an approximate replacement in a skinny, sickly Swiss girl, on whom he doted, as he practiced his old veterinary and incipient human medical skills on her many infirmities. In class, he slipped me notes that said such things as "The sooner you realize you cannot own a man, the happier you will be." He was surely right.

I tortured myself with jealousy when, in the middle of the night, he would solicitously cover me and ask, "*Hast du genug platz*," worried about my comfort in a language he and I never used. I could not shake my helpless infatuation with him, in spite of the devoted efforts of all of his and my friends who would tell me that he was bad news, not bright, and would be a terrible physician.

Eventually, he provided the watershed to my hapless medical student career. Alone at home for a long weekend to study for a crucial zoology exam, I became tired and went to see a movie. Standing in line was Harris, with his fussy Swiss date. *The Corn Is Green* played that afternoon without me and has acquired an everlasting black mark for me. I went home, scrubbed my room, wept, scrubbed some more, and eventually pulled myself together and hit my class notes in the short time that remained. I had barely passed my preliminary oral exam in physics the previous week; it had always been a hard subject for me. Zoology was a favorite of mine, but just remembering the lectures was not an adequate knowledge base. Passing this second exam would have required a good three days' cramming. The examining professor smiled, as I knew the answers to his first few questions. When shortly thereafter, we happened into territory I had not had time to revisit, he frowned and said in his characteristic Bernese drawl, "You are not stupid. I think you have to work a little."

There were four preliminary exams in all: I didn't show up for the other two. My friends refused to believe me when I said I failed. "It's really true. It really happened," I said. While I certainly could have taken the exams again the following semester, this failure, an experience to which I was unaccustomed in my academic endeavors, signaled to me that it was time for a change.

It was 1947, three years after the end of the war, and the reality of a resurrected home had finally settled in. The Czech government had taken notice of my existence and replaced my provisional passport, issued during the war by the government in exile in London and recognized by no one, with an internationally recognized document.

My family filled out lengthy forms forwarded to us from Prague, where the new Czechoslovak government was working hard at cobbling together a republic from the fragmented constituencies that existed after World War II had ended. The questionnaires we were completing pertained primarily to the concept of national reliability, trying to recognize and weed out people whose behavior during the war would have compromised them, most likely those who had collaborated with the occupying Germans.

And then, suddenly, I was no longer stateless. I found myself the proud owner of a brand-new passport. A feeling of great relief and happiness overcame me.

This was in stark contrast to the circumstances that made me the legitimate, albeit brief, holder of a passport issued by the German government in 1942. At that time, I was summoned to the German consulate in Zürich, which was located on the Predigerplatz, a beautiful square in the old town. My uncle Leo came with me, and when I entered the door, which was marked by the vivid red, white, and black colors of a swastika, my breath almost stopped. I felt as though my life was at risk.

The Swiss authorities had insisted that I get this document as a condition for my continued stay in Switzerland. The passport was marked with a big letter, "J," for Jew and made out to Kitty Sara Fischer (all Jewish women were Sara and all Jewish men were

Israel), and I was declared a citizen of the German Reich. In less than two months, the German consulate recalled the passport with a comment indicating that Jews were not entitled to German citizenship. The Swiss authorities no longer bothered me after my German passport was revoked, but I never for a moment lost the awareness that I was an ill-tolerated refugee, who could be expelled from the borders of Switzerland at any arbitrary moment.

I had a wonderful new passport, fresh in my hands, and the time was approaching when we would prepare to leave Switzerland and return home to Czechoslovakia. A continuation of my medical studies seemed a renewed possibility, as we believed that some of our family property might be returned to us. My father kept telling me, challengingly, teasingly, but also pleased to have found a way out: "You want to study medicine? Like your brother? Well, you will be able to do that in Prague." My father, unlike my mother, did not feel at home in Switzerland. He was eager to return to Czechoslovakia as soon as possible.

In the summer of 1947, my mother, brother, and I made an exploratory trip home. I cannot make sense of the fact that my father wasn't with us. Perhaps he had gone on a brief exploration earlier, or, more in keeping with my parents' relationship, would go later, after my mother had determined the situation. Between the two of them, she was the optimist, the doer, the darer. My father tended to defeatism, to pessimism; he mourned his home, his culture, and his family. He had loved the comfortable, cozy, slow pace of Moravian small-town life, spiced up as it was by the proximity to Viennese culture and the addition of a glamorous foreign wife.

It was our first venture out of the confines of Switzerland, which had been mine and my brother's prison and safeguard since 1938. Trains had begun regular service through rubble-strewn Germany. The trip for us three, in a first-class railroad compartment, cost one and a half packs of American cigarettes handed over directly to the German train conductor. We traveled from Basel through Karlsruhe, across Germany toward the Czech border at Cheb and on to Prague. The train sped through a landscape devastated by war. I specifically remember that Karlsruhe, our first major stop, was in ruins. These images were new to me, although we must have seen photographs of bombed cities in newspapers and newsreels.

But the visceral reality of the destruction had not been brought home to us as is done today by ubiquitous television coverage. The contemporary broadcast media brings images and sounds of carnage and destruction, often live, as they are happening on the ground, by combat-embedded reporters, aerial views from overflying planes, and, at times, even pictures taken by the combatants themselves. These reports unfolding in our living rooms in the middle of our lives shock us, inform us, and, by and by, become known, accepted, and eventually fade into unnoticed background. It's hard to remember that before television settled into our living rooms, we only knew the reality we had actually witnessed. The occasional newsreel, photograph, and personal communications provided just slivers of distant happenings, perhaps like photographs illustrating a story.

In Germany, we entered a world that appeared caught in a time warp. Three years after the hostilities had ended, the bombed-out landscape through which we passed appeared as if the destruction had barely halted. There was rubble and desolation everywhere. The very idea of Germany had been so frightening to me that I had not managed to learn German geography in school, or managed to withdraw my thoughts from any excursion into the country that had brought apocalyptic terror to the world, that had annihilated my home and murdered much of my family. So, as I looked out the train window, what I felt was a huge relief, like facing a slain monster. Nevertheless, the lasting feeling was one of chest-squeezing, breath-obliterating anxiety, as though a dead tiger could still kill the careless gazelle.

After we crossed the border into Bohemia, the character of the traces left by the war changed. There were only occasional spots that spoke of violent destruction. Instead, we observed damage caused by shortages, neglect, weather damage, loss of morale, and different priorities that had been established by the occupying power. Roads were in disrepair, pitted and rutted, paint was peeling off houses, windowpanes broken, land untended. In contrast to the terror and awe engendered in me by the German landscape, the train trip from the Czech border to Prague brought just sadness and desolation.

Once we arrived in Prague, we felt lighter. Golden Prague had not been damaged, only run down. And there were signs of repair and refurbishment everywhere. Some houses had been repainted, and the National Theatre had been restored. We took rooms in the second-best hotel in Prague, although Mother had hoped for the Alcron, then the best. It seems to me now, and the memory of that trip is dim, that we each went our own way. I remember having a wild time trying to forget my unhappy love affair by carrying on simultaneously with two men of the New World, a Czech who had returned from London to be part of the new government and an American medical student. There seemed to be shortages of everything except luxuries: no water in the room, threadbare sheets and towels, but we lived on roast chicken and champagne!

We met a friend of my brother's who had spent the war in the British army. He wore the frequently seen attire of paratrooper boots and khaki uniform pants, denoting a person who had participated actively in the war, on the winning side. He was in possession of a jeep and offered to drive us to our native village, some 150 miles southeast of Prague. We stopped overnight in a hotel, where I awoke with my back on fire, covered with bumps and splotches, my first acquaintance with bedbugs.

Part of me felt like a returning partisan, part like a guilty imposter, a shirker of the rigors of the long war years. When we arrived in the village of my childhood, we barely recognized it and had trouble finding our house. From a modestly elegant little country house, it had been converted into a cement box having a number of uses, among them as Gestapo headquarters. Our deep wine cellar that tunneled some 200 meters under the hill behind our house had served as a political prison. The only bomb that had hit the small town found the Jewish ghetto, but left the synagogue standing. It now served as a storage facility.

The house and garden where I had grown up were unrecognizable by depredation and neglect. People walked up to greet me, some seemed glad to see that I had survived. Others showed by their expression that their feelings were mixed, complicated reactions, since some had appropriated things from the homes of Jews and feared and resented a possible accounting that might occur if the former owners had, in fact, survived. I don't remember what was said about so many people dead: the Jews deported and murdered, some Czechs dead in the war, the many Germans who died in battle and others who were expelled right after the end of the war.

I inquired after Marenka, my beloved nursemaid. She was overjoyed to see me. She hugged me, cried, and said, "Now I can die. I was only waiting to see you again." Her daughter added, "She has been speaking so much about you, it's as if I knew you." I sensed that her feelings must be mixed too. It must have been difficult to have a mother who pines for and extols some absent love.

I also started to ask around the village about where I might find my second nursemaid, Edith. From the answers I received, I got the impression that she was among those whose behavior during the occupation had not been good. People shifted their gaze from my face when I asked about her, and said things like, "You might find her at her old address, but she might not be around" or "She might not be home" or "She might not open the door." It seems she had been among those who had helped themselves to possessions left in our house after everybody had fled.

When I found her, she at first refused to open the door, and then she asked, "What do you want?" When I indicated that I just wanted to say hello, she relented and opened the door a crack, but did not ask me to come inside. The fun-loving, beautiful, black-haired girl that I remembered, with whom I had such good times, had turned into a mean-looking woman with a huge, dark wen on her hairy face. Her expression barely softened when she decided she would talk to me. "You are a good girl to come and see me," she said. "I am busy now. Good-bye." Then she closed the door.

The images and specific memories of this first post-war visit to Miroslav are no longer clear in my mind. What does remain strongly held in my recollection is the feeling I had, upon finding myself in that no longer familiar, fundamentally altered place, that no matter what, this was the place where I belonged. Here, no one could dispute that fact; no one could question my right and entitlement to be here, to claim it as home. I think it was a moment of healing from the ever-present implicit, and often explicit, attitude that existed in Switzerland. As ubiquitous as the air we breathe, it was always there: You are a Jew and we don't like you. You are a foreigner and we don't want you. You have no say here; you have no rights; we tolerate you, for now.

I was eager to take the plunge and return home, leave Switzerland behind, and resume my medical studies. But returning to live in this sad village did not occur to me then. Prague, on the other hand, was a city full of promise, and I inquired about the possibility of living there and continuing my medical studies. Friend after friend advised, for a variety of reasons, to wait until the following spring. "You know no one here. You are not accustomed to the hardships of life here: there is no heat, food is sparse, you have no connections" or the more informed warning, "The political situation is unstable. People would not trust anyone who voluntarily exchanged the comforts of Switzerland for the rigors of Prague." These voices were those of Czech friends. An American friend who had joined us for a couple of weeks in Prague emphatically supported that view: "You don't want to come back here now, Fischer. It doesn't look promising."

When I got back to Switzerland, a strange thing happened to my memory of the visit: It became immediately distant, unreal, fuzzy, and joined my pre-war memories with no time space between them, as if a bead had been added to a necklace and pushed to adjoin those already strung.

Geneva

In the fall of 1947, I found myself back in Switzerland with no immediate plans. Working was out of the question, as I lived there all those years as a tolerated emigrant who was not entitled to a work permit. I felt dispirited. I had registered for the fifth semester in medical school, but it made no sense to me to try to continue. I stopped going to classes. My attention had shifted, and I had settled into a waiting mode. I would let the winter pass and move to Prague and enter medical school there. In the meantime, unfocused and emotionally dislocated, I decided to explore what was to me a heretofore-unknown part of Switzerland, French-speaking Geneva.

Before I left, my mother tried to be helpful to me, and it was one of the few times I remember when she tried and I accepted. Much of the time we were at terrible odds. She was unable to understand and validate the difficulties I encountered in trying to find my way and could not comfort me in the distress I felt.

I imagine Switzerland represented the happy years of her childhood. Her inability to understand how different my situation was made me reject and rebel against her. To this day I am left feeling that I am not entitled to my own unhappiness, *others had it worse, it could be worse, it isn't worth attending to it.* I was among the luckiest of the ill-fated ones; what right did I have to expect better? I felt very much on my own, unguided and unprotected. Free to find my own way, to stumble, to pick myself up or not.

My mother's advice came in the form of an introduction: "My best friend, Nelly, lives in Geneva. Give her a call when you get there; perhaps she could help you. Please mind your manners, and don't be impolite." I did as suggested and called Nelly not long after arriving. I had been successful in renting a room, and a chance meeting on the beach with an American businessman led to an off-the-books job. I was pretty well set. Nelly was friendly, if a bit cool. She was leaving for Paris that weekend but invited me to a salon held every Friday night at her apartment. Nelly described it as an open house, where refugees, artists, journalists, family, and friends gathered. She told me just to show up. And added that I should not be offended if her husband took no notice of me.

"He has his own friends and is concerned with his own things. He's not always welcoming to young people."

I remember the dress I wore that night, which is unusual since clothes were not often memory markers for my experiences. But that particular dress, a strong royal blue with a deep V-neck, fitted at the waist, with ample batwing sleeves, drew the host's attention. I saw Nelly's husband, E., engaged in deep conversation with another man. E. was a short broad man with a big head wreathed in white curls, animated and intense. He came over, asked who I was, complimented me on presenting a lovely appearance, and included me during the rest of the evening in his various conversations. He walked me home that night and saw me each day after work for a couple of weeks. Eventually he became my lover.

I had registered at the University, which was a requirement if Switzerland were not to deport me, and found a roommate, Lida Smejkalova. I met her by sheer accident, when I found myself standing next to her in the line that formed waiting for the early edition of the *Tribune de Geneve* to come out. It was there that you looked for rooms, and where students found affordable housing. I was wearing a duster in a lively color that approached cobalt blue.

In its small lapel I sported a round, red, blue, and white pin, representing the new Czechoslovakia.

This friendly, tall, rather drab-looking woman standing next to me looked me over, and then smiled as her eye noticed the pin. "*Ceska?*" (Are you Czech?) All things Czech meant recovered home and love to me at the time. Immediately, Lida and I decided to look for a room together, becoming close friends. We found an oblong room in an old building, and placed our beds catercorner to each other, thus providing privacy. We seemed totally compatible and got along very well. She asked me how it felt to wake up and find a white-haired, balding head next to me on my pillow. I remember my answer: "I don't mind it at all. There are so many interesting thoughts in his head." When one is young, fear of age is not an issue.

I quickly discovered that E. had no money of his own and was supported by his wife. I felt shy about using any of their money. We settled into a modest way of spending, and I usually paid my own way. When Nelly was in town, I spent evenings kibitzing with them while they played bridge at the international club. I thought for sure that she knew what was going on with E. and me, and that she didn't mind. She would often finish playing around 10:30 at night, get up, and say, "Well, I'm going home. E. will see you home, Kitty." I realized Nelly was running out of money when their winnings became important to them. Eventually, she took a job.

E. was a very good lover, using what was his best talent, his language. He complimented me extravagantly and made me feel wonderful about my participation. "You make love like a queen," he would say. "Like the Queen of Sheba. And I am your slave." He knew the arts and history and music and gossip about famous people. Whatever the official story, he knew what had really gone on. At one point, he suggested that we go to Canada and bring suit on behalf of Indian tribes that had been robbed of their territories. He was a half-century ahead of the times!

When I was with E., I practiced a rather idiosyncratic form of birth control. Immediately following orgasm, I would jump up and wash. Amazingly, this method, when diligently applied, always worked for me, although I wouldn't recommend it. One evening, on a double date, I flirted with a young man and, without intention, deeply offended E. I felt terrible and tried to make amends. We made love, and I did not permit myself to jump and wash him out of me. I somehow felt I had to hold and contain him. Within a few weeks, my pregnancy was confirmed.

E. went crazy and started talking about leaving his wife. We would run off to South America together; he would make a pile of money; make another baby with me and stay with me for a few years. Then he would leave me a well-fixed single mother and disappear from my life so that I would not be saddled with an old man. This talk scared me. I had always rested comfortably in the knowledge that his marriage was steady. Suddenly he was talking nonsense. He earned nothing. How would he suddenly make me a fortune? I was a romantic, but not a total fool. I sensed his urgency, his wish for a child of his own, but I remained unmoved. The idea that he would break up his marriage and desert his wife seemed unseemly and embarrassing. It was not difficult for me to decide: I would not have this child. I had to find a physician who would help me terminate the pregnancy.

Abortion in Switzerland was legally permissible if the physical or emotional well-being of the woman was endangered. A psychiatrist had to attest to my emotional risk, and an official state psychiatrist had to OK the report. I found a competent gynecologist who agreed to help me and referred me to a psychiatrist. The psychiatrist was an earnest man who listened to my anxiety about my condition and understood my total lack of readiness to parent a child. He declared me anxious and depressed, and agreed that carrying the pregnancy to term was contraindicated. The official state certifier was another story, he made me undress for the examination. Then he asked me to walk up and down his office, felt my skin, wondered aloud whether all Jewesses had such soft and beautiful skin. He inquired how the lovemaking had gone, whether I had enjoyed it. And he suggested that I insist the pregnancy was the result of a one-night stand. It was quite a horrible experience, and perhaps its bad taste spilled over onto my feelings toward E.

We had one last encounter. In his effort to stop me from leaving him, he had written a poem. Would I listen to his reading it? I was flattered and agreed. Then he added, "I hope you don't mind the name in the poem is not yours. It is Annemarie, because it fit the cadence of my thoughts better." A moment earlier, I was conflicted, and felt affection and regret, but the notion of a poem addressed to Annemarie stopped all those feelings. It was over. I was certainly not jealous of any Annemarie, but the note he introduced was so false it put everything not just into question, but out of the question.

The story of E. is an experience I knew I would eventually need to record, but not at the time. For as long as the main participants were alive, it was something that required secrecy and discretion. Its importance to me is not major, but I am sure that like every close encounter with another human being, my link with E. has had consequences. The other day, I began to wonder about the meaning of the word *sordid*. I used it to describe the ending of the Geigei infatuation, and then I thought that the transformation of our relationship into a caring connection lasting many years made the word *sordid* inaccurate. I think an experience risks becoming sordid when its reality is in variance with its public description; when, slowly, its private description corrodes; it is no longer coherent or justifiable; and is continued out of weakness and with self-deception. By this definition, the E. affair was not sordid. Why am I then compelled to explicate it?

Decades later I had a visit from Marion, Nelly's daughter. We had not seen each other for 33 years. Throughout my childhood, Marion was held up by my mother as a model of perfect behavior. "Marion wouldn't be so rude. Marion would behave *comme il faut*. Marion would not be naughty." Nelly came from a family of well-established, well-to-do Swiss Jews. I don't know how long the Weills (spelled with two l's, which added a couple of notches in status) had, in fact, been in Switzerland, but certainly longer than my mother's family had.

They had immigrated to Switzerland from an area that had been alternately Lithuania, Poland, or Russia, around 1899, when Mother was around three.

My mother was the eldest of five children, three of whom survived; one boy died in infancy of an infectious disease, the other at 12 of kidney disease. Perhaps because her mother was grief stricken at losing two sons, my mother became closer to her father and served as the family's link to the Swiss culture. She became, to use a term coined by family therapist Judy Landau, a go-between child. It became her job to connect the family to the Swiss local community, a task she did exceedingly well. Her skills were aided by her father's generosity in equipping her with "only the best," and by her extraordinary beauty and charm, by her tenacity. And it was that tenacity which would later save us during the German takeover of Czechoslovakia. When she arrived in Switzerland during the middle of the war, to a considerable degree, she could still draw on her former friendships with Swiss Jews and non-Jews, and thereby help rescue my father from an Auschwitz-bound deportation train.

My mother always held it against me that I failed to win social acceptance in St. Gallen, where all my friends had been from nonsocial families. Switzerland was a country in which anti-Semitism increased with social status, which was, I believe, quite the opposite in other European countries. As I think back to those times, this principle operated daily in school: Those children who were open to me, who were friendly, interested and available to socialize, all came from lower-status backgrounds. Higher-status children instinctively backed off, and on a couple of occasions when they did include me in some invitation or activity, their parents made them retract the invitation. Even if I had wanted to fulfill my mother's expectations, it was simply not possible. And I don't think I wanted to. Sour grapes? Hurt pride? Who knows? It was better to think that I chose my friends actively than that I accepted what was left over.

As I mentioned earlier, Marion came to visit me years later. Marion was not only Nelly's daughter and E.'s stepdaughter, but also the cousin of the man who had become my first husband, Edgar. Edgar had come to Geneva from Palestine a few months after my affair with E. had ended. By then I had gone to work for Marion's husband, a journalist who afforded me the opportunity to become a stringer for *Time-Life*. It was delightful to meet with Marion again after all those years. I found our connection easy and familiar. During our time together, the narrative of my long-ago life captured me, and I was stuck on it like a fly on old-fashioned flypaper. I couldn't get off it, but I could move it along.

As we talked about bygone days and bygone people, I was seized with the irresistible urge to tell Marion about my involvement with her stepfather. She had talked about her mother, whose guiding wisdom had been like a sundial, noting only the sunny hours. Toward the end of her mother's life, they had established a mutual closeness that allowed her to forgive her mother for never having paid attention or listened to her. I probably should have left things alone. Instead, I said to Marion, "I want to tell you something, but I am afraid it might really spoil things between us. Yet, I want to chance it."

"It's up to you; do what you want," she said. "I don't get seriously upset about many things."

So, I told her that I had been involved with her stepfather for a number of months and that I always had believed that her mother had known. When I told her of the pregnancy, she understood.

He had been the live-in tutor to Marion and her two brothers in their childhood. "I often wondered how he felt about having no children of his own," she said. Then she burst out laughing. "Imagine, you would have been my stepmother! And perhaps also given me another sister."

The Annemarie episode must have reached some deep resentment in her. She couldn't stop laughing, saying, "That is just like him!" and "You've got to write this story!" So I have, too long and yet not long enough. Often when people ask me a simple question, such as "Where did you go to college?" or "When did you come to the States?" my answers are long, involved, and colorful. Usually I hear, "You must write this." Now I wonder whether the relationship of the telling, the animation and the curiosity of the listener, make for good writing? I tell my life from the point of view that much of it was coincidental. It just happened to me. Or, as an astrologer put it more elegantly, "You have a heavily fated life." Now as I write, I am entangled in a few of the many fragments of my sexual/emotional coming of age. It seems in this arena, I made choices quite often that were not always sensible ones nor were they unhurtful. If I wasn't always in control of my feelings, at least I struggled to align feelings and actions.

Before long my roommate, Lida, had a boyfriend, the son of one of Geneva's patrician Calvinist families. The young couple prepared themselves to deal with the obstacle of her Catholicism, but life took a different turn. In February 1948, the Prague government was taken over by the Communists. Jan Masaryk was killed by defenestration, and things changed. Lida wept with frustration that she had not been home in Prague to participate in this most glorious of all events. She had identified herself to me as a member of the Catholic Communist youth movement. Within one week, she volunteered with the Czechoslovak embassy in Berne for administrative duty, relinquishing her studies and abandoning her boyfriend on the spot.

Left without a roommate, I was lucky to run into a friend, Elsi, the daughter of a small hotel owner from Lucerne who was studying at the Interpreter's School at the university. She invited me to live with her in a comfortable flat near Rondpoint de Plainpalais. Elsi and I each paid an equal share of the rent. She was on a stipend from her hotel owner father, and I was earning an acceptable salary as a secretary. We had taken in a third roommate, Josie, a high school friend of Elsi's who was studying law. Her father was a janitor and her financial situation was dire. She paid about 20 percent of the monthly rent for a small room, which probably had been a maid's room. Elsi had the bedroom and I turned the comfortable living room into a makeshift study-bedroom.

Josie taught us how to live frugally. I remember learning to make an omelet for three people by using one egg and two heaped tablespoons of flour and milk. Josie went on to become the first woman elected to the House of Representatives in Switzerland (Women received the federal vote in Switzerland only in 1964!)

A few weeks after I moved in with Elsi and Josie, the phone rang in the apartment. The call was from the Czech Legation in Berne. The consul general wished to see me, and I was asked to present myself at the offices in two days. I learned that Lida had given the consulate my name as her possible replacement. "She is not political," she told them, "but she is a decent, reliable, patriotic person, and, in addition to Czech, she is fluent in German, French, and English."

It was a fair description. My fervent love of my home country, which had permeated my being when I was a small child, had gone underground but not disappeared during the hopeless war years. That whole childhood world had begun to resurface as the tides of war began to make an Allied victory first possible, then probable. I was readying myself to return to Prague and resume my medical studies there. Only the serious entreaties of friends during our Prague trip in the summer of 1947 caused me to remain in Switzerland. I felt happy and was thrilled and impatient to re-enter the world of my childhood.

With the summons to Berne, the fervent Czech patriotism of my childhood burst into flame. I rushed to the embassy, anxious to be of service to the new country. I arrived at a rather nondescript-looking building and was readily admitted to an office, where two young men were eager to talk to me. They reviewed my qualifications and especially my multilingualism. I made a passing comment about the absence of any political involvement on my part. They declared themselves satisfied, that I would be an acceptable replacement for Lida. Very happily I accepted their decision. "I can start in a couple of weeks!" I beamed. "My semester is almost over."

With eyebrows raised, they shook their heads, and looked at each other. "We are not interested in your studies," one stated in a markedly chilled tone. "We need you here now." Something in the tone alerted me to inquire further. "Couldn't I finish my studies first?" I asked. The senior of the two men was clearly put out. "What are you doing here studying anyway? How come you are in Switzerland? How come you are not home? We need people like you. The diplomatic service needs people like you. Either you appear for your job here as needed, or we will ship you home."

I wish I could say I was politically savvy, and that I was staging a protest against a dictatorship, but I could say no such thing. I was in delayed adolescence and taking orders didn't sit well with me. I don't know what happened to my fervent love of my homeland. I don't think I had stopped to figure out that a homeland under totalitarian regime was in no way the homeland I had left 10 years earlier, and to which I had dreamed of returning. Although I had been in possession of my Czech passport for a paltry year or so, and was proud of having it, I took it out of my purse and tossed it onto the desk. "Here. I no longer want it." In refusing an offer that was in fact a command, I relegated myself again to the miserable status of statelessness. Any thoughts of medical studies in Prague went out the window. An uncomfortable, if diffuse, threat of being on the Czech blacklist took its place.

For decades after, I feared that somewhere in the files of the Czech Republic, there was a black mark against me, and that they would get me if they could. I avoided any thought of traveling there, although my parents made repeated trips to explore possibilities for return. It was not until 1987, as part of a delegation of U.S. family therapists organizing an East-West conference in Prague, that I risked entering Czechoslovakia. Even then, I first rang the State Department, which referred me to their Eastern Europe desk. They reassured me it was safe for me to travel, and that the American consul in Prague would assist me should I encounter any difficulties.

In my heart, I thanked my Prague friends, who in 1947 prevailed on me to wait until the spring to return home. I stayed in Geneva another year, holding a number of part-time, off-the-books jobs, and dating Edgar. I had been fired from my journalist's spot because, when asked by my boss, I could not in good conscience say that to be a journalist was what I wanted most in the world. I wanted to be the one doing things, not the one writing about other people's doings. He told me that if I was not fully dedicated, he would not spend the time and energy to train me. For a while, I subbed as a telephone operator file clerk at the Geneva ORT office, an international Jewish organization devoted to the rescue and settlement of refugees. It was a dreadfully boring job. I entertained many thoughts about the misuse and abuse of working people, feeling terrible for the woman on vacation whom I was relieving. She was anxious when she returned after four weeks.

"Didn't you just love the job?" she gushed. "I was so afraid you would not want to give it back to me. You are in on everything, on the phone with Paris, and Warsaw and London, and read and file copies of all the correspondence!" I assured her that I had no intention of stealing her job from her.

I had a lot of fun in another vacation replacement position in a law firm, where I somehow managed shorthand in French, German, and English. I also spent time on the phone with the Swiss government offices in Berne and got much pleasure from imagining what their reaction would be if they knew that the law firm they were doing business with was represented on the phone by a stateless person without a working permit.

Edgar was a pleasant companion. Even though he rarely had money, he always had a lot of time and was devoted to me and proud of me. Geneva had a diverse, active international community, and he was very skilled at meeting people. By then, I had upgraded to a shared apartment, whose lease signer, albeit an illegal one, I became. The people Edgar would bring home for lunch included visiting American congressmen, high functionaries of the International Labor Organization; three particularly elegant young women, Greek and Hungarian, to whom he was a comforting escort; and an assortment of other exciting people. In accordance with local customs, my lunch break lasted three hours, enough to walk home, put on an economical but pretty lunch I had devised based on red vinegar rice salad, and act the charming hostess. I'd rush back to work, and around seven o'clock, would meet Edgar in the local café, where he was usually accompanied by some of our friends. I worked hard, paid for everything, and had fun. I don't think I resented the uneven distribution of tasks and responsibilities. Only once did my bubble burst, and I experienced a very unpleasant situation.

My apartment, which I had taken over from two American girls who had returned to the States, was a beautiful mansard space, a four-story walk-up, situated on top of the old city wall, at 4 rue Beauregard. It was imaginatively furnished, with playful decorations and exquisite antique pieces. There was a hallway, a bathroom, three rooms, and a large kitchen. The rent was affordable if divided three ways, and utilities were split evenly. Since we were all usually out and also on tight budgets, the utilities bill amounted to very little. Tenants came and went; for a while, my friend from Lucerne had one of the rooms, an Alsatian student occupied the other.

When the Alsatian roommate left, someone sent an American couple, and without much thought, and certainly without pertinent information, I agreed to rent them a room. Even as I remember it now, my blood begins to boil, and I become enraged all over again. They moved in, and the wife proceeded to play "little homemaker." The husband, Wes, shielded his little Audrey from all contact with us. He spoke for the two of them; firmly, roughly, decisively. She, in the meantime, did her wifely things: cooked breakfast, cooked lunch, cooked dinner. Since she was home all day, the place had to be heated more adequately. Within a couple of months, it became clear the arrangement did not work. Audrey hogged the kitchen, burned up all our coal, did not speak to us, and referred us to Wes when we tried to come to some arrangement with her. He would prove his love for her by barking at us and comforting her. Actually, he barked at me, because Edgar had no official standing and no unofficial guts. I felt demeaned and humiliated.

When the utilities bill arrived, it was four times the usual amount. I tried to reason with Wes, to explain to him that we could not afford his domestic ways. It would be fair if he paid the lion's share of the bill, since Audrey cooked all the time. He insisted that living like this was his right and that he owed us nothing further. In the middle of the argument, they moved out suddenly, owing not only utilities but also rent. In Switzerland, there is a legal requirement of at least a month's notice before moving out. It was a universally accepted rule, and no one would consider breaking it. Wes and Audrey's pre-emptive action left a serious deficit in our meticulously calibrated monthly budget. It was the worry about how to make up the shortfall as much as my fury at the two of them that made me want to hold them accountable. Maybe I felt envious that Audrey had her Wes to protect her.

I knew Edgar was of no use as a protector. Instead, I turned to a dear friend of ours: tall, comfortable, bearlike, Joe Zasloff. When I told him the story, he immediately felt as outraged as I did, maybe a little more so since he was ashamed of fellow Americans behaving badly when guests in foreign countries. I could not take recourse to local courts because I did not have a legal leg to stand on, holding, as I did, an illegal lease. Joe suggested we seek mediation through the American consul. In retrospect, I realize that the duty of the consul is first and foremost to help and protect American citizens, and that no consul would ever side with a local person against an American citizen. Nevertheless, the consul agreed to see us, and Wes, without Audrey, agreed to attend.

The consul spoke fairly, kindly, and wisely, advising Wes to abide by local custom and pay what he owed. Wes appeared reasonable, agreed to the terms, and even gave a friendly goodbye. When I arrived back home, the police were waiting for me, having been alerted by Wes to my lease status. I felt angry, sulliedc and deserted by Edgar. I was envious of Audrey for having a creep like

Wes protect her while she played helpless. I experienced the events as a collision between straight dealing and treachery. For years, Wes remained the most hated person in my inner cast of characters. I often hoped that he would go back to being a military pilot and that his plane would crash in flames.

The Swiss police were kinder than expected and only gave me a verbal reprimand. Somehow, I managed to make up the financial shortfall, but Geneva had lost its appeal. Simultaneously, Edgar immigrated to the United States, where he had family. I went back to Zürich to stay with my parents, who by then had moved to a small town nearby after my father was hired by a chemical company and given a work permit.

Author's Mother, Aunt Fanny, & Uncle Leo, c. 1910

Swiss Fraternity Life, c. 1914

Author's Father, Austro-Hungarian Army, 1916

Author's Mother at University, St. Gallen, c. 1916

Author's Parents, 1917

Author's Parents—Wedding Picture, 1918

Cousin Annemarie & Brother Fred, 1924

Family—Grandparents, Mother, Aunt Fanny,
Uncle Leo, Brother Fred & Author, 1932

2nd Grade Class, Miroslav,
Teacher's left hand on Author, 1935

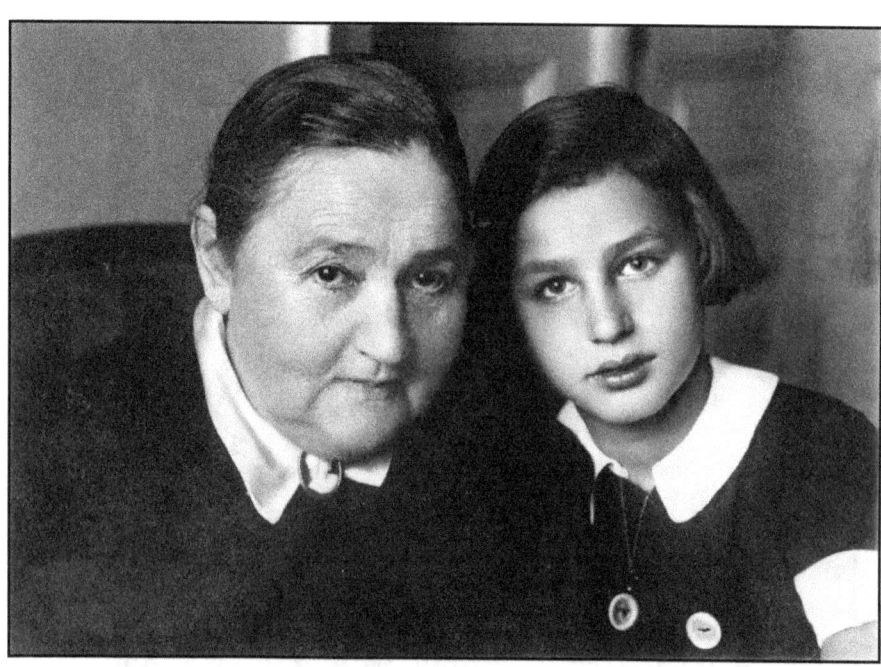

Author with Grandmother Fischer, c. 1937

St. Gallen, Rosenberg, c. 1938

St. Gallen with Bridges over the Sitter;
Saentis Mountain Range in background, c. 1938

Girl Scout Troop, c. 1940

Author with Aunt Fanny, St. Moritz, Summer, 1941

Dressed up for Dance Class Formal, Spring 1941

A1A Class, (Geigei, back row with glasses; Cordelia, 3rd from Left; Author, extreme front right), Spring, 1942

Elly, Selling Celebratory Pins, c. 1943

Author's Father, after Rescue, with Children, c. 1944

Newly Arrived in America, 1950

Connecticut College, Class of 1952

Edgar Frank, 1952

Wedding Picture with Art, 1956

Author's Family Welcomes Melanie,
Switzerland, July 1960

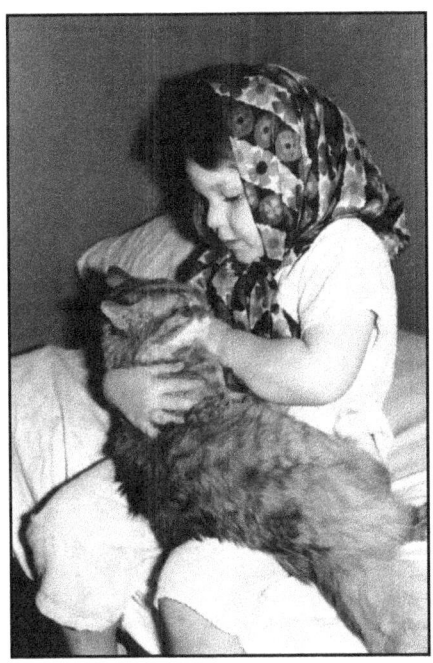

Melanie with Ginger c. 1963

Nathan W. Ackerman, Director, The Family Institute, c.1969

Family Home, Turned Industrial, c.1970s

Miroslav, A Village Street, c.1970s

Miroslav-Topography, c.1970s

The Kahn Sisters' House c. 1970s

Melanie with Chipmonk, 1971

Melanie, 1976

Founding Board Members of AFTA, 03-12-1978

Al Scheflen, c. 1980

Author & Larry on Beach with Polly, 1999

Author & Larry, 2000

*Getting Started
in America*

A Not-So-Soft Landing

Filled with eagerness and anticipation about the unknown world I would soon encounter, I boarded the SS America in Le Havre, France, on March 5, 1950. The sense of adventure pushed aside any apprehension I might have felt. Perhaps I didn't feel any. I was confident I could manage with my three-month visitor's visa and a small amount of money, less than 100 dollars.

My accommodations were then called steerage, bottom deck inside cabin. There were four bunks; I managed to claim one of the top ones. My bunkmate below me was a young French girl sailing to America to marry her G.I. boyfriend, whom she hardly remembered. She was tearful, timorous, and early on attached herself to me. We were about the same age, but looking after her made me feel grown up and worldly.

Crossing the Atlantic in March could be rough. Considerable sea legs and a strong sea stomach were required. Strong winds and high seas extended the length of the crossing from nine days to 13. Many were seasick. It was challenging to navigate the vomit-spattered cabin and hallways without surrendering to the strong urge to join in the general malaise. The first few days I found refuge in the swimming pool on a lower level, where it seemed somewhat calmer. On the third day the ship moved so violently that the pool's water flooded the changing cabins. The pool was emptied, and the facility was shut down. My next strategy was to spend as much time as possible up on deck. I was advised to watch the horizon, and, indeed, by doing so, eased my ever-threatening nausea. I hooked arms with my French charge and forced her to walk the deck with me. My concern for her health, as well as my determination to keep her from falling apart, strengthened both my sea legs and sea stomach. At the same time, I successfully diminished her terror at the thought of marrying a man who was all but a stranger to her.

In the dining room, bad weather table boards were put up to prevent the briskly moving plates and glasses from flying off the table. As I sat in the increasingly empty dining room, the dinnerware would take leave of me and bump against the board, only to return in a few seconds with the next wave. Most people had stopped coming to meals. But a few of us; obstinate, hardy, or simply unaffected souls, stuck to the mealtimes and ate. Lying in my bunk at night was an exercise in fortitude. My three cabinmates were miserable, groaning loudly as they brought up what little food they had earlier managed to force down.

Our cabin steward, a pleasant young Chinese man, tried his best to clean up the mess. At night he stood by my bunk and gave me the most wonderful back rubs, which eventually put me to sleep. It made me think about my father, whose expression of affection often took the form of sitting at my bedside and rubbing or scratching my back. In this way, he had provided me with a lifetime resource for soothing and pleasure.

The ship finally docked in New York. The immigration officer looked at my papers and mumbled something. He looked up at me and, with a twinkle in his eye, said, "So, you were born in Czechoslovakia? Just make sure you don't let that happen again."

Taking in the straight-up skyscrapers, my first impression of New York was one of awe. My friend Edgar came to meet me and took me to the smallest house I could have imagined. He was renting a room on Woodhaven Boulevard in Queens and had found me a room in the neighboring house. They were like twin dollhouses: each had a tiny entry, a small living room decorated in pastel colors, tiny bathroom, tiny kitchen, and two tiny bedrooms: one for the widowed owner, one for the tenant.

Our landladies were extremely kind, making us comfortable, providing occasional breakfasts, and tidying our rooms, which, like the rest of the house, were decorated in pastel colors. Mine had a mint green bedspread and curtains. Edgar's room was done in shades of matching blue. It was sweet, friendly, and, at only 10 dollars a week, affordable. Yet, somehow I sensed almost immediately this would be the briefest of stops in my new life. I had to look for a paying job. As a student in Switzerland, as here, I had lacked a work permit, but had managed to find people willing to pay me off the books. I thought that in New York, so much bigger and more anonymous than Zurich or Geneva, it would be easier to work unnoticed by the official watch dogs.

I had not considered a basic reality: Employees in the United States are required to have a Social Security number to submit to their employer. Obviously, I didn't have one, and couldn't obtain one legitimately. I didn't ever consider resorting to any devious strategy. I wanted my presence in the New World to be in order, pristine. Edgar's uncle, Emil, a distributor of foreign films, provided me with part-time secretarial work. I felt oppressed and that I was the recipient of his charity as I assumed the role of a newly arrived and needy person. I began to search for other options. Perhaps I could apply to a school, where I might qualify for a stipend. I found the address of an organization called The International Institute of Education. I walked into their office and asked to speak to a counselor. She was extraordinarily unkind. In a sharp, dismissive voice, she addressed me as if I were learning disabled, or maybe just stupid.

She said, "The name of this organization is The International Institute of Education. *International*, do you know what that means? That means among nations. I see that you are stateless and, therefore, you are not a member of any nation. How could you think that 'international' might apply to you?"

Such a remark might have devastated me, and maybe it did, deep down. But throughout my years as an unwelcome refugee, I had grown a protective shell. Insults, threats, and rejections all tended to slide off me. This was true when rude and prejudiced behavior came from an institutional source or had political motivation, but also when the rejections and cruelties were relational. In personal situations, my ability to shrug off diminution and insults tended to mask the long-term damaging effect. My protective membrane permitted me to stay in painful and offensive relationships. Not only had I turned in my weapons of self-defense, I also had furloughed my survival strategies of self-respect and protection.

Through some acquaintances, I got in touch with an immigration lawyer, who was charming and offered to help. First, he told me how attractive I was, and how much he admired my courage. He stepped closer to me, kissed me, and caressed my back. Within seconds I was enveloped in my rescue-needing, home-seeking fantasy. *What a nice man. He really likes me. Perhaps he will marry me....* Instantaneous delusion. A look around his office with its photographs of his wife and children jolted me back to reality. The whole flight of fantasy lasted less than a minute. I thanked him for his interest and concern and lied when I said I would call him in a few days to find out if he had any specific suggestions for me.

I found my way to the offices of the Jewish Refugee Organization on Park Row. A kindly, rational, somber lady explored with me the reasons I had chosen to come to New York. She ascertained that I had not fled personal peril and acute persecution, and that I had not been thrown out of Switzerland. She said perhaps there were other options I had failed to consider. Staying in

New York on my own would be difficult, she mused. I would likely be better off if I returned to Switzerland.

Through an ad in *Vorwaerts*, the Jewish weekly, I secured a job as an au pair. A middle-aged couple with a three-year-old boy needed a babysitter. They were barely emerging from the trauma of flight and rescue from war-torn Vienna. They ran a dry-cleaning store on nearby Cabrini Boulevard and were hard-working people, small, quiet, grey: it was as if any loud word, any colorful scarf, any intense wish might precipitate their annihilation. They did not question why I would want such a modest job. A previous potential employer had done so, suspicious not only of my motives but also of the likelihood I would stay in the job.

The couple and their son, Paul, lived in a one-bedroom apartment in Washington Heights, about six blocks below Fort Tryon Park. The husband and wife slept on a pull-out couch in the living room, while the boy and I shared the bedroom, he in a crib, and I on a couch, without so much as a night table or reading light. This was particularly difficult, as I was expected to go to bed around the same time as their son, about an hour after they came home from work, usually around eight.

The first day I gave Paul his lunch, I discovered he was still drinking from a bottle. I did not know much about childcare, but a bottle at three years old?

I said, "Come on Paul, you are a big boy. Here is a cup. Let's give it a try." Paul drank from a cup. He found it neither difficult nor traumatic. In fact, he was proud. As little as I knew about childcare, I gave even less thought to the parents' need to keep their son a baby. When I had Paul show off his newfound skill of drinking from a cup, his mother became very upset. She said to me, "I hired you to mind him, not to educate him." Later, I learned that they had lost one child (I never found out the circumstances) and that Paul was their whole life. They wanted nothing as much as to protect him every waking moment from any possible peril. I was very dense; it made no sense to me. I wanted Paul to enjoy himself, to learn new things, to be adventuresome rather than a fraidy cat. As the days went on, Paul came to like and trust me.

Living under these oppressive circumstances, I gradually became uncertain of myself. My employers would say to me, "Here is a dollar. Go to the store and buy a pound of Red Delicious apples. They will cost 38 cents. Bring back the change of 62 cents. If they don't have these apples, come back home and I will tell you what to buy instead." I began to doubt my ability to count, to add and subtract, to think. It felt like I lost 20 IQ points during my time with them. To make matters worse, I have never been a good housekeeper. I didn't possess the skills that would have made me appear competent to them. I had cooked and ironed only when I couldn't avoid it, and even then, just barely. Because of my shortcomings, I was not expected to do any household chores. My employer even ironed my blouse when she saw how deplorable my own efforts were.

In the middle of all this drudgery, a wonderful event occurred. Herb, a medical student with whom I had carried on a brief dreamlike affair, stretching over ten snowbound sparkly weekends in the Swiss Alps, arrived for his summer vacation. His parents lived in Syracuse, his sister in New York. While he was visiting her, he made the time to come to see me. Since I was taking care of Paul, Paul and I included him in our daily outings to Fort Tryon Park. Herb, a handsome six-footer who looked like Lil' Abner, joked around with Paul, gave him piggyback rides, and roughhoused with him. Herb nurtured Paul's self-confidence, helping him become a lively little boy. Herb also fed my romantic dream of what a wonderful father and husband he would make.

My pay was modest, customary for an au pair, and also appropriate for my low level of domestic skills, even though my hours were long: essentially every day, all day, except for Saturday noon to Sunday night. I must have obtained a three-month extension of my visitor's visa, although I no longer remember how and when. Slowly the six months approached their end and my visa would expire.

When I woke up from what I now think of as my dissociated idiot state, I realized I probably would return to Switzerland. Before returning, I accepted an invitation from Herb's parents to visit with the family in Syracuse. The visit turned out to be painful and humiliating, but it did help snap me out of my stupor. On the day I arrived, Herb's mother said, "Well, we have other commitments, so you will be in the house alone. Here are the keys; there is food in the refrigerator. We will be back in a couple of days."

The letdown I felt upon learning of their departure, which included Herb, was hugely overshadowed by the sense that they trusted me. They gave me their house keys! They did not think I would leave the gas on, forget to lock the door, burn their pots and pans: all the worries my New York employer voiced. What a release it was. In the end, I luxuriated in the quiet solitude of the house. I even located a nearby stable and went for a three-hour ride on a lovely and obedient horse.

I was overjoyed to welcome Herb upon his return home. When we found some time alone, instead of being the tender and enthusiastic lover I had known in Switzerland, he acted awkward and strange. Although we had full privacy, he avoided me. When I inquired as to what was going on, he mumbled that his father had admonished him to be prudent and cautious, since surely I would scheme to entrap him by becoming pregnant so I could stay in the States. His father was worried this would put an end to his medical studies. It was one of those most hurtful interludes I otherwise might have shrugged off, but it infuriated me. Herb seemed to knuckle under his father's intrusive sexual instructions and seemed ready to ascribe such despicable machinations to his "darling kitten forever and always." I did recognize that the family were refugees themselves; the physician father spent five years preparing to retake his medical exams. They doted on their son and were afraid for his future, just as my father had been for mine.

I was strengthened by the experience and felt more myself when I got back to my au pair job.

Before returning to Europe, I wanted to see more of New York than just Washington Heights. One Friday afternoon in early August, with my week's pay of 30 dollars, I did the forbidden thing: Paul and I boarded the A train to mid-Manhattan. We got out at Columbus Circle and walked into Central Park. It was a particularly hot afternoon, and the park was crowded. I decided to splurge and give Paul a special treat. I had heard about Rumpelmayer's, the Vienna-style conditorei, on Central Park South. I felt wonderful as I found us a table there. I hadn't realized just how homesick I was, not just for the gracious pleasures of Europe but also for my old competent self. Paul had a banana split with hot fudge sauce. I ordered an iced coffee with whipped cream. We both enjoyed the feast, which took about a third of my weekly pay.

Happy and satisfied, we left Rumpelmayer's and turned west to go back to Columbus Circle. Suddenly I heard someone calling my name. Who would know me here? I thought the call must be for another Kitty, although there weren't many of us around. I looked and saw a woman waving directly at me.

"Kitty, what are you doing here?" was Barbara's greeting. For a moment I couldn't place her. Then I remembered that we had met two or three years earlier, when she had been a member of a Smith College group spending their junior year abroad in Geneva. I had made friends with some of them, notably Marjorie Church, a Wellesley student whose father was a U.S. Congressman from Evanston, Illinois.

"I have a job as an au pair," I replied, "and this is my charge." I pulled Paul close. Then I added, "This is just temporary, and it's coming to an end. My visa is running out and I am thinking of returning to Switzerland."

"I thought you were going to resume medical studies?" Barbara countered. "What happened?"

"Well," I stammered, feeling embarrassed, not at my au pair job, but at my lack of resourcefulness, "I had hoped to find a way of studying, but I have no money."

"No money? Don't you know that there are no financial restrictions between the U.S. and Switzerland? How careless of you to leave without making proper financial arrangements."

At this point, I began to stammer. I vaguely recalled that Barbara came from a wealthy Baltimore family. Her father was in the oil business, or something like it. Was it possible that she didn't know some people had no money?

"I was clumsy," I replied. "I couldn't arrange things."

"How nice to have run into you," Barbara said, smiling. "Where can I reach you if I want to call you?"

We exchanged addresses and phone numbers. I gave Edgar's number in addition to my workplace, and we said good-bye. Our return home was uneventful. Paul and I had had a good day.

The following week, when Paul and I came in from our Saturday morning walk, his mother greeted me with a suspicious look. "There was a phone call for you from Connecticut College. What is that about?"

I had no idea. I told her so and got dressed for the evening to meet Edgar. I was going to be out until Sunday night. That afternoon, another phone call had reached Edgar, and the message was clear. "Connecticut College called you," he told me. "They want you to come up for an interview."

"Connecticut College? Where? What? And what should I

wear?" I attempted to calm down. I learned Connecticut College was in New London, less than three hours by train from New York. The interview was scheduled for Monday. On Sunday, I asked Edgar to go to my employer's home and return with a suitable outfit for a daytime interview. a grey skirt and a white blouse. He would tell my employer that I had taken ill.

Edgar came back with a terrible story. During my absence, my employers' living room ceiling had collapsed, and a piece of plaster had strafed Paul's forehead. He had a huge white bandage around his head. Fortunately, the gash underneath, while long, was only skin-deep. The household, understandably, exuded both tragedy and fury.

"Yes, I am sure she is sick," my boss said to Edgar. "What do you take me for?" He described how she had eyed him almost menacingly. "Yeah, Connecticut College, clothes for an interview." Despite her anger with me, she went into my room and came back with a suitable outfit, including daytime flats.

I felt terrible when Edgar told me what had happened in my absence. My first thought was that I was well out of there, as I might have been hurt. My second thought was about Paul and how frightened he must have been. I felt compassion for his parents, who had tried so hard to shield their son from the lurking dangers that await us all.

Paul's mother sent a message that I should come and get my things. And that I owed her the money she had paid me while I was away in Syracuse. She had no intention to pay for a vacation when I no longer worked for them. At that moment of truth, perhaps she saw far more clearly than I did that my life was about to change dramatically.

Becoming a College Student

I arrived in New London for my interview on a warm August day. I was puzzled and confused, but nonetheless excited. I still wasn't sure just what a college was; my prior experiences at the universities of Zurich and Geneva offered little or no help. The Connecticut College campus and its surroundings resembled a park with expansive lawns, quaint houses. Was it a resort town, perhaps? I had no idea what awaited me.

The taxi had deposited me in front of a building somewhat larger than the others. I couldn't orient myself to the layout of the houses. Certainly this couldn't be a university? I could not escape a sense of unreality. I floated into the building and up the stairs. Eventually a friendly and soft-spoken woman greeted me in a reassuring and maternal manner. She invited me into her office and gently involved me in a conversation about my circumstances. I told her I had entered the United States on a visitor's visa, and therefore was unable to gain access to any school where I might consider applying. There was always a person at the door who would ask for my visa before I could be granted access to an admissions officer.

I also told Dean Burdick, with whom I was speaking, that no opportunities were open to me in Switzerland either. I did not have a work permit and had no financial resources to continue my studies. I told her that the Swiss authorities wanted me out. At some point in our talk, Dean Burdick informed me the college had a scholarship set aside for me in the amount of one thousand dollars, which left 650 dollars for me to pay for a year's tuition, room, and board.

I never inquired where the money came from, how they found me, or why they had called me. I discovered much later that Barbara's father gave 500 dollars on my behalf, inviting the college to match it. (Barbara's father was Jacob Blaustein, and he became a major benefactor to Connecticut College.) In the midst of my floaty state of disbelief, I could feel myself pull away from the offer. I had my reasons: There was no medical school to continue the studies begun in Zurich. I would be one of the oldest students at the school (in the past, I had always been the youngest).

I was ashamed even to admit it silently, but I did not want to attend an all-women's school. There was, of course, a simple and practical way to win this argument with myself and reject the offer. I did not have 650 dollars to cover the difference. "Thank you very much," I told Dean Burdick, "but I don't think I can accept your offer."

"What are your plans?" she asked.

"I think I will return to Switzerland and go from there."

She looked at me intensely, in order to capture my full attention. "Has there been any change in the conditions there?"

It was a simple and clarifying question. "No," I said. "Nothing."

"Then you don't have much choice," she replied. "You've had a difficult time. We would love to offer you a year's respite. A room, your meals, a library, and no compulsion to attend any classes, if you don't want to."

I didn't then understand the incredible generosity of the offer. Nevertheless, I saw no way to accept it. I couldn't begin to see myself in that beautiful place. The insurmountable obstacle of my personal financial deficit made any further examination of my feelings irrelevant. I thanked her and said good-bye. I returned to

New York and began to look into booking my passage back to Europe.

Less than a week later, I received a phone call from Connecticut College informing me that I had received a full scholarship. I was summoned back to New London, asked to arrive in time for the beginning of classes, in approximately one week. The decision had been taken out of my hands. I immediately decided to turn it into my own choice. I didn't stop to recognize how relieved I was to have a focus and structure. I hadn't admitted to myself how my unmoored situation had weighed me down. I set about preparing to enter college.

I searched for someone who might give me some hints about what was ahead of me, who might offer advice. There wasn't much time, and the choice of suitable mentors was extremely limited. I remembered Aunt Martha, a distant relative of my father's, who had immigrated to America in the late 1920s. A retired schoolteacher, she lived on the Grand Concourse in the Bronx. During the war years, there had been some tense, ultimately unsuccessful communication between her family and ours after they had been unable, or perhaps unwilling, to provide affidavits that might have assisted our exit from Europe. Despite this, with a solid plan in place, I felt comfortable contacting her.

She welcomed me in a friendly and warm manner and invited me to her apartment. Upon my arrival I met her nieces, young women also in their 20s, who had gathered to greet me. In contrast to Aunt Martha, who was calm, quiet, and grandmotherly, the younger women seemed curious, but a tad unfriendly, perhaps jealous. They looked me over and then commented that I was headed to a fancy school. I sensed disapproval in their voices and expressions. I suspected they lived in modest circumstances and wanted to make it clear there wouldn't be help coming from them.

Fortunately, Aunt Martha didn't share their sentiments. She suggested we go shopping to purchase the necessary clothes. This task required a major expedition into Manhattan. As I would be leaving for school within a couple of days, our shopping adventure occurred almost immediately. Neither Aunt Martha nor I knew what the required uniform would be, but she took me to Klein's on 14th Street. We chose a black and white tweed skirt with velvet trim on its faux pockets, a pair of grey slacks, several sweaters, and a sophisticated fitted red cocktail dress. As I recall, the total amounted to about 20 dollars. More than 60 years later, I still am touched by her generosity.

At college, I quickly saw that my new clothes did not match the customary style of dress, but I wore them anyway. Everybody else wore jeans, men's white shirts, and saddle shoes. During the two years I was at Connecticut College, I never adopted the popular attire. The constraints of my extremely limited budget forced me to wear what I had brought. My clothing marked me as odd and different, but also gave me the ability to observe the underlying differences in my cultural values compared with those of my fellow students. The other girls wanted to wear the same things. It was a statement of belonging, being included, and knowing what the score was.

In photograph after photograph from that time, there I am, wearing my slacks, sweater, and loafers. I never felt ashamed. I don't remember longing to dress in the prevailing campus style. It seemed somehow appropriate and fitting that I should look different. Growing up, I was taught that it was important to be an individual, to value uniqueness in spirit and temperament, and to dress as individually as possible. Perhaps I believed that I was the truly enlightened one at college. I didn't grasp the concept that having arrived in this new country, it was my place to adapt.

I got my first shock the day after arriving on campus. Four or five enthusiastic and friendly girls had met my train. They greeted me effusively with hugs and welcomed me to Connecticut College. The whole gang of us drove to the campus, where they helped install me in my room. I felt overwhelmed. I was usually more reserved and did not immediately open up to strangers. I did not have much small talk to offer. It took me a bit to warm up to them, but then I did, and they won me over. My God, so many girls wanted to be my friends, to know me, and to be with me! I came across them walking together on campus the very next day. I was eager to identify them. Would I remember their names? What would I say?

It was wasted anxiety. Their mission, to pick up the foreign student at the train station and settle her in the dorm. had been successfully accomplished. They didn't bother to greet me again. I was shocked and hurt. The process of learning about the different kinds of American relationships began in that moment. There were those that are person-specific, and chosen with some deliberateness, which might grow and deepen over time. Then there are those that are function and context defined: We are friends and relate to each other as long as we are involved in a common task or program. When that is completed, our connection ends.

My status as a foreign student gave me the privilege of living in one of the very few single rooms. It was sparsely furnished, as most of the items that made a dorm room look cozy and comfortable usually came from home to supplement the basic necessities of bed, desk, and chair. Someone gave me a spare lamp, and from somewhere and someone else a spare pillow appeared. I didn't know who provided what, but in no time I was settled in and felt at home. Residing in such a stable, solid, and beautiful place that had an air of permanence, power, and affluence gave me a sense of security. I felt uplifted and nurtured that there were people who cared about me, so much so that I became infused with new energy. I wanted to join in and participate in whatever programs were happening. I inquired what other students at Connecticut College were studying and was told that everyone was working toward their Bachelor of Arts degree.

I immediately decided I wanted to do that as well. I learned that the course of study consisted of two basic parts: courses that represented the core requirements, which had to be met by everyone, and courses chosen individually, which added up to one's major course of study. I requested a meeting with Dean Burdick to ask how to proceed. Her warm and non-condescending manner had won my full trust. The first obstacle to planning a course of study was the fact I had no transcripts, nor any proof of completed academic work. I had assumed the lack of official documents would present an insurmountable problem. As I prepared to meet with her, I was ready to concede defeat before I began.

Dean Burdick offered a solution both simple and generous. "Do you know what you would like to study?" she asked. "Why don't you look at our program and decide which courses might interest you? Then speak to the professors who are teaching them and ask permission to attend." Filled with both relief and gratitude, and without a moment's hesitation, I energetically embarked on this plan. I chose my major by process of elimination. I did so without any advice, which was undoubtedly available and might well have been helpful.

As a beginning medical student in Switzerland, I had studied science, and believed I did not need any more of what I imagined would be beginning-level basic science. I felt similarly about languages. I was drawn to political science, but after my dismal experience as a stateless person with other educational institutions, I couldn't imagine a career in the public domain. Increasingly, the study of psychology appeared to be a good fit, primarily because when I was studying medicine, mind-body connections had interested me.

I was able to fit the core requirements into two years and received credit for some of my prior studies. My Swiss schooling had prepared me well; my first year's grades were excellent. Connecticut College extended my scholarship for a second year, allowing me to stay until graduation. At some point during the first year, with the college's assistance, my visitor's visa was converted to a student visa. I felt cared for in a way that I hadn't been in a very long time.

My basic expenses were covered by the scholarship: room and board, as well as tuition. It was my responsibility to earn enough money for books, toiletries, and other personal needs. Fortunately, the college had a work-by-the-hour program, which many students used. It puzzled me that well-to-do girls desired to work for pay. At home in Europe, students definitely did not work at menial jobs for money: to do so was considered socially demeaning. In any event, no such jobs were available at home. At Connecticut College, I had to compete with all the other girls for dining room service and kitchen clean-up slots. The college paid one dollar per meal, and we were relieved from the requirement of dressing for dinner and spending an hour sitting at the dinner table.

The other available campus jobs paid 65 cents an hour. I was thrilled by the variety of opportunities open to me. I spent many hours working at the biology lab, feeding and cleaning the cages of a group of field mice, housed in individual cages. Some were from the mainland and the others came from nearby Block Island. The research hypothesis was whether the groups of mice represented two separate species or were simply geographic variations of one species. They were wild, and too old for taming. Nevertheless, I gave each one a name. I wasn't present the day the critical part of the experiment took place, in which, in an effort to discover whether members of the separate groups would mate, they were introduced into each other's cages.

In the morning when I arrived to take care of the mice, a shocking sight awaited me. Each cage held one dead mouse and one live and victorious mouse. I have since learned that mice are extremely territorial, and do not accept newcomers into their areas. I wonder whether the researchers knew about and considered both gender and territoriality, whether the females were ready for mating, and whether the males had to be brought to the females or vice versa. I was devastated. My next lab job was gentling rats for learning experiments. They were especially bred docile young white rats, and the more you handled them, the tamer and friendlier they became.

Eventually I was chosen to act as secretary to Dr. Louise Holborn, a professor of government. She was thrilled to discover I could correspond in German, French, and English. Her reliance on my skills added to my self-confidence. Later on, the experience with Dr. Holborn led to my being in charge (with much assistance by the faculty) of organizing an intercollegiate United Nations conference (together with Wesleyan College) of workshops, panels, and discussion groups. Also in that first year, I was elected president of both the Psychology Club and the International Club.

In spite of all my involvements and activities, a deeper connection with my American classmates did not happen, not even when I landed one of the leading roles in the senior melodrama, as a villain with a foreign accent. The casting highlighted not only a difference, but also a deficiency in elocution. I was pleased and humiliated simultaneously. Ultimately, the play was judged unsuitable because the text contained innumerable puns derived from cocktail names. At the last minute, the administration canceled the performance.

Around this time, I was beginning to feel constricted, confined, and alienated from myself. I had lived on my own since I was 17, and the 6:30 curfew the college had in place was intrinsically confusing to me. I obeyed the rule but had trouble accepting it as a statement about the truth of my life. None of these shadows had made their appearance when I first arrived at college.

Early on, two girls connected with me. One was Marne, who sought me out specifically. She moved easily between her rather large group of friends and a budding friendship with me. She felt a kinship with me, as she also considered herself somewhat an outsider. She was the daughter of a single mother. Whether never married or divorced, it did not make much of a difference in those days, both conditions were cause for shame. She came from a remote and impoverished branch of an affluent family. An uncle, whom Marne considered her benefactor, paid her tuition. He was a distant figure, but one she felt was due respect and gratitude.

We were both recipients of others' largesse, and thus in a different category than most of the students, who came from wealthy families. It was an impression reinforced throughout the year when the weekends rolled around. An equally stylized and unvarying attire of cashmere sweater sets, pearls, and fur coats replaced the daily uniforms of blue jeans and men's shirts. Often chauffeur-driven cars arrived to drive girls home for the weekend. Marne and I formed a friendly alliance as outsiders spending our weekends on campus and developed a friendship that lasted a lifetime. Our bond only ended with Marne's death from cancer in her mid-seventies.

A few days after my arrival, a group of girls in the dorm told me, in that excited and mysterious manner usually reserved to announce a pleasant surprise, that they had such a surprise for me. They couldn't wait to see my pleasure. With curiosity and total absence of wariness, I followed them into a nearby room, where another foreign student had just moved in. They announced with lively anticipation, "This is Annemarie; she is from Czechoslovakia too. Aren't you happy to have a friend?"

I looked at Annemarie, and Annemarie looked at me. We returned tight, polite smiles. There was a problem. Annemarie was a Sudeten-German. Her people had undermined Czechoslovakia and then invited Hitler into my homeland, which they claimed as their own. They were the ones who had spread anti-Semitism and

National Socialism, had been instrumental in assisting the dismemberment of Czechoslovakia and the deportation and subsequent murder of the Jewish population. In turn, after World War II, they were expelled from Czechoslovakia. Annemarie and I were defined enemies. But Connecticut was neutral ground, and the other girls, who obviously were unaware of our differences, were friendly to us both. Annemarie and I were speechless.

Astonishingly, before too long, Annemarie and I became best friends. We both felt alien to American culture. Our sensibilities were middle European, much more alike than different. I remember Annemarie telling me at one point, "No, Kitty, the rules don't apply to you. You are different and above the rules." I felt pleased to have some of my "exceptionalism" recognized. Annemarie, a German, was willing to admire a person perceived as outside of (or above) everyday rules. What joint delusions we must have shared.

The college prided itself on its program to admit foreign students who had suffered during the war and its aftermath. They wanted the community to be aware of our existence. I was sent on many outings to speak to community groups about my experiences. I went as a college emissary and tried to do justice to the task. I don't remember anyone prepping me for it and had only a vague notion of what I was doing. In Switzerland, following my father's injunction not to be seen or heard, I had lived on the margins. I had no sense of having a place in the mainstream, or even that it would be a safe place to be.

But off I went, undeterred, if not a bit dissociated, feeling not quite myself, developing a different persona. At one point, I arrived at a gathering of the elders of the Unitarian Church, held in an ancient house located on a beautiful stretch of shoreline in a cove in Niantic. The room was dark, formal, and forbidding. About a dozen women, all of whom seemed ancient to me, were seated in a circle on straight-back, dark wooden chairs, silent and solemn. It gradually emerged that they thought I was the daughter of missionaries. They had expected me to speak about my mission work. Instead of standing up for who I was and saying, "I'm Jewish! I don't know about mission work" or at least identifying myself as a foreign student at Connecticut College, I tried to oblige them. I quickly refashioned myself into my friend Cordelia, whose parents indeed had been missionaries in India, and later in Switzerland. I spoke to them as Cordelia. Not only can I not remember a word of what I said, but I probably did not know what I was saying at the time either.

At another point I was sent as a college delegate to a meeting called the Junior Republic, which convened in Hartford, at the offices of the Aetna insurance company. I sat silently on a panel, where I met the then-governor John Davis Lodge. That same day I also met Eleanor Roosevelt in an unusual way. In the public restroom, I opened an unlocked stall door, and walked straight in on Mrs. Roosevelt! I was mortified and petrified, but she said, in a very relaxed and kind way, "That's all right. I'll be out in just a moment."

This intimate encounter remains my most vivid recollection of the entire Junior Republic meeting. There she was, Mrs. Eleanor Roosevelt, a large and relaxed woman, friendly and reassuring, even in a most awkward situation. While it is true that famous people are only human, like everyone else, they are not at all like everyone else in their poise, kindness, and ability to put one at ease. Mrs. Roosevelt seemed totally unconcerned and didn't show a trace of embarrassment.

The environment and experience of Connecticut College greatly shaped and influenced my view of America. It played an enormous role in my acculturation, and in my understanding of the fundamentally different assumptions held by Europeans and Americans about the nature of life. The generous and welcoming reception the college afforded, the care and support extended, were all in sharp contrast to the difficult times I had endured in Switzerland. The compassionate and gracious way the college enabled my progress came to represent the United States as a whole.

Whatever alienation I might feel when people connect in superficial ways, whatever I might wonder about those who consider happiness not only a right but a normal daily occurrence, who think that a person who sees life as hard and tragic is just a depressed kook, I try to hold on to the view of life I learned at Connecticut College. Nothing can really shake my fundamental and almost childlike faith in America as a benevolent country, one that means well, tries to function sensibly, rationally, and lovingly. I sometimes find I clutch this view desperately, even angrily, especially given the current harsh immigration policies, which flies in the face of my faith in this country.

In addition to giving me many opportunities to participate in off-campus life, various faculty members also tried to enlighten me about more mundane American ways. "Never toot your own horn! Never boast! Always find someone else to do that on your behalf!" was one such maxim. After a particularly insistent political debate at the time of the Korean War, I took a liberal, anti-interventionist position while the seven other people at the dinner table all took the opposite view. I was reprimanded. "It is not polite to disagree and not just because you are a guest here," I was told.

I didn't understand why their disagreeing with me was fine, but my disagreeing with them was not. Similarly, I got into trouble in a sociology seminar when I took passionate issue with a classmate's presentation. She had based her report about the education system of India on a single source, a British report written years before India achieved independence, a topic I had learned much about from my friend Desai in Zurich. Once again, I was sternly reprimanded. One must not criticize one's classmates. Nowadays, I agree that to disparage someone's opinion is not the best way to engage in discussion. I don't think that was explained well to me. I certainly did not understand it at the time. In European schools, the tradition of sharp debate was highly prized.

I spent the summer between my junior and senior years in New York City, working as a proofreader for the Research Institute of America, a job I found through a newspaper ad. With the change in my visa status, I now had a work permit. It was uplifting to work in the open; it helped me feel less like a sneak. The person who hired me explained that people who had a foreign background and had learned English as an additional language were much better spellers than Americans. My work consisted of proofing, rather than actual editing, so his assessment of the usefulness of my skills was quite accurate.

My apartment, which I found the same day as I did my job, was a 10-block walk from my work. I shared it with a nurse, who had advertised for a roommate. It was a pretty one-bedroom apartment, and I slept on the couch in the living room. She had a plan whereby we wrote down what we spent on a list tacked onto the refrigerator. At the end of the week, we would add it up and split the expenses. She was a professional woman, earning a comfortable salary. I was a thrifty and impecunious student who had very little money and bought very little. When she realized how disparate our weekly expenditures were, she shrugged and said, "Let's just let it go."

That fall, when I returned to Connecticut College, she sent me off with riding britches and boots, among other items of sports attire. I don't remember her name, but I think of her kindly for having taken in a stray cat and looking after it so well.

My second year at Connecticut would be my last. It was becoming harder to ignore and tolerate the disconnect between what

I felt the college expected of me and who I really was. Before coming to Connecticut, I had lived on my own for almost five years. While I had experienced many hardships, I maintained a sense of personal cohesion and integrity. At the college we were all assumed to be virgins and under parental supervision. The college did their best to fill this role for me. Before vacations, they asked whether I had a place to go and whether I needed money. They encouraged me to get medical check-ups and dental work so they could pay for it while I was a still a student. When I graduated, they found a way to give me a Phi Beta Kappa graduate scholarship to help me financially.

Yet, I could not balance the external with the internal. Senior year was a time of engagements. It seemed everybody was sporting a diamond ring. In heartache, in homesickness, and with a sense of isolation, I thought about Edgar, and decided I would marry him. In February of my senior year, I went to New York and we were married in a Jewish ceremony in a rabbi's study. Neither his family nor anyone from mine was present. My college friend Marne was my witness, maid of honor, and moral support; she was my family. Being a good Catholic, she needed her Monsignor's permission to participate in a non-Catholic ceremony. Edgar and I spent a three-day honeymoon at the Lighthouse Inn in New London, Connecticut, after which he accepted a job in Puerto Rico. I already had one foot out the door of Connecticut College. I joined him in San Juan as soon as classes finished, not bothering to wait for commencement.

In another example of my tendency to place myself on the margins of situations, 50 years after graduating, I received the Connecticut College Medal, largely through the efforts of Jo Vanderkloot, a Connecticut alumna and professional colleague. The medal acknowledged my long road from stateless refugee to nationally and internationally known professional woman. I felt I did not deserve it. I had not remained significantly involved with the college, with the one exception of an unsuccessful attempt to convince my daughter, Melanie, to go there.

First Marriage

I had done well in my studies at Connecticut College. In a long discussion with my English professor, Dr. Rosamond Tuve, I compared a German translation of a Shakespeare play with the English original. I came down unequivocally and passionately on the side of the German translator, who, in my opinion, had presented stronger sounds and images. In a particular passage describing a wild windswept landscape of trees, I pictured the scene of a forest in a storm much more vividly when it was mediated by the power, imagery, and auditory resonance contained in the German translation.

Only much later did I fully realize that the language acquired in childhood imparts an everlasting richness to our linguistic experience. In childhood we simultaneously learn about the world and how to name what is in it. This is an experience not easily matched by the meager and skeletal vocabulary of a foreign language learned later. When we learn words in a language other than our mother tongue, it takes many years to accumulate the associative experiences that can give the words depth and personal meaning.

It was May and the campus was in full bloom. Wherever you turned, the beauty of the meticulously tended landscape nurtured the soul. When not in class, I had been able to spend time horseback riding whenever I managed to have enough money for an hour or two of riding fees. Connecticut College was a sustaining, nurturing environment—why was I so eager to be done with it and leave? My studies were completed, and I would receive my bachelor's degree. I had revalidated my competence as a good student.

During my senior year I had applied to graduate schools. My faculty advisors cautioned me against choosing the universities of Iowa, Minnesota: anywhere away from the Eastern Seaboard. They were concerned I would not fit into American midwestern culture. Thinking back, I suspect my professors did not understand the cultural abyss I had already navigated on a daily basis. I was Jewish, liberal, an intellectual, and stateless, as well as *homeless*. I often felt ill at ease. Young as I was, the previous events from the turbulent life I had experienced had turned me into a complex person. I needed to contain the rebellious, battered, uprooted survivor within the friendly and placid dailiness of an American student.

My advisors were probably less attuned to (or concerned with) such inner tensions than they were cognizant of one simple fact: I did not behave like an average American girl. They may have believed academic intellectual environments on the East Coast would be more forgiving and tolerant of my style, an outspokenness that veered toward the argumentative and possessing only a rudimentary set of social skills, which led me to argue for what I perceived was the truth, rather than expend effort to make the other person feel good. I prided myself on my distinctiveness. When I tried to conform to the prevailing norms, I felt contempt. I certainly was unaware of social rules that were gender-specific, where men spoke, and women listened quietly, raptly, adoringly, or at least respectfully. I suspect it never crossed my mind that I would be unable to fit in if I moved away from the East Coast.

My plans for the following year fell into place. Yale University offered me an assistantship in its graduate psychology program.

With a landing place for September secured, I turned toward Puerto Rico, where Edgar had a position at the San Juan Hilton Hotel. I spent little time deciding that I would skip the graduation ceremonies and the social events attached to the conclusion of college. What seemed of paramount importance was that I leave two and a half weeks earlier than the other graduates.

Why didn't I want to attend the ceremonies? Why didn't I want to walk with my class, stand up and receive my diploma? At the time, I didn't stop to consider the reasons. Of course, I didn't have knowledge of or direct experience with graduation ceremonies, nor did anyone choose to inform me. In truth, I didn't inquire about the specifics. It was also true I had no family who would attend and participate in this rite of passage. More fundamentally, I had built up a strong defense against the pain of exclusion. I did this by adopting a sour grapes defense: *Who wants that anyway?* This began when I was 11 and newly arrived in Switzerland, with the status of a barely tolerated immigrant, a category of personhood defined by exclusion from participation in the general Swiss community.

My brother had dealt with the pain of Swiss rejection by keeping his adolescent left-wing leanings. He thought himself a revolutionary who was contemptuous of all things bourgeois. He had read Karl Marx's *Das Kapital* from beginning to end and his records of *The Threepenny Opera* made me identify with Pirate Jenny and love Mack the Knife.

Before any of these events found their way into our family history, I had assigned my brother a parental role. He carried out this role not in a caring and loving manner but in one that was rather bossy and instructional. He taught me to be dismissive of pop culture, to distrust and eschew all the ways a young girl might develop her femininity by trying to dress and look and behave to be attractive. He once said, scowling, "You put that paint on your face. Who would take seriously anything you have to say?" Or "Take that nail polish off your fingernails. You want clean hands." This particular message echoed one my mathematics teacher gave me in school. Upon noticing pink polish on my fingernails, he sent me home and ordered me not to return to class until I had "cleaned up."

During the years in Switzerland, my teenage head swirled with an ill-defined mixture of left-wing politics, gender protest, and the attempt not to long for social events from which I was already excluded. These teenage struggles with social identity persisted in the perceptions of my surroundings at college, perhaps merging with my attempts to understand the fundamental differences between my European worldview and the underlying American way of life that I sensed around me. Given that, it was neither difficult nor painful for me to choose to exclude myself from the graduation festivities and so I boarded an airplane instead.

Edgar had rented a room with a bath from a Puerto Rican family living at Parada 17 in Santurce. It was my first trip to the tropics. The fragrant, heavy air felt like liquid clinging to my skin. The blue ocean; long, pristine beaches; palm trees; paneless windows; two-inch-long palmetto bugs creeping in through the slats to the kitchen or into the shower; warm damp air against the body; tile floors in the apartment: all were part of a mysterious, relaxed new world. Edgar had made friends with two Americans, and our social life revolved around going out with these two unattached guys. It wasn't long before I noticed money in our household was scarce. Edgar often managed to arrange that the others picked up the checks.

His work wasn't going well. He was employed at the then-new Hilton Hotel. It was classy, touristy, and elegant. Edgar carried himself as if he were the director. He conducted a personal telephone life during working hours, stepping out as he pleased for coffee or a drink. He was probably only an assistant to the assistant to the second bookkeeper.

Our relationship was not thriving either. Our sexual connection had never been close to a romantic one. And I had never been in love with him. I found him comforting and anchoring, especially during the second year of college, when everyone was getting engaged and I sensed I was losing my solid footing. At that moment, the idea of marrying Edgar had represented a lifeboat.

Early one evening, Edgar arrived at our apartment. When I opened the door, I saw behind him the shadow of an intriguing man. "Art and I teach at the Benedict school together," Edgar explained to me. Edgar taught languages, English, maybe Hebrew and maybe German. Art taught English and medical nomenclature. Art became our steady companion. I learned that his wife was in the process of leaving him and was taking Darel, their three-year-old son, with her. Art was extremely sad, an obvious sense of loss surrounded him, which he tried to diminish with the help of numerous rum and cokes.

Edgar and I were close to teetotalers. Perhaps Edgar saw Art as a strong macho American. I regarded Art as a strong, but deeply wounded soul. One afternoon when Art took me to a sailors' bar called Chain Locker, I watched him put away 35 rum and cokes in the course of about six or so hours. It speaks volumes to my total naiveté about alcoholism that warning bells did not go off in my head. Instead, I admired his capacity, and compared Edgar unfavorably to him, thinking, *Edgar never even has one drink. What a boring man.*

Another person who occasionally hung out with us was a woman in her early 30s. The story was that she spent her 20s in Hawaii working as a hooker and had saved quite a bit of money and was now searching for a husband. She cast her glance at Art. I told her in my best proto-therapeutic manner, "I agree that he is a very attractive man, but he is terrible marriage material. He is just divorcing his second wife. He has no money and he drinks." She took my advice and turned her attention elsewhere. It's very hard to explain, but a few years later, I would find myself married to Art.

Within approximately five weeks of my arrival from the States, I had applied for an immigration visa at the American consulate in the Dominican Republic, a short airplane hop from San Juan. (My marriage to Edgar had made me eligible.) My immigration status was determined by my birthplace, Czechoslovakia, which, had I applied in the United States. would have required a wait of many years. The Dominican Republic, on the other hand, had two free Czech slots, which became available after July 1. On the morning of June 30, I made my way from San Juan to the Dominican Republic.

While getting ready for this short, but important and somewhat stressful trip, Edgar intimated that he might need to look for a new job. The evening before my departure he gave me a task. "The Normandy Hotel is looking for a manager," he informed me, "and the owner lives in Ciudad Trujillo. Why don't you contact him and see whether you can talk him into giving me the job?" Looking back at my level of innocence and lack of judgment at the time makes me more tolerant of what seems to be the uninformed stupidity of many of today's young people. Surely, the young woman I was then could compete with them.

In 1952, the Dominican Republic was under the nasty dictatorship of Rafael Trujillo. When I arrived at the airport, only two other passengers disembarked. Wherever I looked, there were barbed wire barriers; soldiers stood at attention with machine guns and long bandoliers strapped across their chests. I found a taxi to the Hotel Jaragua, a luxury hotel that seemed devoid of guests. I ventured outside and saw a wide promenade with monumental statues on either side proclaiming the presence of some kind of Übermensch. There was not a soul in sight. It was eerie, like a science fiction movie. I fled back to the putative safety of the hotel, clutching the phone number Edgar had given me, hoping for a little human connection when I called his contact.

The conversation should have given me pause, as it promised anything but ease or reassurance. But as was my wont, I did not stop to think things over. Perhaps it would have been terrifying to consider seriously my situation. I pulled out the slip of paper with the phone number of the man I was to ask for a job for Edgar. And not just any job; Edgar wanted the director's position at the Normandy Hotel.

The operator dialed the number for me: A gruff male voice answered. A servant, I thought, or perhaps the big man himself? I explained the purpose of my call. I told him I wanted to speak to him about a job he might have for my husband. Might I come to see him that afternoon? After a short pause, he said, "Come to my house at eight o'clock tonight." When I inquired about his address, he said, "Just take any taxi and give him my name." Ominous and possibly dangerous; that is what I should have thought. Instead I read the situation as "a powerful and well-known man on a small island."

At 7:30, I set out in a taxi. When I gave the driver the name, he looked at me a little strangely. Then we set off on a drive through the unlit countryside. I was rehearsing what to say, and so was not particularly observant about where we were going. In any event, it was too dark to notice any landmarks, and I had no familiarity with the island's geography. We drove in silence. Was I imagining an uncomfortable silence on the driver's part? Suddenly, he stopped the taxi, seemingly in the middle of nowhere, turned to me and said, "*Aqui.*" (Here you are.)

I got out. As my eyes became accustomed to the dark night, I saw a plastered wall with an inconspicuous unmarked door. I rang the bell and pounded on the door. After a while, I heard some steps, and then the door opened. I faced two German shepherds on a leash held by a man, whose other hand held a gun pointed in my direction. Undeterred, I said, "I am here to see Mr. X." He waved his hand and said, "Come in."

He led me into a large living room. The first thought I had was of Mussolini; it was the living room of a dictator. A massive two-story fireplace with a beautiful mahogany armature defined the space. The room was opulent, with a double-height ceiling, books in large bookcases, sumptuous red leather sofas and armchairs, and hand-woven carpets. I felt intimidated but was also curious. I sat down and waited and waited and waited. Much later, I finally heard what sounded like shuffling steps on the stairs. I looked up and there was a little old man wearing khaki shorts descending the imperial staircase. His spindly legs were stuck into a pair of delicate pink mule slippers. He said nothing; I said, "Hello," and quickly informed him that I had come to talk about the possibility of employment for my husband.

He waved my words off and growled, "Later." He made himself comfortable in an armchair. He looked at me and then pointed to a bar that stood next to one of the bookcases and commanded, "Scotch and soda, with ice." I got up and found a glass and served him a Scotch and soda with ice. By now, I was extremely ill at ease. Somewhere there had been a complete failure of communication. I did not know what he had in mind, but it was creepy. If he had made a straightforward proposition that I have sex with him in exchange for at least a job interview for Edgar, I might have considered it. What occurred to me is that he thought I was a prostitute. In any event, he was going to treat me as one.

It was a dangerous and perverted atmosphere. What could this dried-up little man possibly want from me? What would he do to me? Would he hurt me? All the good sense I neglected to pack earlier suddenly jumped into my throat and converted itself into utter panic. I said, "I need to leave." He said, "No, no. What's your hurry? Sit down. Come over here. Rub my feet."

No courage situated itself in me. All I wanted to do was get out. After about 15 minutes like this, his irritation rising, the little man apparently got bored. With an angry look, he abruptly walked out of the room. I sat there wondering what would happen and what I was going to do next. Some time later the man with the gun and dogs reappeared. He looked at me with disgust and spat, "Get out. Now." He pointed to the door, waited for me to pass in front of him. I stepped out; he closed the door behind me. I stood in front of a blind wall in the middle of the black night. I could just dimly see that the wall was topped with broken glass and barbed wire. I surely had no idea where I was.

There was nothing to do but wait in the hope that a car might drive by and that I could hitch a ride back to town. Quite obviously, that happened, and it must have gone without a problem, but strange as it sounds, I can't remember it. I only recall how terrified I was once I got back to the hotel, and the feeling lingered into the next morning. I was due at the consulate first thing to collect my visa. I packed my bags and took them along with me, fearing that somewhere along the line, this spurned man might take his revenge and have me hurt or killed. Once in possession of my visa, I went straight to the airport, where I waited many hours for the plane to arrive. It was not until I was airborne that I turned against Edgar.

Edgar and Art greeted me upon my arrival. Edgar was eager to hear how the job request had gone. Did I have good news to report? Art, on the other hand, asked about the visa, and then told me all kinds of bits and pieces he had learned about my history in Switzerland, such as, "You lived at Rue Beau-Regard, didn't you?" It seems he had a friend in the FBI, who had looked up my folder and told him about me. Later that day, I learned Edgar had been fired from the Hilton. We would be returning to New York in two or three weeks.

What on earth would I do in New York? I had no money; my Yale program didn't start until September. Even worse, I would arrive in New Haven to begin graduate work without any nest egg. Art was going on leave from the Coast Guard to New England at the end of August. First, he would be meeting a girlfriend in New York, where they were going to spend a few days at the Commodore Hotel. That information wasn't particularly relevant then, and I must have filed it away. Later I reached back in my memory to retrieve it.

Upon our arrival in New York, Edgar and I found a room somewhere in Queens. It was hot and we had no money. We needed to find jobs. I went out and, within a day, found employment cutting samples in a plastic factory. Edgar found it was too hot to get out of bed. The first week passed with me working and Edgar still trying to muster the energy to mobilize himself. He did nothing. Our love did not flourish. A critical moment occurred that might have hammered the final nail into the coffin of our barely begun marriage. One Sunday morning, Edgar's aunt called and said, "Listen, you kids. How would you like to come for brunch? We invited three couples and one just canceled. The two of you probably haven't had a decent meal in days. Why don't you come?"

Instead of feeling grateful or relieved, I was enraged. Do I now have to play the poor, schnooky relative to these people? No way. I thought it likely they were happy that Edgar married me because he needed a firm hand. Well, I had needed an anchor. I realized that I was insufficiently resourced to pull him along. We went to the brunch, and when we came back, I said, "Edgar, I think this is it."

I picked up the phone and called the Commodore Hotel and asked for Art's room. When a lady answered, I said, "May I please speak to Art?" Running from anger and confusion and the mess I'd made of my situation, I made a date with Art. We decided to spend a week on Block Island. In those days it was quite undeveloped. We found lodgings within our price range, Mrs. White's Cottage. We rented two bicycles and had a blissful week. Art taught me about New England culture. I had clam chowder and ate my first lobster. We looked at dunes and the tall grasses that grew everywhere. When the week was over, we chartered a small airplane to take us to New London, Connecticut, where I still had a small savings account. It was just enough to pay for the plane and see me back to New York.

I said good-bye to Edgar. He was visibly shaken and had consulted a therapist. He asked that I join him for a session. The therapist was kind and helpful. He inquired whether I loved Edgar. I responded that I didn't know. He suggested that this would be a good time for me to leave. Edgar would come to terms with my departure. Helped by a push from this sensible therapist, I put guilt aside and got ready to start my first year of graduate school at Yale.

When I abandoned Edgar, his family viewed me as if I were the Wicked Witch of the West and cut off all contact with me. Edgar and I stayed in touch and saw each other occasionally. I met his second wife whom I liked. The two of them developed a close, loving, childless marriage. At one point, he wanted her to go into therapy with me. At another point she turned to me to help her get Edgar to a dentist since his teeth were rotting and he was afraid to go. I was able to help out with some stern words. Eventually we lost touch. It wasn't until Marion, Edgar's cousin, told me Edgar had died ten years earlier of a heart attack that I learned of his death. She reported he had become portly and mindless of his health. I also learned that Edgar's widow grieved him still. Theirs had been a happy marriage. The entire family had conspired successfully to protect her from the knowledge that Edgar was a compulsive liar. None of his stories were true, but his wife believed them all. They lived on her salary and a trust fund her parents had left her. Like his uncle E., Edgar was spared the need to earn a living.

Yale: A Road Not Seen

I was looking forward to going back to school but had no real sense of what a special place Yale was. Perhaps I didn't understand that any better than I had understood what an important entry into American life Connecticut College might have presented, had I found a way to make use of it. I saw my access to these first-rate schools as a particularly lucky break for me. Only much later did I realize that they served as definers of one's position within the American social hierarchy. I still felt I was a tolerated interloper. I didn't know how to claim full ownership of the situation in which I found myself.

Indelibly and fundamentally, I perceived my life as taking place on shifting ground, lacking predictability and firmness. I jumped from island to island, avoiding the treacherous storms and chasms in between. To this day, when I lose heart, I almost expect to be swallowed by a crack in the sidewalk or drift off into the air like a balloon that escaped a child's careless hand, in either case, not to be seen or heard from again, my departure unnoticed.

I felt that good luck had rescued me from a series of situations that could well have brought about my physical death, such as those that befell so many in the world of my childhood, or, at the very least, a personal stifling that surely would have happened had I remained in Europe. While it is true that I escaped many a trap and survived harsh circumstances, I had not attached the word *survivor* to myself. I believe that it was my general view at the time that life is full of hardship and toil and that some people survive better than others. Much later, I began to wonder what life would look like if the primary task was one other than surviving and mastering this or that threatening situation, *What would people feel? How would they spend their time? Would they find things to do, to strive for, without the pressure of assuring their survival?*

I never formulated a coherent personal philosophy of life. I firmly disagreed with sayings like: "You can be anything you want to be." Or "You're the captain of your boat and the master of your fate." Or "Reinvent yourself as who you want to be." I considered these ideas evidence of American self-deception. I saw myself playing defense against the assault of life. I was happy when I was successful in averting or escaping the assault. When I found myself in situations that were hugely better than I might have imagined, I was grateful to fate. This perception did not lend itself to the idea of choosing a direction a plan, setting a goal.or learning the steps it took, one at a time, to reach where I wanted to be. I might have this or that fantasy, but I never defined any steps I might take to bring it closer to reality.

It was a sunny afternoon in East Hampton, when I was in my 60s, that I finally realized that I somehow expected a rich man would appear in my life and provide me with one of those gorgeous oceanfront properties like those I was seeing. No matter its absurdity, the certainty of it had lived underground and unarticulated, but was there nevertheless. On several occasions, the fantasy held me back from buying a small house.

In retrospect, my inability to set and then pursue a specific goal may appear to have been a real drawback. But at the time the ability to remain open enough to utilize opportunities as they presented themselves was also proof of my resilience and flexibility. Perhaps I honed these traits in my childhood family, when nothing much was expected of me as a girl, nine years younger than my bossy brother. As I was growing up, whatever I thought, my brother had already been there and had thought it better. He wiped out whatever I came up with and proved to me how wrong I was. I capitulated and accepted his view of things. In a manner of speaking, he defined the path. Although I may have walked on that path, I didn't accept total responsibility for completing it. My brother and I were caught in a competitive dynamic for the entirety of our lives, and my mother remained loyally and devotedly on his side.

Later in life, I found myself caught in replications of this sibling dynamic, where it remained more painful than funny and badly handled by me. Two examples come to mind. After watching Nathan Ackerman, the founder of Family Institute, interview a family, I voiced an opposing opinion in the discussion that followed. Dr. Ackerman, who criticized freely but brooked no dissent in return, admonished me, "I am 30 years older than you are. Whenever we have a disagreement, you better believe that you are wrong." Another time, Al Sheflen, a then-famous and hugely creative social scientist, with whom I was in a relationship at the time, dismissed a particularly interesting connection I thought I was making, saying, "Anything you could possibly think of, I have already thought."

How did I help generate such absurd exchanges? From time to time, I would tell the story of my life to friends and colleagues. At a particular meeting of women family therapists in the 1980s, one of the young attendees said to me, "They have to make a movie of your life, and you have to play the lead." And I remember thinking, "That movie with me in the lead has already played." Then someone said, "You are a real survivor." That was the first time I noticed how the act of surviving had become a noun: *survivor*.

All my life I have been able to make the best of things, to find the hidden pearl. One of my husbands once said, "You could fall into the gutter and come up with a new suit." He also complained, "It is difficult to argue with you; you always give yourself excuses. You never feel bad about things." That ability to prevail, to adapt, to get to the head of the class, to rely on my competence, to rely on being smart enough, all those assets I never listed but always counted on seeing me through, suddenly soured when the word *survivor* was applied to who I was.

"Wow, how wonderful she managed to survive" being turned into "She is just a survivor" to me meant that I was seen as sort of crawling along on the bottom of things, making sure I didn't go under. When seen like that, where is the creativity? Where is the vision? Where is the accomplishment? Where is making the most out of yourself and your situation? Where is enriching life, reaching for things that are new and emergent? The label of *survivor* began to eat at me, and I stopped thinking of myself as one.

In the last active decade of my professional life, I achieved much more than I had ever dreamed possible. I loved my work, was a successful clinician and a well-loved teacher. I was known throughout the then-small field of family therapy, locally, nationally, and internationally, and people respected my opinion. I was not a star; I had neither the driving ambition nor the intense energy nor the greedy ego needed to battle for and maintain high visibility. I didn't write and publish much. I couldn't find the right tone to formulate what I knew without making it rigid and thereby obsolete before it appeared.

My vision of myself as a solid, serious, data-documented, evidence-based thinker in family therapy wasn't strong enough to push me toward the hard work that would have been required. Things had come easily to me. Digging in and slaving away in the service of success and self-promotion were neither attractive nor possible for me. At the same time that the label of *survivor* eroded my pride at having survived, the peak of my professional life had come and gone. I was faced with adjusting to the diminishing rewards of near-retirement.

This was made more difficult by the enormously changed landscape of gender discrimination. When I had started on my professional path, hardly any women were on that road with me. In my Connecticut College graduating class of some 200, only two went to graduate school. There followed the decades of battling the barriers that women met everywhere. It was a battle that fit right in with my world view that things out there were difficult and that you had to prevail.

At that time there were many factors that made it more difficult for a woman to achieve real professional success: there were fewer places in graduate school, less financial support, widespread sexism throughout the faculty, only low-level positions in universities, difficulties combining the requirements of private family life with the requirements of the job. I remember a particular argument with a woman who did not consider herself sexist, who said, "I think women can do the work just as well as men can, but when a woman has to go home to look after her children or her husband, her work suffers. So, I propose that responsible, professional positions be given to women who agree to remain unmarried and childless."

Different strengths were required to find one's way into that professional atmosphere, and, perhaps as a result, I fully admit that conversations with men in the 1960s and the 1970s were more interesting than the conversations with women, which tended toward babies, recipes, and suburban living. Against all of those obstacles, my ability always to be self-supporting and to achieve a respectful professional position was very satisfying.

Once the next generation of women came along, their path, while not totally cleared of impediments, was vastly more open and more supported by changing relationships with female colleagues.

Women had learned to be friends instead of competitors to each other. Women's accomplishments burst forth and spread, allowing them to flourish in many areas of life. This is what happens when survival is not at stake, when you can take for granted that the basics of life will remain available to you and you can devote your energies to imagining new worlds. There remain times when surviving is of the essence. If it doesn't happen, all ends, and therefore, where relevant, it must be acknowledged and celebrated, recognized and remembered.

Nowadays, the atmosphere in our world—climactic, political, and social—is such that the preciousness and value of surviving is once again deeply relevant. Without survival, all else stalls.

When I think of my short year at Yale from September 1952 to May 1953, I see mostly a whitish fog. Somewhere outside the fog dwell all the things I learned in class, enough for the first half of the doctoral orals. The stern mandate not to make any statement that cannot be proven at the .01 level of statistical significance burned itself into my superego and throughout my life has stopped me many times from venturing my opinion. Similarly, the requirement that presentations to the colloquium be defensible against criticism and that the task of the listener is to find weaknesses and mercilessly expose them remained in my repartee far too long. On the other hand, my assistantship with Dr. Irving Child, which consisted of summarizing relevant literature published in German and French, taught me that my opinion counted. An important part of the Yale experience was that the faculty regarded us as junior colleagues whose thinking was worth listening to. I felt quite wonderful being a member of the graduate school of psychology. I remember a similar feeling in the first year of medical school in Zürich seven years earlier, where a class of some 200 students, among them just six to eight women, was welcomed into a special community of future physicians.

When I peer more deeply into the slightly milky fog, a little place clears to show the apartment I shared with Florence Riddle. It was a three-room railroad flat on George Street, a five-minute walk from 333 Cedar, where the psychology department was housed. Drunks would often sleep in our doorway, and the short block of Davenport Avenue was Hooker Row. Florence was an English major from Reed College. She was slim, blonde, pale, and very protective of her living space. She needed this to be able to tackle the two or three enormous papers the English department required of its first-year students.

The door to our apartment opened into a middle room, which had no windows. To the left was the room that looked out on George Street. To the right was an eat-in kitchen with a shower and toilet. Florence felt her space would be invaded if I had to walk through it each time I came and went, so she chose the outside room with the windows. She painted it a light, sunny yellow. The main piece of furniture was a cot covered with a red tartan wool blanket. She had a wooden table and chair and a small bookcase. My room, on the other hand, was dark, with a brownish-green, plush velvet armchair, chenille bedspread on a sagging bed, and a nondescript rug. The furniture had come with the apartment, but it quickly came to absorb and reflect our distinct personalities.

I dove into graduate school social life with abandon, though I did my work and often stayed well into the night at the statistics lab. This was the era of calculators, long before there were computers, and we sat crunching numbers for our experiments. I loved those nights. The work was mindless, meditative, and satisfying, especially when you got good results. Between late lab nights and party nights, I often slept in. My room began to seem shrouded in discreet penumbra, exuding vibes of relaxed indulgence, unpredictable schedules, and unforeseen guests. I did the best I could not to impinge on Florence's lifestyle, but she became increasingly distraught by what she felt emanating from my room and seeping under the door into her pristine monk cell. Each time she had to pass through my room, which, of course, was often, as my room provided the only access to hers, she felt clinging to her the miasma of troubling mystery my room had come to represent.

Around Christmas, I returned from class one afternoon and found Florence sitting in the kitchen with Art. His arrival was a total surprise. He had been accepted into an officers training class in New London and had left Puerto Rico. He had arrived that morning and had spent the day scrubbing the kitchen and bathroom. It was indeed gleaming. "We sailors are clean," he announced.

When I walked through the door, he was wearing a checked lumberjack shirt with rolled-up sleeves, drinking a beer. His arms were tanned and strong. The top buttons of his shirt were open, and he looked the picture of raw, male sex. Florence, across the table from him, was drinking a cola. Her face was animated; she seemed to be enjoying herself. Art stayed for two or three days.

After Art left, Florence's difficulties intensified. She had no friends and didn't date. She finished her first assignment on *Moby Dick* with difficulty, but, ultimately, with success. She now was approaching the poetry of Yeats, and whatever she encountered there, combined with the stresses she experienced in her life, pushed her toward an increasingly unbearable edge. With the help of a therapist, she and I decided to dissolve our roommate status. She moved out, but I don't remember how I managed without her rent contribution. The rent was 60 dollars a month and between the two of us, we spent about eight or nine dollars a week on food.

I knew nothing of New Haven. I never made it to the beach, never walked around the commons, and had no sense of where it was located.

Sometime in March or April, Art washed out of the officers'

training program. He was unable to do the math. We decided that I would leave Yale and that we would be together. We wanted to avoid his being stationed at a seaport where he would have ocean-going duty. Our inland choices were St. Louis and Colorado. He was planning to go back to school, so we chose St. Louis. I contacted Washington University, where I was accepted. I gave no thought about what I was giving up by leaving Yale. When I informed my professors that I was leaving, they seemed nonplussed. The following week, I received a lovely letter from Claude Buxton, the department chair. He expressed the faculty's regret at my leaving and said they would be willing to have me return within a reasonable time period should the occasion arise, adding, "We don't usually send this kind of letter." When I think back, it's as though a part of my brain was missing, as though the implications of my decision were unknown to me. Had my IQ dropped by half? What was going on with me?

I had latched onto Art as my anchor. It was in this kind of situation where the primacy of survival really messed me up. I couldn't imagine living without such an anchor, which I believe came to represent my lost home. Having a home to be rooted in was a priority unequaled by anything else in my life.

At Yale I had absorbed a great deal of information in my classes. A year of double sessions two or three times a week with Neal Miller left me with a lifelong grounding in learning theory. Dr. Irving Sarasen's interest in test anxiety formed the baseline for my careful use of psychological and other test results. Quantitative thinking had always been difficult for me, and so I looked forward with trepidation to statistics with Dr. Fred Sheffield. As luck would have it, in one of the first classes I had with him, he was demonstrating a puzzle board and commented that it was truly difficult to solve. I was in my usually fidgety mode while he was speaking, and, in what seemed like an accident, solved the puzzle.

I raised my hand to show the solution. Dr. Sheffield praised me. From that day on, I became the bellwether for the class's understanding in statistics. If I didn't understand, it wasn't well explained.

I sailed through those two semesters happily and successfully. I had no extracurricular interests, except for a period when I served as circulation secretary for a small student paper promoting peace. Of course, later on, because of that, I ended up on some kind of blacklist.

I had another weird experience. I went out once or twice with a medical student. On our second date, I stopped by his room to wait for him to get dressed to go out. He sat down on a chair. He said, "Come sit on my lap." As I revisit this scene, I am puzzled by the fact I must have been wearing a skirt, not slacks. With one hand he encircled my shoulder and with the other he was doing something, but I wasn't paying particular attention. The next thing I knew, with lightning speed, he had pulled his penis out and put it in me. By the time I collected my wits, it was over: the whole incident was maybe two seconds. I remember saying, "What was that all about?" It seemed totally pointless. I did not feel raped or disrespected or injured. I thought instead, "What a foolish boy." Following that experience, I did become a bit more careful.

These few distinct events form most of my memories of Yale and New Haven. I must not have been aware of the power, the resources, and the support that an institution like Yale might have extended to me. I think they were quite willing to help me in the development of my career, but somehow what they offered never connected with what I needed.

When I finished my second term, it was time to join Art in St. Louis. Again, I didn't wait for graduation. I packed up and disposed of the meager household goods I had by giving them to another needy student. I remember getting rid of my skis, my ski boots, and other sporting equipment as if I were giving up any further thought of resuming any aspect of my former Swiss life.

I recalled how I evaded graduation at Connecticut College, leaving as soon as classes and exams were over and rushing to join Edgar in Puerto Rico. I was doing a similar thing now. Then, to complete the trifecta, I later chose not to participate in graduation ceremonies for my Ph.D. I really don't now remember why this third omission occurred. Perhaps by then it was my expected norm.

Uncharted Territories

Art and I sat down and discussed what life together might look like. It was our nod to reality. He wanted to continue his education and earn a bachelor's degree. I intended to continue on the path toward a Ph.D. in clinical psychology. We needed to find a Coast Guard station that would permit him to attend night school, which meant only inland locations were acceptable. In the spring of 1953, there were openings in St. Louis and in Colorado. Why did we pick St. Louis? Was it a simple toss of a coin? Perhaps it was the romantic history of the Mississippi River? Maybe it was St. Louis music? Who knows now? I was happy enough when I heard from the psychology department at Washington University that they had accepted me. I was not going to participate in Yale's graduation ceremonies but didn't rush off to St Louis. Instead, I paused and spent three or four days in a no man's land of reluctance. And then I geared up for an adventure into an unknown America.

The long bus trip to St. Louis lacked any comfort. It was yet another kind of transition, but not really a hardship. During part of the journey I was seated next to a man who identified himself as William Carlos Williams, the well-known American poet. I did not believe him. Why would a successful and famous poet take a cross-country bus journey? Before disembarking he gave me a signed volume of his poetry. It was the first promising sign and broke through my state of haze. I was traveling toward poetry. I was traveling toward love. I was traveling to find fulfillment with a man with whom I was madly in love.

The truths of Art's situation had receded in my mind almost to the point of invisibility. He was a sailor who had washed out of OCS training. He was twice divorced and didn't have a nickel to his name. All of that had faded, blotted out by the brilliant light true love had cast over my being.

As far as leaving Yale for Washington University, in my head, one university was like any other. Nobody had sat me down to explain the American landscape of institutional academic education. Eventually I became aware of the differences on my own, but by then the die was cast.

Art had promised to pick me up at the bus station in St. Louis. I arrived three days later than I had originally indicated but had informed him of the change. Nevertheless, as I stepped off the bus, there was no sign of Art. What should I do next? I had no idea where he lived, or how to reach him. I was without resources in a strange place. Perhaps he had jilted me? Before there was time to fall into real despair, a tall man in a noncommissioned officer's uniform appeared.

"Hello, Kitty? I'm Harry. Art is sorry he couldn't meet you. He expected you three days ago and got so impatient waiting for you that he walked off his post while on watch. They put him in the brig. Let's go see him." It was a lot of information to absorb. But what else was there to do but go with him?

I have no memory of where we drove but recall a kind of holding pen with jail-like bars. The bars were spaced wide enough apart to permit holding hands. With our youthful athletic prowess, it was possible to exchange passionate kisses. Further physical expression of passion was not possible, although it's likely we tried. Art had to remain in the brig another four days, which gave me time to cool down and deal with reality.

Afterward, Harry drove me to the apartment on Delmar Boulevard that Art had rented for us. It was comfortable with a kitchen, a bath, and a bedroom. It was pretty basic but felt luxurious to me, holding as it did the budding shoot of our future together. I settled in and waited for Art's release. It did not occur to me then that while he had been waiting for me, Art had probably gone out and gotten drunk, which was likely the real reason for his lockup. It would be quite some time before I saw his drinking as a calamity, before I would accept his abuse of alcohol as a potential threat to our life together. At the time, I still viewed it as an enhancer of the joy and fun we were having.

We lived in the Delmar apartment for a few weeks. Art's work with the Coast Guard was like a regular office job, every day from 8 am to 4 pm. While he was gone, I played housewife. I put my studies out of my mind and immersed myself in our rather seedy honky-tonk neighborhood. The apartment was above a jazz club, one of three or four within a few blocks. Jazz was big in the St. Louis of the 1950s. We were not married, but I tried on the identity of a working-class wife. I did the housework and fed us on our meager financial resources. On Sundays we explored the bars along Olive Street, which stayed open in the otherwise dry St. Louis and sold 3/2 beer.

These places were the refuge of drinkers who couldn't go a day without alcohol, and who didn't have the wherewithal to purchase supplies on Saturday that would last until Monday. Many seemed poor and depressed. There was an inordinate number of disabled people. In my confused state, what I saw unfolding before me were adumbrations of post-World War I Berlin. It was a low-down, dirty, exciting, and mysterious milieu. Quickly, though, the haunting jazz sounds turned into excessive noise, and the freedom of the down-and-out became unappealing. This awareness coincided with the realization that I was a graduate student and needed to prepare for the academic year. We moved into a rooming house on Pershing Avenue, renting two single rooms, but mostly we slept in one single bed. We cooked on a two-burner hot plate. I managed to produce meals delicious enough that our landlady complained with exasperation, "They're cooking with herbs, they're cooking with herbs."

Art registered for night school with the intention of studying economic geography, or perhaps anthropology. My initial visit to the psychology department went well but confirmed the disappointing reality of what the psychology department at Washington University was then. My transcripts from Yale were excellent. Yale had granted me my master's degree just before I left New Haven. My professors said, "Why don't you take the master's so that you will have something official that shows that you attended Yale?" The system at Yale allowed me to finish half of my requirements during the short two semesters I was there.

Washington University by contrast worked on the quarter system requiring 120 credits or 30 per year. According to the psychology department's calculations, I had earned only 30 credits at Yale, leaving me with a huge deficit. I requested permission to begin taking courses during the summer to make up some of the shortage. The department chair said, "Why don't you begin by studying for your language requirements? You will need them for your Ph.D." My answer was "I really don't need to study these languages. I could teach them. I am totally fluent in French and German." The chairman gave me a dismissive look and replied, "That's what they all say, and then they flunk their language exams." Sometimes a very short statement is worth volumes.

The difference between the psychology departments at Yale and Washington University became clear in those two simple sentences. I spent the rest of my time at Washington University struggling to make up credits and taking any independent study and extra credit courses I could find. I also discovered it was a department that favored experimental psychology and the male students. As a female graduate student interested in clinical work, I was very low on their totem pole. Nevertheless, I did manage to fashion a satisfying and sustaining graduate program by seeking out professors who themselves were considered marginal to the psychology department. The support of Dr. Jane Loevinger was invaluable. She became my dissertation chair and later a dear friend. Dr. Loevinger, a brilliant researcher and statistician, had been denied a suitable university position due to the discriminatory rules of the day. Her husband was a full professor in the chemistry department, which severely limited her employability with the University or elsewhere. She became an adjunct in one or another clinical program.

Dr. E. James Anthony, a renowned child psychoanalyst, was also on the faculty; he came to St. Louis from the Maudsley Hospital in London. Brilliant and internationally recognized, he was the big man in charge. He occasionally sat in on staff meetings. I particularly remember his contributions to the diagnostic sessions held at the Municipal Child Guidance Clinic, where I also worked. He would encourage the presenter with a great display of interest and attentive focus. He would summarize the relevant data in a manner that implied that the presenter's work exhibited remarkable insight while at the same time delicately and imperceptibly decimating him or her. In listening to Dr. Anthony, I understood how closely linked sexual and intellectual excitement were for me;there's no turn-on like that of a brilliantly presented argument!

I was also encouraged by a married couple, Doctors Quentin and Naomi Rae-Grant. The Rae-Grants were the director and co-director of the Child's Psychiatric in-patient unit at the Jewish Hospital, where I worked with them. I enjoyed a nostalgic revival of my European debating skills as Quentin appreciated a spirited argument. "We are so lucky to have you, Kitty," he would say. "We can't get anybody here to debate with us."

Living with Art without the benefit of marriage made my social situation awkward. The domicile we found after leaving the rooming house was a good example. The tiny apartment was near the St. Louis State Hospital, where I was to do my internship and other clinical work. Our rental had been created out of a tiny garage attached to a small single-family house. A barber and his family occupied the extremely modest home. It was in a quiet lower-middle-class neighborhood, where we didn't even make it into the main section. The apartment measured about 15 by 25 feet, and included a tiny kitchen and bathroom, with a sitting tub we painted black. Upstairs was the then-ubiquitous door mounted on two sawhorses that served as a desk, table, and all-purpose surface. Next to that, there was a full-sized mattress and a high window, which let the moonlight shine into the room.

I had mixed feelings about this place. My feelings for Art still had the glow of new love, giving something of a charmed hidden cottage appeal to this abode. But in the light of day, its pitiful inadequacy outweighed the pleasure and convenience of its proximity to the hospital. Unwed cohabitation was not something that occurred in 1950s St. Louis. I cannot say it was regarded unkindly; it just wasn't regarded. It was discreetly omitted. In the official life of the school, I was probably considered single. Among the friends we did make, I was seen as whatever people needed me to be.

After two years of living together, Art said, "It's high time I made an honest woman out of you. Let's get married." Ruth, one of my close friends, took me aside and said, "Art is a charming, interesting, and exciting man. For all I know he may be a wonderful lover. Why don't you keep him as that, and not turn him into a husband? He will not make a good husband." I looked at her with incomprehension, lover yes, husband no, what on earth is the difference? I didn't understand. If you love somebody, you live together; you marry. As I write this, my abysmal lack of basic common sense knocks the breath out of me, but those were my feelings. I thanked Ruth for her caring thoughts. Then asked if she would be my maid of honor. She said yes. She and her husband gave us the wedding.

I was living a more or less regular student's life. Art was going to night school. In my private life I felt like a working-class person. Perhaps I felt a bit like our maid in Czechoslovakia, or my Czech school friends, whose parents were farmers. Something of the little girl in me remained, the child who looked up to Mother as an elegant lady from the upper class, while I was only a street kid. Much of it had to do with the fact that Art and I had absolutely no money. Sometimes we had to choose whether to use 40 cents for a bus ride, a movie, or supper. We became good friends with Ruth and her husband, Jack, who was also a student. They were the first couple that accepted Art as a normal social connection.

One Christmas holiday they said, "We're going away; would you like to borrow our car so you can drive to the country?" I was overwhelmed with gratitude that they would entrust us with their car. Some part of me saw myself as some kind of *untermensch*, which was also the result of living for 10 years in Switzerland as a barely tolerated persona non grata. That had dug deep into the core of my psyche, joined with the early childhood message that my mother valued my brother more than she valued me.

Art became more civilized. He entered therapy. He tried hard to drink less. His behavior around my friends, and especially around other psychologists, became less provocative and outrageous. We moved into an apartment where we could entertain friends and live a more regular existence. Shortly after we married in January 1955, I got what was then referred to as first papers, the equivalent of today's green card. These new papers allowed me for the first time to consider returning to Switzerland for a visit. When I left Switzerland five years earlier, it might have been for a short duration, but due to many fortunate circumstances, coming to America turned into a life-altering immigration. I had been in relatively infrequent contact with my family, with only weekly letters and brief telegrams on very special occasions—a notice of my first marriage to Edgar and one of my second marriage to Art.

I think often about the tenuousness of these connections. Phone connections did exist, but Transatlantic phone calls were so expensive nobody with a budget like ours would ever consider them. I don't think I called my family even once during those first five years. With my papers in order, I made plans for a four-week stay. After visiting my parents, I would visit friends in Zürich, Lucerne, and Geneva. I worked out the itinerary in my head. Importantly, I would borrow my father's car, which would enable me to fit these visits into two weeks. During the time I stayed at my parents' house, we had only a day and a half without rain. The eagerness to slosh around a grey Switzerland quickly disappeared.

In addition, my welcoming scene was significant. Sitting in the living room with my mother, father, uncle, and brother, I told them of my plans and asked, "Dad, may I borrow your car? It will be easier to do all my traveling if I have a car." My father looked at me. "That's not possible. I need my car to go to the office every day." "Come on," my brother said. "It's a 10-minute walk." My father replied, "I like to drive."

At that point, my brother spoke up. "You are a fine father; your daughter hasn't been here in five years and the first thing you do is refuse to lend her your car?" My father, not to be abashed, looked directly at my brother and said, "You're a fine one to talk. If you hadn't dilly-dallied in your studies, you would be finished by now and would have a car to lend her." As I listened to them, I sensed a sudden great release in my soul. I understood why I had left the family nest. Any remaining guilt vanished.

Back in St. Louis, Art and I were beginning to settle in. My studies were going well. Art was close to receiving his degree but again felt restless, imprisoned by the three or four remaining years of his Coast Guard re-enlistment. He wanted to earn some money. At that time, there was a great drive to lower military spending. Legislation was being passed to reduce the size of the armed forces. I remembered Marjorie Church, whom I had met in Geneva. She told me that her father, who had been a Congressman from Illinois, had died, and that her mother had taken his congressional seat. With Marjorie's permission, I contacted her mother and explained that I was married to a man in the Coast Guard who wanted to be released from the remainder of his enlistment period. Since there was a reduction of armed forces in the process, perhaps she could offer some advice?

Through her, we reached New York Congresswoman Lenore Sullivan, who was involved with the budget commission on military spending. With her intervention, Art received an early release and was then free to look for different work. With his bachelor's degree completed, and his master's barely begun, he was offered a position with the Orinoco Mining Company, which would take him to Venezuela. Art was proud that his salary would be almost triple of what he earned in the Coast Guard. The job required a six-month probationary period. He would live in Venezuela alone during this period and I would stay in St. Louis. My vision of life with Art as a romantic fairy tale had suffered several scratches, dents, and bumps, yet I was shocked at the thought of living without him for six months. How could he do that? Wouldn't he feel bereft and incomplete without me? It never occurred to him that there could be a problem with the arrangement.

It was shortly after we married that my idealized vision of the marriage suffered its first serious blow. Lying in bed one night, Art said "I hope you don't mind but I think I'll always love Ruth [his first wife]." Then he added, "You and me? We are really a *mariage de raison*. I could not have done any better in the world than to marry you."

It was a cruel obliteration of my vision of eternal love. Was he insane? If I were in touch with my reason, would I have married Art? What was he thinking? It was certainly never wise nor smart nor easy to be married to Art, but still my connection to him was an important part of my sense of security. Believing that he loved me as much as I loved him had made all the difference to me. In time I began to understand Art's position. No matter how much we struggled, for a long time I felt settled and contented in the marriage.

His "marriage of reason" required he find a woman who settled and steadied him, who inspired him to finish his education and encouraged him to move up in the world. It was the antithesis of his French-Canadian cultural message, which shouted, "Who do you think you are? Don't get too big for your britches." The concept of being undeserving, of knowing his place, of being modest was divergent from the general American invitation to be all that you can be, to be your very best self. Since I had been raised with a similar mindset, perhaps some restraint and modesty may have formed a bond between us.

With Art away in Venezuela, I moved ahead with my studies. I also purchased a houseful of furniture, the secondhand kind found through newspaper ads, some of which had exotic origins. With each purchase I imagined the life I would encounter in these foreign lands. With only a dark bamboo living room from the Philippines as a stimulus, I pictured myself joining Emile of South Pacific or a Surabaya Johnny of Indonesia. The rest of the furniture was plain, suitable not particularly for the tropics, but for the tedious and somewhat boring life we would be leading.

Some four years before, when I had decided not to give up Yale in order to join him in Puerto Rico, Art began a relationship with a young woman named Amparo, who was 17 years old. When he was accepted to OCS, he dropped her, and we resumed our liaison. Nevertheless, I was almost certain that sexual fidelity on his part was not a guarantee and was probably not on my part either. It was important to me to have the state of fidelity or infidelity equal for both of us. I became involved with schoolwork, with planning a household, and making purchases I had never made before, and so time passed quickly.

As the date for me to join Art in Venezuela approached, I began to look forward to it with mounting expectations of happiness. The company he worked for paid for packing and shipping; they even provided first-class airfare. I had quite an adventure smuggling our two cats into Venezuela, first into the overnight hotel at a stopover in New Orleans, and then into Venezuela, which turned out to be far more difficult. My arrival occurred a few days after President Nixon had been pelted with eggs in Caracas and YANKEES GO HOME banners still hung in the air. I was beside myself that my brand-new American passport, of which I was so proud, quickly brought me the trials and tribulations of being an American in the world. Already I was seen as rich and had to pay $200 at customs for each of our two alley cats.

Art met me at the small airport in Puerto Ordaz. My arrival did not fit into his evening plans. We went home for a hurried supper, after which he excused himself. "We have men's bowling league tonight, and, no, you cannot come."

What change had taken place? We were moving from an academic world defined by colleagueship into an expat working world defined by strict company hierarchy and separate rules for men and women. I was not any good at that kind of life, and I did not like it. We made a few friends, but at the same time we drifted apart.

In Venezuela, Art's drinking did not stand out. Alcoholism, or at least heavy drinking, was rampant among the men, and many of the women. Nobody thought anything of it. It was the tropics and it was hot. What else was there to do in your leisure time other than drink?

That first half-year in Puerto Ordaz was a letdown. Art and I were probably more distant than at any time before, mostly because we didn't have much in common. I found a teacher from Spain to teach me formal Spanish, as well as to help me pick up a bit of the local dialect. I did not want to be like the other American women, who after eight years, still could barely speak enough Spanish to say good morning to the maid or ask her to make the bed or to do some kitchen work. It would have been impossible for me to live in a foreign country without, at the very least, making an effort to familiarize myself with its language and customs. I didn't recognize myself. I had lived in Switzerland as well as in the United States without ever fully belonging, but the campo of Eastern Venezuela represented a very different challenge.

We lived in the middle of a wide-open landscape. The Caroni Falls, as yet unmapped and unexplored, were nearby, and a four-wheel-drive truck was sufficient to get us there. The Orinoco River was large and mysterious, full of heavy-teeth baring fish. The river supplied the below-sea-level life of Puerto Ordaz with its daily mist and moisture. The food supply was spotty. Every two or three weeks, we had to make a 150-mile trip to reach an oil company PX to stock up on groceries. If one had the resources, the time, the equipment, and the know-how to explore this largely uncharted expansive land, it would have been possible to live an adventurous life. But we were not adventurers or explorers. We were held in the grasp of the time requirements of Art's rather pedestrian job, classified as lower management.

All the Americans who worked for Orinoco Mining were considered management. Natives, a designation that encompassed all non-U.S. citizens, including the Europeans, held the non-supervisory positions. It was an abrupt introduction to the mixture of class and race. For me it was strange, but probably not an unusual caste system.

Most of the Americans were holdovers from the earlier construction days. They had worked in the exploratory phase of the mining enterprise for construction companies like Bechtel and Halliburton. They were a tribe of expats for whom working in Venezuela, or anywhere overseas, represented a privileged state. It was better pay than at home, no taxes, personal freedom, none of the usual laws and regulations that governed community life. You could do whatever you wanted to do. The company provided housing, rigidly allocated according to employment status, and the camp service provided amenities, from replacing broken refrigerators to screwing in new light bulbs. Within the confines of geography and relative isolation, life was comfortable and unfettered.

Besides the abundance of drinking, there was a great deal of sexual partner–sharing among the couples. For the single men there was an ample assortment of whorehouses.

Wives started to play bridge at 8 am, before it got really hot. For those of us who were more ambitious, there were frequent outings on horseback into the uninhabited, untamed countryside. I was happy when my time there came to an end.

Several months in, we had decided that I should return to St. Louis to finish my degree. Once there, I found a place to stay and a job to support myself. The estrangement from Art weighed on me considerably. I went into a depression of the kind that had befallen me from time to time, beginning in my late teens. I had terminated the therapy that had been part of my professional training and needed to find another therapist. Through recommendations, I found an analyst who agreed to see me for the low amount of five dollars, which was the fee for students at the time. Each time I arrived for a session, before lying down on the couch, as was the custom in analytic treatment, I took a good look at my therapist. I was comforted that he seemed calm but was not attractive. His speech was homespun and slow.

As we got further into my treatment, I perceived that he was not familiar with people like me. At one point, I stated that the ability to understand things was one of my most essential needs. Later he told me I had deeply impressed him, a woman with an inquisitive mind. Also later on (yes, there was a later on) he confided that his parents deemed everything he did was wonderful. They did not encourage him to work harder. When he got to college, he discovered there were many people who were much smarter than he was. He became upset and struggled to make up for the discrepancy.

About the *later on*. At a point when loneliness and depression were weighing me down, I said in the course of one session, "I can't bear going home to an empty apartment. When I walk out of here, I might invite the first man who looks at me in a friendly fashion to come home with me." It was a silly statement, equal parts absurd, provocative, and bragging. I meant it as a comment to be dissipated into thin air. As I prepared to leave, it became clear my statement had found an interested audience. My therapist said, "You don't have to go out and find anybody. I will come to your place." I was startled but nonetheless went into automatic mode and wrote my address on a piece of paper. I left his office, headed for a liquor store, and bought a bottle of bourbon to have something to offer him. I called a friend who had intended to come over for a visit. I asked her not to come, saying something unexpected had come up.

That is how the affair with my therapist began, and it offers much food for thought. First, the basics: A therapist does not sleep with a patient. When I became his lover, I stopped being his patient. It would not have occurred to me to go back to his office, or heaven forbid, continue paying for sessions, as I know some people have done. Whatever this infraction represented for him and his career, in my own therapy it represented a badly timed interruption. On many levels, it was an unacceptable affair. Aside from the professional taboos that were breached, he was married, the father of five children. And I was married as well.

I did not have a guilty conscience about Art. I knew he did not adhere strictly to monogamy and marital fidelity. At one point, when he and I discussed these matters, he said his infidelities were nothing, only one-night stands. "I get drunk and I go to bed with someone. The next day it's over. On the other hand, you get involved and bring emotions in. So your infidelity matters because it's an emotional infidelity, but mine don't matter because it's just a bodily function." I certainly don't agree with that dichotomy. And that wasn't an accurate description where Art was concerned. Over the years, I observed him become involved emotionally with other women.

My involvement with my ex-therapist was something I could justify to myself, but I wasn't ready to justify it for him. I thought he should go back to his own analyst to get help about this form of acting out, which was a professionally devastating behavior. Deep inside, I was humiliated by the required sneakiness that came along with the arrangement. Yet I also felt somewhat gleeful that I could pull it off. We carried on our affair in broad daylight. We went out to eat at the best restaurants in town. We had lunch outings. We even had an occasional evening out on the town. It was as though something in plain sight was not suspect. I did not feel guilty about his wife. I didn't think I was taking anything away from her. I had no aspirations to steal her husband. I didn't want him on a full-time basis.

On the whole, the affair was a good experience, despite the dubious ethics. He was a reliable man who cared about me. To the extent he could be, I felt he was there for me. The results of this liaison were twofold. At first, I decided to separate from Art because I did not feel a strong enough attachment to remain married. But as the affair progressed and I felt comforted and somewhat healed, I began to feel more optimistic about sustaining the marriage. I came to believe our estrangement was largely my fault. If I changed, things would be good again. This is a mistake I have made often in relationships, not only with Art. When things are difficult, I see the times I could have been more loving, more wise, more forgiving, and more understanding. By now, I have had sufficient experience to recognize the fallacy of that assumption. One partner's change does not necessarily lead to an improvement in a relationship.

At the beginning of the summer, I left for Venezuela in good spirits. I was looking forward to putting my newly found love and equanimity into action. Once again, like my first arrival in Venezuela, what greeted me was not what I expected. It was as if Art had gone through his own journey of estrangement. He was suspicious and furious. Before I even fully entered the house, he looked me over with an accusatory expression, and proceeded to interrogate me about my misdeeds, which he was sure had transpired. Either he had a sixth sense, or I was very transparent. At the end of a grueling 14-hour interrogation that lasted until the next morning, I finally gave up and confessed the affair.

The next two months in Venezuela were horrible. Art drank and raved. His son and a friend were visiting, which lent a little bit of safety and security to family life. I can't remember anything other than pain, anger, and distress, and lots and lots of drinking on his part. I can't drink. I get sleepy; then I get sick, so that particular avenue of solace or oblivion was never open to me. At the end of that summer I decided to leave for good. I was sure the end of our marriage had arrived.

I was an awkward and unhappy wife attempting to fit into a small company town situated at the confluence of the Orinoco and Caroni rivers. My marriage was unsuccessful. I certainly was not a good fit with any of my expat neighbors. In St. Louis, to which I was commuting during the first two years of our time there, I lived quite successfully as a working clinical psychologist and graduate student, busy collecting data for my dissertation. Each time I returned to St. Louis, I had to find a new place to live and a job. And each time I left, I gave up my living quarters and passed on whatever job I had to a younger colleague. It was an exercise in many-faceted impermanence, for which my life up to that point had well prepared me.

It was this professional life that I was prepared to resume full time when I returned to St. Louis in August of 1959. But events took a different turn. Shortly after a scant three weeks after I left Art decided to follow me. We reconciled and I became pregnant. Art and I saw the future that lay ahead of us fairly clearly. Art had two divorces behind him and had often said that he would hold on to our marriage because he did not want to be a three-time loser. I wasn't ready to let go either. We decided Venezuela was an unsuitable place for me to go through pregnancy, as the obstetrical medical facilities were non-existent. I stayed in St Louis until the middle of my eighth month of pregnancy, collecting dissertation data and continuing my work as a psychologist in a child psychiatry unit. I presented a great teaching opportunity for our inpatient children, who watched me get big and bigger, asked questions, felt my belly, and listened as they learned where they had all come from.

Art returned to his job in Venezuela. My work life was happy and satisfying, and my friends were supportive, but pregnancy was hard on me. I often felt depressed in the morning, unbearably tired by late afternoon, and scared and nauseated at night. I became hugely needy, dreaming of someone coming by and fixing me a cup of tea. And then marveling at the miracle of someone having enough energy to make not only their own tea but also an extra cup for another person. My women friends, and even my past therapist, tended to me wonderfully.

But when a decision had to be made about where the birth would take place, I felt too alone in St. Louis. I decided to return to my parents' house and have the baby, whom my friends and I had been referring to as Melanie Rachel, see the light of day in beautiful, medically up-to-date Switzerland. A medical certificate permitted me to fly late in pregnancy. I knew a Swiss birth would not confer Swiss citizenship on my child, and also ascertained that a foreign birth would not compromise her status as a native U.S. citizen. I registered her birth with the American Consulate in Zürich.

When Melanie was about three weeks old, Art came to visit, and to accompany us back to Venezuela. With a baby in the house, the focus of our lives shifted, at least temporarily. We did not return to St. Louis for a year and a half, until it was clear Art's employment at Orinoco Mining Company was coming to an end. One of our cats, our brave little Grisha, failed to return one night; we assumed she had been eaten by one of the wild animals that inhabited the region. We found a good home for her daughter, Gwendoline Goldilocks, and somewhat carelessly entrusted our street dogs, Jimmy and Susie, whom we had been feeding and whom we had befriended, to the benevolent care of the remaining community.

When we returned to St. Louis, we found a picturesque but rather ramshackle house in Webster Groves. It was almost like something out of *Hansel and Gretel*.

I was getting ready to settle into a peaceful nondramatic life in St. Louis. I occasionally thought of the two professors, Ruth Wiley and Katherine Baker, who constituted most of the psychology department at Connecticut College, and of their supportive concern in counseling me against living in the Midwest. I thought they would be surprised at how well I had adapted. I had come to fit in quite nicely in the gracious but problem-ridden Southern town that St. Louis was then. Art found a job with McDonnell Aircraft in the spare parts department. It must have been a low-level job, because he was paid by the hour and was entitled to time and a half for overtime. In fact, he earned more than he ever had, but he chafed under what he felt was a diminished status. Art had been a supervisor-manager in Venezuela.

We began to have friends and developed a regular social life, with couples inviting each other for dinners and parties. We were no longer regarded as the oddballs. We belonged.

I finished my dissertation. And not only did the statistical results come out beautifully, but Dr. Loevinger also paid me an enormous compliment: "Here you are, a foreign student, and yours is the only dissertation I have read that's written in decent English."

After working in a number of clinics, I was becoming a well-established psychologist. I knew many professionals in the mental health field and had established a private practice, mostly in diagnostic testing. My income just about equaled that of Art's. Throughout our marriage, without a conscious decision, my income never exceeded his. Shortly after we separated, my earnings rose to a proper level.

I imagined a comfortable and happy life in St. Louis. I began to think about the next step in the American dream: owning a home. Before I could take that fantasy any further, the wife of one of Art's co-workers, who was a real estate agent, called me. "I hear you're thinking of buying a house. What areas do you have in mind?" I thought of the sections of St. Louis that were close to the university, ones that had substantial houses with old gardens and mature trees. I said, "Maybe somewhere in University City or perhaps Clayton," and then named a few other streets. "Are you sure?" she asked, inflecting her voice to dismiss my notion. "Wouldn't you prefer for your children to grow up among your own?" I told her rather pointedly that I would be among my own and I bade her good-bye.

Before I could pursue my dream of owning a home any further, Art came home one day elated, with the news that a headhunter had contacted him about a job with Kennecott Copper Mining Company. The company's headquarters were in New York, and the new job represented a logical and meaningful step upward in Art's career. Once again my desire to stay put so as not to disturb the little bit of equilibrium I had managed to create in our lives was a barely perceived blip. I reluctantly agreed to move east.

I went to see Dr. Anthony and told him about my upcoming relocation. Upon hearing I did not have any plans in place for my professional future, he said there were only two people worth working with in New York, Sybil Escalona and Margaret Mahler. In the early 1960s, hierarchy was respected: Dr. Anthony was a number of steps above me. When he addressed me in such a collegial way, I felt promoted into his world. He invited me to a cocktail party at his home on the occasion of the annual meeting of the American Psychoanalytic Association. An invitation to the Anthony home for an exclusive gathering of an inner circle of analysts was beyond anything I had envisioned. Dr. Mahler would be in attendance.

Dr. Anthony said, "I will introduce you; see what you think. If you can forgive her paranoia, you will learn a lot from her." Dr. Mahler had dark hair and was small and round. I was struck by her apparent sadness and found myself wanting to protect her. I probably experienced her in this manner because I had not yet worked with her. We had a brief conversation at the party, and I promised to call her when I got to New York. A professional bridge to New York had been built with Dr. Anthony's important introduction to Dr. Mahler. The move then became somewhat easier to accept.

Dr. René Spitz, a tall white-haired man then in his 80s, was also at the cocktail party. Years earlier he had studied the development of infants. He became well known for finding that physical contact was as important for infants as food and sleep. This concept illustrated the importance of nonverbal exchange between mother and infant. His name was linked with the concept of *marasmus*—the failure of an infant to thrive. At Dr. Anthony's home, I overheard Dr. Spitz in friendly conversation with other colleagues. He fondly recalled his three-month psychoanalysis with Freud. His eyes welled up; his cheeks blushed. I thought to myself, "There go the theories of resolving transference at the end of treatment."

I was still anxious about the move and shared my anxiety with friends and colleagues. Unlike the incredulous questioning I encountered at Yale about choosing the Midwest for further graduate education, the reaction of my St. Louis friends was one of admiration and optimism. They considered New York as a move into a bigger world. They shared the clichéd sentiment, "If you can make it there, you can make it anywhere." In this instance, my cluelessness was helpful, because I wasn't worried about making it or not making it in New York.

Life in New York

Profession: Family Therapist

Melanie and I moved east in 1962. Art had arrived ahead of us, and rented a house in Stamford, Connecticut. It was spacious, with four bedrooms and a large backyard, located in a working-class neighborhood. It was similar in layout to our house in Webster Groves, minus its charm, but also minus the flying squirrels and chewed-up electric wiring. And without the unspoken understanding that no Jews were allowed. Art commuted to his job in the Chrysler Building in midtown while I worked half-time as Dr. Mahler's research psychologist: her project was located on Horatio Street in the Village. My door-to-door commute took approximately two hours each way. I hired Margaret, an Irish au pair, to take care of Melanie when I was working in the city. I also found a position as a therapist two days a week in an outpatient clinic at Stamford Hospital. There I discovered how much more I liked clinical work than I did the research on Dr. Mahler's project.

Although I had worked as a clinical psychologist for almost a decade, I consider 1962, the year I received my Ph.D., the official beginning of my professional life.

Dr. Mahler wanted me to apply to the New York Psychoanalytic Institute to train as a psychoanalyst. She even explored sources of available funds for this expensive and protracted enterprise. At the time, the Institute accepted non-M.D. applicants, as long as they signed a pledge that they would use their psychoanalytic training exclusively for research and never in clinical work. My life had been constrained by so many unalterable external circumstances that I was unwilling to put voluntary constraints on my professional options. I chose not to apply.

Dr. Mahler's observational study of mothers and infants was designed to elucidate the postnatal development of the human psyche, as it evolved within the mother-child relationship. Her work helped remove me from the reductionism of individual psychology. We were collecting observational data, buttressed here and there by filming, a far cry from today's sophisticated instrumentation. We kept running records of interactions in the mother-child pairs, both in the room as a participant observer, and outside of the room, as a non-participant observer. Dr. Mahler was creative and brilliant, as well as difficult and demanding. But she liked my work. She sometimes used me as her cat's-paw to intimidate other workers. "That La Perriere thinks like a man," she would say in admiration. Dr. Mahler valued my contributions. But it was also clear to me that I was only a temporary associate on the project. I had not yet found my focus.

We observed mother-toddler pairs two or three times a week looking at the harmony or disharmony of their personal rhythms. In another phase of the study, we interviewed the mothers several months later about their recollections of our earlier observed times. The considerable discrepancy between what the researcher observed and noted and what the parent remembered forever impressed upon me the fallibility and unreliability of recollection.

Dr. Mahler was devoted to her work and ultimately published her findings in three well-received volumes titled *The Psychological Birth of the Human Infant*. Eventually new technologies expanded significantly on her early findings. These later advances disclosed extensive information on the inner life of infants beginning in utero in contrast to Dr. Mahler's assumption of a blank slate at birth.

Dr. Mahler worked very long hours. On the occasions when we worked late, I would stay over at her beautiful apartment in the tower of the El Dorado on Central Park West. Perhaps her work ethic was the way she had found to cope with loneliness. On holidays, such as the Fourth of July, or even Christmas, she summoned her assistants. If we chose instead to celebrate these occasions with our own families, she accused us of dereliction of duty. Art, Melanie, and I spent many a weekend at her delightful country estate in Brookfield, Connecticut. While we were there, she and I would meticulously pore over the observation reports, then categorize them and discuss our findings.

I assisted in the writing of some of the research papers. In 1965, I was credited as a co-author in an article published in *Psychoanalytic Quarterly*, "Mother-Child Interaction During the Separation-Individuation Phase." With the publication of this article, my name became known within the psychoanalytic community. I admired Dr. Mahler, and even felt a kind of tender, protective love for her, but she was moody and explosive. In this regard, she was similar to Jane Loevinger whose study dovetailed with some of Murray Bowen's concepts in early family therapy.

I was fortunate to study, apprentice, and work with a number of outstanding people whose ideas informed and encouraged me. The year at Yale taught me how to evaluate evidence and be cautious about generalizations and imbued in me a sense of personal worth as a thinking person. This sustained me when I first encountered obstacles as a clinical psychologist. At the time the profession was not valued by academic psychology and was put down by psychiatry. I also suffered from the ubiquitous gender bias that relegated women to a seat in the audience, but not at the podium. To this day, I remain grateful to my Yale professors, who treated me as a junior colleague and expressed their belief in my professional future.

When I was working on test construction at Washington University with Dr. Loevinger, I conducted a study on the ego development of postpartum women, interviewing them while they were still in the hospital. I got great statistical results, but more notably I developed rich interview protocols. This project marked the beginning of my drift into clinical work. Dr. Loevinger once remarked that she wished I was the clinical consultant instead of Dr. Alex Kaplan, who was a psychoanalyst. She would have preferred he were the research associate. I understood this was a compliment to both of us. In all these situations I paid attention to the factors that psychology, focused as it was on the inner life of the individual, tended to exclude as extraneous error sources. In interviewing the mothers in my study, I found the contrasts in their conditions could not have been more dramatic. The affluent moms were in pretty rooms, surrounded by flowers, care, and loving family members. The women who gave birth on a public ward, six to a room, with basic, mean-looking furnishings received scant attention. From day one, these babies entered different worlds. Which of the test findings were going to be affected by this difference, and what would be the conclusions?

I later looked with a critical eye at standardized tests, supposedly culture-free, purported to measure concepts such as native intelligence. More relevantly, they were utilized as a measurement of the likelihood of scholastic success. Thus, they played a large role in a child's future educational opportunities and options. I particularly remember two cards in a picture completion subtest. One was a comb with a missing tooth, and one a snowy landscape depicting a man and a dog, but only the man's footprints were left in the snow. I thought the answers were a poor person's comb and a snow condition in which the powder had melted and then refroze. Therefore, the surface was strong enough to hold up the dog, but too soft to keep the man from sinking and leaving his prints. The correct answers were a broken comb and missing paw prints.

As I write this, I note how hard we tried to be uniform, to reduce everything to the simplest dimensions. In October 2017, I listened to a radio interview with the author Junot Diaz. He spoke about the impoverishment of ideas that our social and political system must cope with in impending hard times and a setting of diversity. How can we mobilize what resources and gifts are available with the imposition of simple-minded views of people and social structures? As I listened to Diaz, I remembered my earliest encounters of psychology in precisely that way. Unfortunately, Diaz has been discredited by the #MeToo movement.

After a year of living in the Connecticut suburbs, I decided Melanie needed her mother more than she needed a backyard and grass. We moved into an apartment on 72nd Street and Riverside Drive. The current tenants had advertised the apartment for rent. When I went to see it, a flashy woman with platinum blonde hair greeted me. She showed me the apartment, giving an extensive sales talk about its desirability.

A few days later I returned with Art for a second look, but the woman was absent. Instead, we encountered a quiet dark-haired woman, a small boy, and a tall man. They were quite noncommunicative. I wondered who they were. Perhaps they were friends who had come over to show the apartment? When we arrived at the apartment for the third and conclusive visit, we encountered all three adults. It turned out that the tall man and the silent dark-haired woman were the tenant couple, and at serious odds with each other. They had decided to move to California in an attempt to save their marriage. The sexy blonde woman was their au pair. And we then were informed she came with the apartment! As we talked with the couple, Joan and Bob, they confessed that it was at least their fourth marriage-saving cross-country relocation.

Beate, the au pair, came to Connecticut with us to spend the summer. Startled neighbors gossiped about the glamorous young woman who resembled a Hollywood starlet. Beate enjoyed sunbathing in the backyard, unperturbed by what anybody saw or said. She turned out to be a true godsend. She was a perfect housekeeper; she cooked and cleaned, washed and ironed and sewed, in a manner I had not seen since leaving my childhood home in Moravia. We moved into Manhattan as a family. I continued my work on the research project with Dr. Mahler.

One day a few months later, I felt ill and stayed home, not wanting to expose our research subjects to what I thought was seasonal flu. Judy Karelitz, a colleague on the project, called to inquire after me. Initially I told her I felt a little ill, but she pressed me. I described my symptoms: dizziness, the sensation of falling backward, and that I was hot. I concluded my self-diagnosis: "It's just the flu." Judy listened attentively and carefully. She instructed me to call a doctor. It was a Wednesday, and in that era, doctors took Wednesdays off. Undeterred, Judy said I must immediately call her cousin, Dr. Burt Korelitz, an internist. I did. (His wife remains one of my best friends to this day.) He instructed me to come immediately. Lying on the table, I said, with considerable personal authority, that he shouldn't worry about my pulse rate, as it was always slow. He shook his head slowly. "Really? It's 144." I spent the afternoon in his office while he monitored my condition. I asked, "Doctor, is it serious?"

He replied, "I don't know."

I persisted. "Am I going to live?"

"I don't know."

Eventually he sent me home to wait for an available bed at Lenox Hill Hospital, where I was admitted. In the morning I woke up to find a worried Art at my bedside. I marveled at the speed with which he had returned home and wondered who had paid for his airplane ticket from Chile. The final diagnosis was myocarditis. Obviously, it was a mild case, as it was treated only with Compazine and bed rest. In addition, I was given a stern admonition to reduce or eliminate stressful situations.

While I was at home convalescing, a graduate school friend, then living in California, visited New York and dropped by to see me. During our conversation, I learned about an interesting new project. There were three psychiatrists who ran a program for boys at risk and their families at Wiltwyck Institution for Delinquent Boys. One of the doctors, Nathan Ackerman, was in the process of establishing a family institute in New York. He was looking to hire a licensed psychologist. My friend suggested I contact him. Her visit presented a possible solution to my professional dilemma about what I would do if I left Dr. Mahler's research project. And that is really how my professional career as a family therapist began.

I went to work for what was then called the Family Institute. In 1963 we believed we were the only family institute in existence: no further identification was required. The Institute grew out of Nathan Ackerman's private practice. It had recently moved to 149 East 78th Street. A number of Dr. Ackerman's former and current patients formed its board of directors. The Institute operated with deficit funding accounting. At the end of each year, board members were expected to reach for their checkbooks to cover the short falls. We existed from month to month in an ongoing state of penury. Eventually, all of that would change.

In order to obtain a clinic license, the chief mental health disciplines (psychiatry, psychology, and social work) had to be represented on staff. Judith Lieb was the social worker, as well as the administrator and assistant to Dr. Ackerman. I was the psychologist. Dr. Don Bloch, also a psychiatrist, was the head of the research department. Although I no longer remember the specific content of my initial interviews with Dr. Ackerman and Judy Lieb, I do recall vividly that it was essential that my New York license be in place.

What remains memorable is the prologue to my interview with Dr. Bloch. In trying to schedule an initial meeting we ran into trouble finding an available time. He expressed trouble finding a time he could meet with me. It was June, and almost everyone was going off on summer vacations. He asked, "Where will you be this summer? I can come and we will have the interview there." I didn't understand what he meant but replied that I would be in Bermuda. "Oh!" he said, "that is not possible. I am not rated for overwater flights." It turned out he was a pilot and owned a small plane. He lived in Vermont and commuted to New York by plane. Need I say more about the mixture of adventure and the grand sweep and absence of reliability this particular configuration contained?

I learned the family therapy trade primarily from Dr. Ackerman. I observed him work, sat in on sessions, and occasionally received a comment or two of a supervisory nature. "What is your difficulty with this family?" he might ask, or "Why don't you like this man?" Usually, it seemed an arbitrary comment, but it was always spot on. Dr. Ackerman was known both nationally and internationally. Many people visited the Institute to watch him work, and to discuss the field. He was possessive and exclusionary whenever visitors arrived. He would not introduce them, instead ushering them into his office. "Nat has visitors," Judy Lieb would say.

The Institute was transitioning from a private-based practice, where people were welcome to visit, to a more formal institutional structure. There was a small research staff, which included Marjorie Behrens, an anthropologist. A newsletter was published under the editorship of Ruth Perl Kahn, Ph.D., one of the Columbia trained female Ph.Ds. Two people, Dr. Emory Hetrick and I, were identified as externs. Years later, Dr. Hetrick became a highly revered figure in the gay community as it emerged into visibility. Other psychiatrists joined as therapists and supervisors, among them Dr. Paul Franklin and Dr. Wally Sencer. Classes in family therapy were formed for licensed professionals. Most of those enrolled were psychiatrists and social workers. The first of these classes were conducted at the facilities of the Jewish Family Services.

Nat Ackerman was patriarchal. When there was a problem in a family, he always saw the woman as the source of the trouble. If a man cheated, well, "boys will be boys", but if a woman cheated, the marriage was mortally wounded and therefore over. He believed a woman, if satisfied at home, wouldn't want or choose to work. Therefore the women working at the Institute were living evidence of personal domestic dissatisfaction. He liked women to be gentle, flirtatious, and sufficiently well-bred never to challenge a man.

I once confided in Ackerman about my troubled marriage. Art was again drinking excessively. Ackerman waved away my request for a referral to an accomplished marital therapist. He advised me to retain a divorce attorney. While this might be interpreted as a sympathetic and supportive gesture, I think it was something else. In Ackerman's view, for a marriage to be respected, the husband had to be competent, dominant, and superior. Art was not that. Ackerman's dismissal of my expressed desire to go into marital therapy most likely made me stay with Art longer than I might have otherwise.

Another time, I dared voice my disagreement about a clinical situation. He said, "There is no point in disagreeing with me. I have 30 years on you. And you'd better know that whenever we disagree, you're wrong." In the main, however, he didn't bother much with any of us. He conducted his professional life and practice, and we were left more or less free to do the same with ours.

We were a high-energy group. At our weekly meeting we developed a treatment model that might well stand up to today's thinking and requirements. We called it Family House. We proposed to bring a number of families with multiple challenges to live under one roof, with services to be provided on-site. The National Institute of Mental Health (NIMH) viewed it kindly and ultimately approved our proposal but financial cuts across the board eliminated any chance of funding.

I loved being part of family therapy. I thought it offered a perspective that took into account the reality of human connectedness and that far from imposing a particular structure to represent "the normal family," allowed that the normal healthy family could have many structures. I believed therapy should endeavor to find a natural shape for a particular relationship. It was an exciting time. It seemed we were at the forefront of a new age, one in which open, loving, and well-meaning people could discover ways to solve conflict.

Unsurprisingly, the pioneers of family therapy were mostly men. In fact, they were all men, with the exception of Virginia Satir and Carolyn Attneave. Family therapy was a closed club; its exclusiveness was also maintained by the fact that most of the men were medical doctors. Many of the women who found their way into the discipline early on were trained as social workers. They came into the field with the burden of a lower professional status. Some family therapists eased the way for their untrained wives. Then there was me, with a doctorate, banging on doors and becoming furious when excluded.

By the 1970s, the ideas and the practice of family therapy were spreading throughout Europe and the United States. We were proselytizers, teaching the gospel of family therapy as salvation for the miseries of the human condition, with individual therapy seen as but a benighted expression of medieval ignorance. Along with my colleagues, I traveled to lead workshops and participate at conferences. We felt smug and self-righteous that we were in possession of the truths. It seems hard to believe now, but at that time, we were confident we were at the cutting edge of social change, rather than recognizing that practitioners of family therapy were swimming along in what had become the social political drift of society as a hole.

Nathan Ackerman died in 1971, at the age of 63. All the externs agreed to stay on for another year. At first, we were unsure whether the Institute could continue without its founder. But Judy Lieb and I held down the fort. I felt more empowered to shape the Institute into the open, visitor-welcoming place I thought it could and should be. A year later, Dr. Bloch returned and accepted the directorship. I was appointed training and education director, leading me to the mistaken assumption that I would have a role in running the Institute. I believed I would have some power and some say in how things were done.

Don Bloch was no more willing than Nathan Ackerman to share administrative power. While there may have been a bit of glory in being the institute's director of education, there was zero agency connected to it, neither political nor administrative. Dr. Bloch was extremely competitive and was worried I might try to grab the reins from him and ultimately become director. That was far from my mind. I did not then, or at any later point, feel qualified to assume leadership of the Institute, either in professional stature or in establishing the relationships required to expand on and further its development.

Dr. Bloch set about strengthening his position. He had not created any particular family therapy school; he concentrated on cultivating relationships and connections. He became a real *macher* in the field. He networked and traveled and befriended and helped. In these ways he accumulated significant personal power, which made him sought after. He helped create a number of professional journals and served as a consultant to family therapy organizations both nationally and internationally. Don Bloch was known as the man who could get things done.

Struggles of one sort or another bubbled up for me periodically, but on the whole, the decade of the 1970s was professionally gratifying. I ran the training program, brought in many new formats, welcomed many visitors, and maintained our reputation as a warm and nurturing place. We developed summer programs and held conferences, and we traveled abroad, giving presentations to enthusiastic audiences. I worked very hard during those years. At one point, the family therapy group of the Tavistock in London sent one of their members, Rosemary Whiffen, to twin me: She would stick with me for a week, morning, noon, and night, to see how I distributed my work and energies. At the end of the week, she found I had put in 66 hours of interactive time.

Could I have achieved greater power and importance in the profession? Certainly there were opportunities offered or suggested that I failed to pursue. I hardly ever considered rising to greater prominence. I was full of ideas, and aware that my knowledge and judgment were more than adequate. There were many things in my favor that likely would have enabled me to become a more celebrated figure in the field, including having an early presence in its development. But the truth is I am inherently a rather modest, even timid, person. Additionally, my personal life put incompatible demands on me. Added to this was the fact the Institute did not support my outside activities. They either actively opposed my involvement or failed to provide even modest funds. I was not any good at working the system of institutional politics. I surely didn't understand the importance of power and money.

A report by a visiting NIMH evaluation team concluded that our program was the only one they had visited that delivered so much more than its literature promised. At first, I read the report as a compliment. Then I sighed, remembering the treacherous European admonishment of my childhood: *Be modest. Don't brag. Don't make waves.* I then began to realize that under-representing one's work and accomplishments is wasteful and diminishes one's substance, however worthy and solid that substance might be. The trauma of losing my childhood world and living as a refugee in Switzerland prevented me from pursuing power and fame. I preferred keeping a low visibility.

Sometimes an idiosyncratic reminder of my background makes its appearance. I was at a conference at the university in Milan, Italy, standing in front of a large audience, when I suddenly found myself seized with great unease about being onstage. "Someone will shoot me!" I thought. This groundless fear dissipated when the predominantly female left-wing audience questioned me at length about gender politics in the United States. They felt my views about domestic and workplace equality were far beyond what Italian women then saw as possible for themselves. With their questions and interest, my anxieties vanished.

A far less dramatic reminder of "I am just a guest here" occurred during a weekend workshop I conducted at a private hospital in the Midwest. The hospital was having difficulty filling its patient beds. The director and staff were eager for me to come and work with them. Their aim was to facilitate better communication across all staff levels and, of course, fill the hospital's beds. I was happy to accept their offer. Six exuberant people welcomed me upon my arrival at the airport. They told me how much they were looking forward to the weekend. They explained that more people had wanted to come to greet me, but the van seating was limited. At dinner I was seated in the middle of the long side of the table, clearly intended as the place of honor. For a time all went well and the conversation flowed easily. I was fully engaged, until I realized there was conversation going on to my left, and conversation going on to my right. I was sitting in the middle, feeling overlooked and ignored.

The awful familiar feeling of "I don't belong here" or "I am not welcome here" or "No one knows me here" or even "My English isn't really good enough; I don't know colloquialisms and am incapable of banter" all struck me at once and felt like a weight on my chest. I finally stopped myself. "These people brought you from New York so you could work with them. They are paying you to be here. They came to pick you up and competed to sit at a table with you. What is the matter with you?" It took only a second or two for these realizations to filter through my mind. I was able to realize that I had cooperated in my own exclusion. I had conversed with people on my left and then got drawn away to speak with people on my right. After that happened a few times, I lost the thread and was left to my own devices. My own devices in situations like that are woefully inadequate.

When you leave a conversation, then want to come back to it, you must make an effort to reconnect. If you want to make it a general conversation, you must have the presence and the volume of voice to include everybody. That second option is not my strength, but I certainly could carry out the first. I re-joined a conversation at the table in the blink of an eye. It is an experience I have remembered for many years.

Another such event happened as I was defining my place in the family therapy community. In 1975 I was invited to join a small group of family therapists organizing what later became the American Family Therapy Association (AFTA). I felt more than included by them and was honored to be invited as the first addition to the original group of 15 family therapists who founded the national organization. Once the organization actually came into being, I poured my energy and enthusiasm into it. In 1981 the second annual meeting of AFTA was held in Boston. Something stopped me from wanting to go. I believe that I had attended a conference of a competing organization, not competing externally for family therapists, but competing inside me for attention and loyalty. This other organization, the American Academy of Psychotherapists, focused on the person of the therapist, a perspective not highly regarded then by most family therapists who dismissed it as "navel-gazing". Family therapy had begun its journey into fragmentation of many competing theories, each pushing its tenets as the whole truth. Perhaps I was averse to engaging in these competitive endeavors. But what I personally experienced was something else. I thought, "I don't want to go to the meeting in Boston. I don't know anybody there. Nobody will notice whether I'm there or not."

At the last minute I decided to go. Early in the meeting, the members of the nominating committee approached me with much excitement. They asked if I would be interested in running for president of the organization. I was hugely surprised but needed only a little bit of persuasion to accept. From where do these vast discrepancies arise between perception and reality? I marveled how my self-perception tended to sabotage me and keep me from proceeding to places where I am afraid I may encounter difficulties and perhaps suffer pain and defeat.

After I accepted the nomination, three women colleagues—Monica McGoldrick, Froma Walsh, and Carol Anderson—encouraged and supported me along with John Pearce and Frank Pittman. I won the election.

With this striking exception, relationships with my newly feminist women colleagues were not always cordial. I was a feminist of a different ilk, and mostly of a different generation. I had chosen my own path into the working world long before the sweep of feminist theory awakened many women in family therapy to issues of gender discrimination and the pervasive inequalities of patriarchy. They had their own slogans and marching songs. Mine didn't match. My professional experience in family therapy had never included loving and supportive women.

I was the first female education director at the Ackerman Institute and had been the first woman president of AFTA. Later, at two separate meetings of feminist family therapists, one at Stonehenge, New York, and one at Kollekolle, Denmark, the women who succeeded me in either position were celebrated as the first. Both of these events involved women I considered friends. They were shocked and dismayed when they were made aware I had been erased from history. I don't think it was a case of personal rancor. I simply was invisible to them. I was not part of their in-group. Their skipping over me illustrates how rigid adherence to an ideology distorts our perceptions.

My distrust of social rules, as well as an understanding of their cultural relativity, made it difficult, if not impossible, for me to believe in and follow any of the established family therapy doctrines. I saw arbitrariness when Nathan Ackerman declared the *natural family* consists of a mother, a father, their natural-born children, and two sets of grandparents. This was the model family unit upon which he based his research and established his theories. As a working family therapist, it was far more relevant for me to explore the family as I encountered it rather than impose *a priori* normative definitions as posited by this or that theory. Family therapy took much issue with individually based therapies, especially the imposition of psychiatric diagnoses, a process that distanced and dehumanized patients while blaming them for their problems and affirming the power position of the therapist. It was not long before the practice of family therapy began to incorporate the same errors, which found their way into the theoretical construct of family therapy itself.

I saw these problems early and clearly. I never found it possible to construct a family therapy theory whose errors didn't riddle it before it was born. I founded neither an institute nor a school, nor did I write a family therapy textbook. Although early in my career at Ackerman, I did show Nathan Ackerman an outline for such a textbook, which I had prepared at the suggestion of an editor at Basic Books. He barely glanced at the pages before ripping them up and tossing them in the wastebasket. Then he said, "Learn something first." Perhaps he was a master hypnotist, because his out-of-hand dismissal completely silenced me as an author. Nevertheless, I was happy with the career I built and the level of achievement I reached. Over more than three decades, I wrote articles and book reviews, conducted workshops, and presented papers at conferences both nationally and internationally. Now that the world offers fewer obstacles to women in careers such as mine, my achievements, which once appeared like a peak in the Alps, look more like a peaklet in the foothills. I must remember that I walked up that peaklet step by step, before any funiculars speeded up the assent.

On a more personal level, I realized that large audience presentations were not my strongest suit. While I spoke easily and well enough, I lacked the drive and skill to prepare what increasingly became all too often self-promoting performances. During this era, presentations relied on heavily edited tapes. They demonstrated how devilishly clever the therapists had been to discover a way to help this or that family. I watched the making of some of these tapes, and realized the finished product was a construction, perhaps a work of art. But it was certainly not data, and if it were data, it was falsified. Nowadays these considerations seem quaintly old-fashioned.

A therapist might have tried a number of different interventions. Yet he only showed the one that had worked. Did it matter that it worked after a number of failures? Was that information needed to complete the picture? Even worse, therapists began to select patients primarily with a view toward what kind of tapes they could get from them. This kind of pre-selection is appropriate when casting a play or a film, but totally inappropriate when presumably demonstrating the workings of therapy. My disenchantment with the philosophical and theoretical development of family therapy, accompanied as it was by the emphasis on outcome, construction of treatment protocols, and compliance with insurance reimbursement requirements, coincided with what might be seen as my political defeat at the Ackerman Institute. In 1980 I needed to take a personal leave of absence, which was transformed into my demotion as training director. Dr. Bob Simon was almost immediately appointed as my successor.

I resumed full-time work after I had been elected to the presidency of AFTA. I involved myself with the organization for the next few years, while at the same time devoting my energies to building a private practice in family and couples therapy. Private practice suited me well. I was secure in the knowledge that people consulted me out of their own free will and choice. At the Institute, when a family was assigned to me, I was tentative during our "get acquainted" session. I knew I was ready to meet with a new family and able to explore the commonalities we could use to build a connection. But I also felt strongly that because they had been assigned to me, they had not made a free choice. It was only when they agreed to return for a second session that I felt confident it was their choice. This was not rational, but it held strong emotional sway for me.

I have always believed therapeutic engagement to be among the most genuine and precious of human relationships. I felt that people brought their most vulnerable and decent selves into therapy. Whether they lied, pretended, vaunted themselves, or paraded their conceits, all these defensive postures could be examined with the view to understanding them and rendering them less necessary. Brought about by problems, pain, conflict, and despair, the therapeutic encounter, inviting trust and openness to the extent that these are available to the patients, was the kind of human encounter I liked best. My status as a foreigner learning about new lands and customs translated readily into becoming a visitor in the land of each family. Perhaps in some significant way, I was a privileged visitor, with just a tad better speaking rights and the right to question, interrupt, and guide the conversation, and the duty to protect the family members from willful and excessive injury.

After my affiliation with the Ackerman Institute came to an end, I chose to devote myself full time to private practice. I had a reputation as a skilled, tough, but caring therapist. Private practice, by its nature, is a lonely enterprise. Although I tried to mitigate the isolation by joining several peer and study groups, it could not change the fundamental character of the work. I felt strongly about being engaged on behalf of my patients. I did not like the tendency of a number of my colleagues to demonstrate clearly that they wanted to boost their appearance of smartness by expressing how brilliantly they guided their patients. My work nourished me. I felt useful, and often got the best from my patients. They spoke to me from close to the core of their being. I usually was spared posturing, small talk, and evasions.

The risk in my practice lay in the fact that it threatened to take over my entire life. Especially at a time when I was without a partner who could supply a counterweight, I found it hard to set limits to how many hours I worked. I was driven by the pleasure and the intensity of the contacts. And also, although not excessively, I was definitely motivated by my ability to earn a decent living. Like so many others, I began to suffer burnout, a common risk for overextended therapists.

From having conceived of family therapy as a gentle research inquiry into the emotional, social, and economic life of people in relatedness, it was only a short leap for the therapeutic interchange to become my preferred way of being with people. As my practice expanded, the distinction between myself as a therapist and as a private person often disappeared. During the years I was without an intimate partner, the private person was eclipsed.

There are many consequences to such an imbalance of relatedness. The focus is always on the *other person*, the other family in your care. Even when I share this or that bit from my own life, if appropriate and helpful, the main theme must never be mine. As a consequence, I became increasingly silent in what remained of my social life. I had no material for gossip. In spite of the fact that New York is large, therapeutic circles tend to contract to the size of a small town. There are few degrees of separation to protect the anonymity of one's patients.

Since my therapeutic work rarely focused on maneuvers skillfully planned and executed, I could not brag about how brilliantly I had done in helping to achieve miraculous transformations in my patients' lives. I felt the process of therapy was very private, and not to be gossiped about. To this day, I have few small talk skills, and the need to participate in it at all makes me ill at ease. I have little patience for the chatter that eases encounters with casual friends, or for self-promotion that we routinely indulge in as we meet and greet. I don't think being a therapist alone has turned me into a socially reluctant person, but whatever natural tendencies I possessed in that direction have certainly been amplified.

At the most intense phase of my practice, I did up to 50 sessions per week, starting at eight in the morning, and ending around eight at night, with only brief stretch and note-taking pauses along the way. At the end of the day, I was dead tired. On the weekends, if not fitting in patients here and there, I tried to catch up with myself. I spent little time with friends, devoted minimal energy to the duties and pleasures of everyday life.

No wonder I find the idea of giving up practice entirely so difficult to consider. After the death of my late-in-life husband, Larry, I became keenly aware how many of my friends had also disappeared into the various crannies of the great beyond. I was enormously grateful for the patients I still saw. These patients were people to whom my life still mattered. And they were people to whom I owed my most intact self, my wits, my skills, my unflagging attention, and even my acceptable appearance.

As my own ending grows closer, it is my patients who keep me younger by providing the kind of social and personal contact without which we age so much faster, and which now is in short supply in my life, just as it is in the lives of the few other aged friends and patients with whom I share my existence. Looking back on my long life, have I found the right words to describe how I went about becoming a therapist? And what kind of a therapist I have been?

Private Lives

In the previous chapter I traveled the path of my professional life, from my beginnings as a researcher/therapist to my ultimate immersion into the intensive work of a clinician in private practice. I traversed this retrospective road rapidly, outlining main trends, stopping rarely, if at all, at the telling details. I did not overfly the terrain in an airplane, but I did not walk it or even bicycle it. Perhaps I was on an expeditious car trip. I emerged with a strong affirmation that my professional life had never been guided by aspirations to build a significant career, by ambitions to reach power, importance, and prominence. The occasional daydream of this or that outstanding accomplishment foundered almost immediately, perhaps because it lacked a realistic and supportive conviction.

   I have always been more likely to underplay rather than overstate my status in the field of family therapy. At one point, when I was searching for the correct reference to an article I wrote with Dr. Mahler, I happened upon an old curriculum vitae. Upon finding it, I was reminded of my long and distinguished career: of a professional life filled with achievements, accomplishments, and recognition. I was also reminded that my private life was reserved for love, and for plenty of heartache, too, and was captive to my efforts to establish a home with the emotional power that would be strong enough to relieve me of my sense of rootlessness. To complicate matters, it was difficult for me to imagine a permanent home in which I did not have a relationship with a man. It was only after I purchased a brownstone that I was eventually able to feel secure, even while unattached. The pressure to establish a loving and lasting connection with a man was always strong, but the common sense required to evaluate adequately potential candidates for their suitability for a permanent relationship, if not marriage, was totally lacking. Although I surely knew better, it's as if I thought that once a loving and intimate relationship was established, everything else would somehow fall into place.

My other raison d'être was my daughter, Melanie, who has been my lifelong family of one. We had many wonderful and loving times together, as well as adventures, dangers, and conflicts. Now I resort to meditation to find ways to accept the relative estrangement that she has chosen, something I find difficult to accept.

Our relationship was a thorny, contradictory, painful struggle. I grew up with a parenting and educational system that followed rules that were quite different from the American ideal of becoming the most you could be. When and where I was raised, the rules of behavior were rigidly set, and it was the task of the adults to shape, cajole, and, if needed, force the child to conform. I had long since jettisoned all those old-fashioned ideas, only to find they insidiously tinted many decisions I made.

I've thought a lot about how miserable it must be for a daughter to have a mother who always seems to know better (or best); who is so caught up in what is accurate and true; who always finds something that needs correcting in her daughter: a statement, an article of clothing, a pronunciation of a foreign word or phrase.

Melanie was born vigorous and healthy. The supervisor of the baby nursery told me, "Every once in a while we get one of these: She knows what she wants, and she'll always get what she wants in life." I have often recalled this statement.

Art had two sons by prior marriages and had fervently wished for a daughter. When he arrived in Switzerland to claim us, the fate of our marriage was sealed; we were now united in deep love for our baby. Before we were to fly back to Venezuela, we did a bit of Swiss touristing. I acquired a khaki-colored carrycot: not baby blue, not little girl pink; this was Switzerland, it was alpine, sport. Melanie experienced some middling mountaintops early on in life.

I loved the beauty of Switzerland and remembered more of the pleasures of growing up there than the hardships my refugee status had brought with it. But this time, in addition to the security and comfort provided by staying with my parents, the fault lines of the family appeared almost instantly. One sunny afternoon we drove to the Alpine village of Teufen, where we visited the iconic pastry shop Spoerri. Our plates laden with carefully selected pastries, we sat down at a table. At that moment Melanie began to cry loudly. Perhaps she, too, wanted libation. I was a new mother and anxiously tried to calm her. I was keenly aware that her crying was an infraction of the rules of public order. My brother, Fred, the childless physician and psychoanalyst, chided me, "Keep her quiet! Just tell her to stop crying!" Unable to comply with his command, I picked her up and walked outside. That exchange set the pattern for the future of our relationship. For the rest of that visit and during every visit thereafter, I would at first attempt to comply with my brother's patriarchal edicts of how things ought to be. Then I would argue my position. Ultimately this would result in long and futile debates that almost always devolved into rancorous arguments. Finally, I would walk away.

In any conversation or disagreement, my brother always had to win outright. When a draw threatened, he simply raised the volume. I often felt outraged and at my wit's end. In retrospect, I think of Fred as someone embedded in a time warp, which kept him frozen forever in the framework of a biologically predetermined patriarchy. He felt increasingly lost and moved from left-wing idealism to the extreme right. Melanie was untouched by any of these problems. She loved her Uncle Fred and viewed him as a fun uncle, as well as knowledgeable, interesting, and erudite. She had no expectations of him and thought his ideas were amusing, interesting, and provocative.

In Venezuela in the early 1960s, as an American expat baby, Melanie lived a carefree life. For 18 months, there were no pediatrician visits to check, weigh, and otherwise advise or fuss over her development. I relied on my husband, the eldest of 10, for pointers in childcare. We had two bad health moments. When Melanie was almost a year old, a yellow fever epidemic required everyone be vaccinated. When I took her for the inoculation, the technician said she was big enough for the vaccine, but not old enough. I insisted he give her the shot. Later on, I wondered whether her extreme vulnerability to allergies had anything to do with that anxious and perhaps ill-advised early shot.

The other health crisis was when she contracted roseola, with flushed hives and a fire-red rash, at 14 months. Her temperature rose above 105. Art had a fair amount of knowledge about babies, and I trusted his good sense. We put her in an ice-cold bath and wiped her down with alcohol to lower her temperature. But when she suffered a convulsion, we gave in to a nurse's advice to administer an ice water enema. When I recall it, I am distressed at the shock that must have been to her system, but it did bring her fever down and she went to sleep.

Relieved that the worst was over, we sat down to eat dinner when we heard a *waddle waddle*. There was Melanie, coming to the table wanting food. Wanting food is always a good sign. Just as I was considering what kind of light and delicate food I might prepare for her, Art ladled some of our stew into a bowl for her and she polished it off. That was the end of the roseola emergency.

On the whole, it was a happy time. A young girl, who had grown up in a communal long-hut along the Orinoco, helped me with Melanie and the housecleaning. The weather was beautiful, if hot, every day. Although the sky was blue and cloudless, tensions began to subvert our domestic harmony. Art again began drinking more and more. His behavior was in step with what everybody else was doing, but not something I had either the experience or the willingness to live with. Art fit well into the expat working force of the Orinoco Mining Company. My life trajectory pointed in the opposite direction as I was finishing my graduate studies. Most people there worked 11 months a year for the relatively luxurious one-month vacation their jobs afforded them. It is easy to fall into a colonial mindset that conveys a higher social status by the simple fact of having a privileged U.S. nationality. The American employees earned salaries considerably higher than those they would have commanded in the United States for comparable jobs. They were also provided with a private club that was off-limits to those referred to as the *natives*, and that included not only the Venezuelans but also Italians, Germans, Canadians—anyone who was not a U.S. citizen.

Everyone else there dreamed of retirement. I was working toward a Ph.D. in order to begin my professional life. I was not just out of step with the others, but on a wholly different life path. I was on the way up, *toward* a realized life, while they had passed the crest and were descending it. I was unhappy at the prospect of spending much more time in Venezuela. Fortunately, I was not put to the test; Art had a disagreement with his supervisor and, when Melanie was just over a year and a half, decided to return to St. Louis.

Throughout Melanie's childhood, her father loved her with total devotion. He revived his photography hobby and spent hours and hours photographing Melanie and developing the pictures.

Once, turning to me, he observed, "Our baby will never have to sit in a therapist's office and say that she wasn't loved enough." He took her pony-riding; when she was three, he bought her a guitar and encouraged her to sing.

When Melanie and I were in St. Louis together, we spent much time at the zoo, building up her early vocabulary, one that was rich in animal names, like *wawy* for butterfly and *pippa pomus* for hippopotamus. Early on she could tell the difference between a peacock and a partridge, which I never managed. In 1962-63 when Art took the job in New York with Kennecott Copper Company, pulling us east with him to Connecticut, his work continued the separations and absences that had begun when he was based in Venezuela. I stayed put while he traveled, first to Chile, then to Alaska. Unfortunately, the travel demands of his work meant he was away a great deal and couldn't spend as much time with Melanie as they both desired. In this single parent existence, some of Melanie's first significant unhappiness may have asserted itself. She missed her father. As a toddler, she sometimes would go up to a stranger and say, "Would you like to come home with us and be my daddy?"

On location in Alaska, Art had an altercation with a foreman that was related to alcohol and lost his job. This made it difficult for him to find another job for some period of time. Eventually, he landed what turned out to be a grim job with RCA in Thule, Greenland. The work had something to do with maintaining the DEW line, a Cold War defense installation. The workplace was a camp, not a town, and people worked seven days a week. Everyone's health suffered, and Art's in particular. When I met him in Europe, after he had been on the job for 14 months, he seemed to have aged 20 years. His face was flaccid and pasty. In Zürich he got a ticket for driving too slow. This was a man who could never stop himself from speeding.

Back in New York, we had to face the fact that Art's age (close to 50) made him essentially unemployable. At the same time, my career was evolving and I was thriving at my work. I was increasingly comfortable in my New York milieu and by implication more removed from the working-class life Art carried within himself. Each job failure made him hate my world more. With Art unable to locate employment, he was now at home with us full time. I extended my working hours because my income was essential. Art slipped into the role of househusband, before this concept had been named and made socially acceptable. He felt humiliated and emasculated.

Quite often he took over the preparation of our dinner. Even though he was a good cook, and liked to make his favorite soups and stews, he viewed his new kitchen duties with the bitterness of defeat; a reminder that most chefs were male provided no solace. When I returned home from work, he would greet me wearing a little ruffled apron, glass of wine in hand, hissing at me sarcastically, "Your little *wifey* has prepared your dinner." He was drinking even more heavily. Neither one of us were able find a way to diminish the toxic atmosphere that permeated our home.

When Melanie returned from her afternoon classes, he took her with him to a friendly French restaurant-bar, Ile de France, on 72nd Street. The owners befriended Art, and he occasionally helped them out. I was not happy about Melanie spending time in a bar, where she also helped out a bit. But it seemed one way for Art to find some companionship and acceptance. This temporary adaptation was shattered one snowy winter evening when Melanie greeted me with the exciting tale of how Daddy had stumbled and fallen into a snowbank. She had a very difficult time getting him up and walking him back home. In horror, I overreacted and pictured us becoming the family in the 19th-century poem "The Face on the Barroom Floor."

It was the vision of our nine-year-old daughter guiding her inebriated father back into the apartment that finally broke this camel's back. The next morning, heedless of Art's hangover, I gave him an ultimatum. He could no longer live with us while drinking. I suggested everything from a meditation trip to India to going back to sea as a purser. Under pressure, Art came up with a much better solution. He applied, and was admitted, to the National Chiropractic College, in Lombard, Illinois. It was a four-year program. It had always been his dream to study medicine. He did have extraordinary healing hands.

We drove to Lombard together, and I helped him get settled into an apartment. Having disrupted my work life by following him to a number of places, I refused to consider another temporary move. Our separation was only slightly less contentious than the last years of the marriage were. Art stayed sober, while supporting himself working as a bartender. In January 1973, he called and sheepishly asked if I would object to granting him a divorce. He was living with a woman named Marie, another student, who was much younger. She was only 22. Art told me Marie wasn't well and wanted to get married before she died. I agreed to the divorce and paid my share of the legal fees.

About two months later, when Melanie called her father for their weekly conversation, Marie answered and said Art wasn't home. She then asked to speak to me. I learned that Art was *indisposed*, in the hospital for a check-up. I requested the number of his doctor. I called and explained to Art's doctor at the V.A. hospital that his daughter lived in New York with me. The doctor delivered the grim news without mincing words: "If you want her to see her father, you better come this weekend. He is dying of leukemia."

When we arrived at their small and tidy apartment, Art was dressed in his Sunday best. He was pale and icy to the touch. Initially, both he and Marie seemed angry about our visit, not very welcoming. Marie thought we were making too much out of his medical situation, which she felt wasn't that dire. Art was still angry that I had kicked him out three years earlier. He instructed Marie to serve us coffee and cake in the living room. "Get the napkins," he hissed at Marie, using an admonishing French. Melanie, then 12, became upset upon learning they had a cat. She interpreted that to mean she was unwelcome to visit again, as she was severely allergic.

Art and Marie had a nice station wagon, and we went for a short ride together. Marie drove. Art became tired very quickly and we returned home. His complexion was a pale green. The skin on his cheeks hung loosely. I touched him and he was cold. "I am glad you came," he said. And then he added, "I was angry. I didn't want to see you, but now I'm glad you came, and might come back. And I do hope they have use for a good chiropractor up there."

In April 1973, on his 55th birthday, Art died of granulocytic leukemia. It was likely a consequence of his exposure to radioactive material in Greenland. That was a time when nobody paid attention to the dangers of radiation. He died just a few days short of his graduation. The next month Marie called and asked if she could come to New York and live with us. I simply didn't have it in me to say yes.

Melanie entered adolescence around the same time that Art died. One evening I came home from work and found her and a girlfriend heavily made up—eyeliner, eye shadow, blush, lipstick. They were excited, telling me they had been at a bar where they had picked up two guys, a teacher and a social worker, and they planned to them see again. I looked at them, they were 13 years old! I wondered if there had even been a social worker and a teacher. If so, who on earth were they, and what had the men been thinking? Barely a week later, I came home at a similar hour to find a policeman standing by my door: "There are some careless kids throwing water-filled bottles down from the 11th floor. You got any little ones up there?" Sure enough, Melanie and the same sophisticated friend were carrying on like thoughtless, ill-behaved children.

I dealt with despondency and the need for money by working as hard as I could. I carried with me the impression (acquired during my school years in Switzerland) that school engaged the students and looked out for them. In retrospect, I think I was far too laissez-faire. I surely was naïve when it came to understanding teenagers. My relationship with my daughter was a very close one. I always implicitly trusted her and believed what she told me. This fool's paradise was disrupted by the events in our lives. Art's departure, and then, more fundamentally, his death three years later, really destabilized us—my daughter lost her father twice. At the time I remember thinking how small an event a divorce was, compared to death. I looked to my brother to step in some to replace my daughter's absent father, especially since our uncle Leo had been such an enormously supportive presence in both my brother's and my life. That never happened. For many years, my at-best ambivalent feelings toward my brother were embittered by his inability to extend himself in any way, personally or financially.

As Melanie had rushed into adolescence and Art had left for Illinois, I entered into a complex and ultimately mostly unhappy love affair with Al Scheflen. I hadn't realized it at the time, but this relationship contributed to the perfect storm of Melanie's teenage years. Unlike Art, I saw Al as an intellectual peer. He was a man I had long admired, a brilliant researcher. But with brilliance comes quirkiness, and with greatness comes self-involvement, and with success comes arrogance. I first met Al in 1964 at a party given for him at Milton Berger's house, following a daylong workshop to which Emory Hetrick took me. The topic of the workshop had been nonverbal communication, the field in which Al was a renowned expert. He was a fabulous lecturer who demonstrated his points at the podium using both posture and mimicry. At the same time, he made members of his audience feel as though he were addressing each of them individually. I had a very brief conversation with him after his talk and was struck by his power and seductive quality.

Six years later, Al came to the Family Institute for an afternoon of teaching. I was in charge of speakers then. I was again impressed. He was brilliant and creative, despite the fact that he seemed somewhat subdued and sad. I was still taken in by his charisma. After his talk, in a private conversation, I mentioned his apparent sadness. He reported that over the Christmas holiday, his wife had left him. Coincidentally, Art had just left for Illinois. Later in the week I called to inquire how he was doing and suggested we have a cup of coffee. He eagerly accepted my invitation.

I later learned he had mistaken me for Phoebe Prosky, a young beautiful WASP therapist, who was also present at his talk. At some point he said to me, "Phoebe is the kind of woman who gives a man the chance for bittersweet resignation because she is out of reach." *I* was not out of reach. My mother was visiting us when Al came to my apartment to take me out to dinner. In an attempt to keep me from going out with him, Melanie, then 10, decided she had a sore throat.

Al put on his M.D. hat and laid a knowing hand on her forehead. He declared we would go to the drugstore and purchase some medication. We did just that, before proceeding with our dinner engagement. On the way back to my apartment, Al suddenly grabbed me and said, "My God, I am so drawn to you. You remind me of my grandmother." Then he added, "You three women in this apartment are crying out for the presence of a man." Well, it was certainly an unconventional conversation and also the direct application of structural theory to daily life. For the next four months we carried on a tumultuous and half-heartedly passionate love affair: passionate on my part, half-hearted on Al's.

Despite many indications to the contrary, I thought Al would be an exciting and suitable partner for me. He was handsome, sexy, and brilliant. The first segment of our relationship came to an end sometime in late May when he learned that his son had gone AWOL from the army. Al decided to retrieve his absconded wife to help with the family emergency. I now feel an enormous sense of relief and gratitude to be able to look back at that crazy time with a clear head, and with the ability to forgive myself. At the time, however, I lived in a world where feelings were everything and form was negligible. For at least a couple of years, I turned into Niobe, engaged at every suitable, and unsuitable, moment in my task of weeping. This was not a totally unfamiliar state for me. I do regret to admit I had experienced similar attacks previously. I would hate to have to rate them as to their severity.

Al's and my professional life overlapped to some extent. But I had successfully put any reality of a relationship with him on the back burner. Then, in early 1974, one of our colleagues casually inquired whether I had news about Al. He told me Al wasn't doing well. "He lives all alone in his office. Perhaps you might want to look in on him." I went to see him. This time, his wife had left for good and he was distraught. He had fallen on very bad times indeed. He had lost his staff and was living in his office. The place looked like a hovel on Skid Row. I went in and cleaned it up. We resumed our relationship.

In the course of his marital history, Al had acquired a total of eight children. He was not interested in adding another one. He was a little bit friendly to Melanie, especially on that first date, when she was ill. On the whole, though, he declared his autonomy and his desire to remain as uninvolved with Melanie as feasible.

With his own children he had subscribed to the maxim that they should be loved and left alone.

Melanie and I had been close and loving. She told me, "Mom, all my friends envy me because you are such a wonderful mother. They wish their moms were more like you." I considered myself an affectionate mother, responsible but probably overly permissive, and too careless.

I had a bunch of babysitters whom I hired as needed. Did I call references; did I carefully vet them? For God's sake, I was glad to have someone! I was often lucky, and they were wonderful. At one point I ended up with Susan, a 17-year-old who lived in our building. Our elevator man, who acted as our building's social director, mediated Susan's employment. Susan's family was tangentially involved in show business. She had babysat for hip Broadway producers who had paid her wages in pot. What did I know about that world? Zip! By the time she came to us she was a rather habitual pot smoker. At 17, Susan also had a one-year-old baby of her own. Before long Susan, Andrea (the baby), Melanie, and I were living together. Was I a responsible, thoughtful, mindful adult? I don't think so.

Melanie took charge of Andrea because Susan couldn't be bothered. Melanie fed and diapered her, cuddled her, and put her to sleep. And I took it upon myself to parent all three of them. It was not the best of arrangements. I didn't understand about pot. To this day I am tempted to say Susan didn't smoke on the job, but that's crazy. It all came to an abrupt end when Susan ran up an enormous telephone bill during a tumultuous meltdown re-reconciliation re-patch-up with Rushmore, her boyfriend. I recall that the bill was more than my monthly rent, and I was living on a very tight budget. I didn't know then that I could have called the phone company and had the amount taken off my bill. I just paid it. I was heartless and merciless toward Susan. I accepted as payment what may have been her only worldly treasures, six candy-colored stemmed glasses from her grandmother.

Susan was gone, but Melanie's interest in pot stayed. The wisdom of the day was, as President Obama said recently, that pot is less dangerous than alcohol. I really didn't think of pot as being dangerous: It was a lark, it was no big deal, nothing to get all worked up about. So when Melanie changed schools from the small Riverside school to McBurney's, one of among the first six girls to integrate the previously all-boys school, she organized, with my cooperation and permission, a big party for her classmates. I forbade liquor, but I don't think I forbade pot. I don't think I thought about pot. The party was a huge success: A lot of upperclassmen came. I think the whole wrestling team was there, and it almost got out of hand. I asserted myself somehow. I have some horrible thought that I may have gone out for a while, but I hope not. I just wasn't that knowledgeable about how to govern these hordes of kids.

Melanie's place in the social order of the school was assured. Unfortunately, it was assured with the party kids. So often when I think about it, I think that Melanie graduated not from McBurney's High but from Hurrah's, the disco next to McBurney's, which was in those days on 63rd Street. The druggy ride for so many teenagers of those years had begun for us. I was of the firm belief that my daughter wouldn't lie to me, that we had an honest, open, loving relationship. When she looked at me and said, "Mom, I just smoke a little pot every once in a while, I would tell you otherwise," I believed her. I was a family therapist; I must have been so anxious to affirm that I had parented well that I could not conceive of a daughter who lied to me.

By that time, Al and I were deep in the process of looking for a home to purchase. For him, the idea of having a woman without a house was unacceptable. When he suggested we look for a house together, I understood that it represented some form of personal proposal. Not marriage, but surely an intimate relationship. Further conversations led to my purchasing the brownstone on 95th Street. Subsequent events clearly brought to light that Al had had in mind not a personal proposal, but a business one. He had longed to have a house to renovate; he loved playing contractor. He also wanted to offer a job to his son, who was learning to be a contractor. Money was very tight, but I managed to scrape together $30,000 for the down payment and obtained a 30-year mortgage.

Immediately following the closing, Al took all his money, also about $30,000, and hastened to buy a tiny house on Eastchester Bay, on the water, as he had always wanted. It was his refuge, his security against too much involvement, and was enhanced for him by his anosmia, which enabled him to be unaware of the intense reek emanating from the garbage dump a few short miles away. Given certain wind conditions, people with a normal sense of smell had no defense. We occasionally spent a weekend at the house. Melanie was always invited but habitually refused to come. Left to my own devices, I would not have gone; I was uncomfortable leaving her alone in the city. Al, on the other hand, felt adults should not permit adolescents to determine their lives. She was invited, and if she didn't want to come, that was her business.

At 16, this was not a good idea. She became too accustomed to living her own life, and I became accustomed to not knowing what she was doing. She became somewhat remote with me, avoided letting me in. At times I felt she was really high or otherwise under some drug influence, but I got nowhere when I asked her. Perhaps I didn't want to know badly enough to find ways to track what was going on. Remembering the example of my own adolescence, where self-reliance had been essential, I did not want to be heavy-handed. More than that, I thought she would work it out. And indeed, she did well in high school and graduated.

It had been my great desire to spare her the many hardships I had encountered in my growing-up years. I lacked parental guidance and support. I lacked financial resources. More perniciously, I had to struggle against an adverse political climate and ubiquitous anti-Semitism. It was of paramount importance to me to make things easier for her. My thinking went something like this: I got to a pretty good place despite all the obstacles I faced. Just imagine where she will be able to get when, instead of obstacles, she will have support and encouragement. I don't think I was driven by the truth or perhaps the fallacy of such a statement. What weighed on me was the fact that she was the only surviving child in my family. Everyone on my father's side was dead. My mother's brother and sister, as well as my own brother, were without children. It's as though I had this solitary precious hatchling in my care, and I wanted to preserve her and give her the best I could.

I thought it would be wonderful if she also went to Connecticut College. I had gone there without choice, on a scholarship without any supplemental support. She, by contrast, could choose to attend and would be welcomed as an alumna's daughter. She went for an interview, and they were willing to have her. I tend to want to avoid anxiety in my life when possible. Who wants to ruin their college years by fretting and trying 15 places? Here was Connecticut College. In the meantime, that same miserable wrestling team that had shown up at her freshman party were now juniors at Franklin & Marshall in Pennsylvania and invited her to come and visit. She did, and while she was there, applied to the college. They accepted her early decision right then and there.

When I heard from Connecticut, asking, "What about your daughter? We're waiting for her application," I had to reply, "Sorry, that train has left."

Almost 30 years ago, Melanie rented a tiny (12 by 12) studio in New York. She painted the walls black and the front door a dark color, something other than the uniform silver-grey of the building, against the building's rules. It looked as though she could face eviction. That would have been most unfortunate; the ever-so-tiny nest was rent-controlled. Fortunately, at that moment the owners of the building began the co-op conversion process. As an insider, I was able to sidestep a possible eviction by putting an offer on a small penthouse in the building, which was somewhat larger than the studio. And Melanie has resided there ever since, in a one-bedroom pent-hut with roof space overlooking the Hudson. I always feel comforted knowing she has, and always will have, a roof over her head, one with fresh air, sunshine, and a view. I imagine that she, too, has derived comfort and ease from this space that she truly inhabits, despite that she has, at times, accused me of having clipped her wings and made it difficult for her to leave New York.

When Melanie was a little girl, Art spent a great deal of time away for work assignments. Melanie and I spent summers away, three times with friends in Bermuda, and other times in Switzerland. When Melanie was 10, we took a trip to the Seychelles Islands. It was a fabulous journey to an as-yet largely untouched island group. I marveled at how mature Melanie was. She would look around and say, "Mom, that lady is traveling alone. Do you mind if I go and have lunch with her?" When a call went out in the afternoons for a fourth for bridge, Melanie presented herself. I would find her playing, presumably acceptably, with three elderly folk.

When she was 15, she did well in a four-week French language university course. I can't say how Melanie remembers these trips, or what they meant to her. I registered them as mounting evidence of her competence in life. At 16 and 17, she traveled to Greece, Italy, and Israel with friends. Perhaps it was around that time that things on the home front became cloudier. What had seemed like positive parenting, encouraging a competent daughter's exploratory travels, became uninformed and negligent when the presence of drugs could no longer be denied.

She had wanted to go to school in a warm climate. I was against it. But now she thought Franklin & Marshall would be wonderful. She had always been interested in science and was good in math and physics. At first, she was going to major in ethology, the study of animal behavior in natural habitats, but she acquired an allergy to fur. She shifted her interest from animals to marine biology, and then acquired a severe sensitivity to cold water. It seemed that whatever area of interest she chose to pursue, sooner or later, an adverse reaction blocked her path.

The promise of Franklin & Marshall quickly faded. The high point was a rock concert, where she sang to excellent reviews in the school paper, which compared her to Blondie.

Later she described the college experience: "Mom, it was like they dug a hole in the ground, stuck me in it, covered it, and stomped on it."

Over Christmas of 1978, Melanie and I went to the Bahamas. It was one of the Christmases when it snowed in the Bahamas. Al and a friend of Melanie's joined us; we were having a good time. The vacation was disrupted when Al learned his ex-wife was seriously ill. He returned home just in time to attend her funeral and caught a bad cold.

When Melanie and I returned home a couple of days later, I found Al extremely ill. It was clear he needed to see his physician. He went to his doctor, who examined him and took chest X-rays. When Al called for the results, the doctor asked him to come in on Monday. Al said, "I know what that means. He doesn't want to tell me on the phone on a Friday that I have lung cancer."

That's exactly what Al had. It was the beginning of a really bad time for everyone. That spring Al's cancer took center stage. He noted that many members of his family had succumbed to some form of cancer around 60, including his father. Perhaps because Al was a heavy smoker, he held the ironclad conviction that smoking had nothing to do with lung cancer. "Oh, all these fashionable causes that befall us: 'You are what you eat,' or 'Your genes are everything,' or 'It's sin that makes you ill.' Now it's all about cigarettes giving you cancer. Nonsense!" He continued to smoke.

Not long after his diagnosis, the decision was made to operate. Neither the size and extent of the tumor, nor where the cancer had spread, was clear. (Technology has moved ahead tremendously since that time.) The surgery was performed at New York Hospital, and it was discovered the tumor was inoperable. It was a tennis ball-sized mass, located in the lower lobe of one lung. The cancer had metastasized into the mediastinum and wrapped itself around the aorta and the esophagus. As I walked into the recovery room following his surgery, I was thinking what I should tell Al. He took one look at me and said, "I know it's bad, because if it weren't, you would have come in smiling, and said, 'Guess what? It's all behind us!'" Such are the risks of being an expert in nonverbal behavior. After the surgery, there was a course of radiation to shrink the size of the tumor. At that time, no appropriate chemotherapy was available.

Al became preoccupied with possible alternative interventions. There were all kinds of ideas that related the body's susceptibility to malignancy with particular psychic trauma, such as being cut off from family, among others. Attempts were made to convene large family gatherings, to access the healing of a connected, loving group. We watched a documentary on a ritual performed by desert Aborigines. They placed a member of their tribe, who had supposedly suffered a heart attack, into a closely linked circle of bodies. They performed a long ritual of hypnotic, rhythmical bodily union, somewhere between a dance and the movement of a coiled snake. At the end of their dance, the patient was healed.

During this same time Melanie had returned to college but had no interest in remaining there. She wanted to apply to a program the college had in India, but learned it was only open to seniors. Perhaps that's how the idea grew that she wanted to travel in India. Melanie had been an enthusiastic and competent traveler, so her wish to set out into the world did not surprise me. She went to work at a travel agency owned by her friend Ganesh. While working for Ganesh, she learned everything necessary to plan the trip.

Ganesh made some introductions. And we also had friends who had a close friendship with a Kumar family. Equipped with the addresses of these contacts, she set off on her adventure. She left in autumn of 1979. It was impossible to stay in touch with her; I had no address for her. As it was in the time before cell phones, there were few options. An occasional letter would arrive without a return address, usually delivered weeks after Melanie had written it.

In the meantime, Al and I traveled to California. He was intent on finding healers, particularly the bloodless-surgery shamans, who came out of a Philippine tradition. It was a form of healing that Gregory Bateson supposedly had undergone. While we were traveling, Al decided he wanted to live in a warm place, and he chose Florida. He went there alone. I continued my practice in New York. He quickly ran into trouble, experiencing severe stomach and intestinal pain. I explored what could happen if a mediastinal tumor became active. The possibilities were terrifying. I went to Florida and brought him back to New York. While staying in Florida he shaved off his full beard and mustache and also trimmed his hair. This 6'4" man, with an impressive lion's mane of white hair, was suddenly revealed as a slight, frail man, whose long body was topped by a small head. He had always been self-conscious about his receding chin; that's what all the hair was intended to cover.

That February I received a phone call in the middle of the night from a ham operator somewhere in Iowa. He had picked up a distress call from someone in Kashmir who had my phone number. He said, "Do you have anybody traveling in India?" *Do I?* Needless to say, I panicked. I was frightened, and wondered what catastrophe had befallen Melanie. I struggled to find a way to reach her. I managed to get back to the man in Iowa. It was through him that I was able to contact the American embassy in New Delhi, which put me through to Melanie in Kashmir. What happened? Despite the fact that she had left for India with her fairly substantial savings, she had run out of money and needed financial assistance. A series of packages had begun to arrive at the house, all shipped from India. Each had a marking "10% paid, 90% due" as well as an American customs bill of collection. Many of the packages contained pretty little Kashmiri rugs. Others contained colorful papier-mâche goods, trays, bowls, and plates. I contacted the rug merchant and informed him, "Please! Stop sending rugs immediately! Nobody here is going to pay anything on them!" After a while the shipments stopped.

When I spoke to Melanie by telephone, she said, "Mom, I would like to stay here. I found a very nice man, a veterinarian who is going to help me get registered at the university." Without any thought, I dismissed that plan: "No, Melanie, you can't do that. I'm having a really hard time with Al. I need you to come home." She said okay. The next day I mentioned the phone call to my friend Joe. "Great idea! She should stay and I'll come with you. We can go to India, and we'll help her get settled." Unfortunately, I was in no position emotionally even to consider his generous and creative offer. Two weeks later I got a phone call from Kennedy Airport; Melanie had arrived home. "I don't have any money to get to the house." I replied, "Take a cab. I'll pay for it when you get here."

It felt as if I had hardly hung up the phone when Melanie appeared. When she arrived, there stood Al, not at all well, making a long face at the imminent intrusion. He was wearing a bathrobe, or something of the sort. He was no longer sturdy. I was very concerned about contagious diseases, and God-knows-what exotic viruses and bacteria that could waft into the house, along with my daughter. At that point, Al and I were living on the ground floor of the brownstone. She was accompanied by two lively puppies, who literally *flew* into the apartment, stunning my dog, Shasta, and my cat, Warlock—*uproar, uproar!* Before I could regain my senses, the entire downstairs floor was wall-to-wall dog shit. The poor dogs had been crated for such a long time. They had held on until they got into the house. It was hardly a felicitous entry.

Melanie was exceedingly exhausted from her long trip. Over the next few weeks, she seemed to be suffering from reverse culture shock. She and her dogs moved into the upstairs studio, just above my office. While I was seeing patients one day, there was a hideous howling-yowling-yelping-screeching cacophony coming from upstairs. Excusing myself from the session, I flew upstairs to see what had happened. The puppies had become tangled in each other's collars. As they tried to free themselves, they were choking each other. Melanie was panicked and crying. This was unlike her. In the past, if there were one person who could deal with entangled dogs, it would have been Melanie.

Shasta and Melanie's two dogs did manage to form a compatible pack. But Warlock was forced to move to a new residence on top of the backyard fence. The Kashmiri dogs were incredibly vigorous: they were healthy, lively, and grew by the day. In no time they dug under the fence into the neighbors' property on the right and devastated their yard. The next day they managed to do the same to the neighbors' property on the left side. And I constantly worried about the impact of this chaos on both Al and Melanie. It was clear the dogs couldn't stick around. My friend Olga said, "Say the word. I'll take care of those dogs."

"What will you do?"

"You don't have to know, but I'll take care of it. I'll have them removed."

I believed the dogs were important to Melanie. She agreed to place them temporarily in a boarding kennel in the country. Sometimes it's good not to remember what one has spent money on during a lifetime. It was an exorbitant price for a luxury country stay for Roxie and George (named after two rock stars).

It became clear I had two unwell people with very different needs on my hands. They had begun to fight with each other. Each felt unfairly burdened by the presence and demands of the other. It was not a happy scene.

I called a friend in Vermont and asked if Melanie and I could visit. She was away, but immediately offered us the use of her home. I took three days off and we drove up to Vermont. Coverage at home for Al consisted of a health aide, a little old French lady, and Elizabeth, the housekeeper/cleaning woman from Congo. She was a good soul, but when given the opportunity, had a real affinity for the bottle, any kind of bottle. Nevertheless, she was willing to stay and cook for Al so that Melanie and I could go to Shelburne, Vermont.

I called Annie, Al's youngest daughter, and let her know her father was more or less by himself. I suggested she might want to call him. What ensued was a black comedy, one that made me think of a Grand Guignol melodrama. By that time, Al was "crazy as a bedbug," as a visiting psychiatrist said. Al made up a story that I had left him to visit my lesbian lover. He reported that I was through with him in his hour of need. At that point Elizabeth, our well-oiled lady from Africa, decided what he needed was female companionship. She crawled into bed with him, offering her body as comfort.

While I was in Vermont, Annie and Willie, her boyfriend, arrived from Pennsylvania. Upon hearing that I had left, Annie felt moved by love and, even more so, by a desire to have more of her father. Annie and Willie packed up this extremely ill man, who could no longer orient himself and could barely walk, and drove him to her apartment in Philadelphia. When I arrived back in New York, Elizabeth was still there, but Al was gone. I barely had caught my breath when I got a phone call from an old friend of Al's. "Kitty, where the hell are you? You need to come down and take care of things!" Apparently, Annie and Willie had stopped at a sports club and bought one-year memberships for each of them. Then they left Al to fend for himself and went on somewhere else.

Al was hungry and wandering the streets. I don't know how he got back to Annie's apartment or how his friend got there and found him. I went down immediately. I didn't bother to take a suitcase, just grabbed my purse and went to see if things were really that bad. When I arrived, it was clear that Al was indeed by himself in Annie's apartment, without care, without food, and without medical attention. I had to stay. But I returned to New York quickly just to get my things and told Melanie I needed to stay in Philadelphia for a few days. After I settled into Annie's apartment, some of Al's other children came and joined me in the vigil. Clearly, the end was just around the corner. Al's oldest daughter, a nurse, helped out with his care. Even with her skill and expertise, and with two of her brothers present, we simply couldn't manage the nursing care Al required. He was big and inert, essentially a deadweight.

Some other action had to be taken. A friend from the American Family Therapy Academy delivered help by putting me in touch with the director of a small hospital, who offered a temporary bed. This avoided the stressful formalities of a full-blown hospital admission. As we rode with Al in the ambulance, I began to feel some relief at no longer being burdened with an impossible caregiving task. Al was installed in a small room off a quiet hospital corridor. Two of Al's sons and I sat by his bed. Al was in a coma, his breathing labored and fast, and his temperature high. He conveyed discomfort, perhaps even panic or pain (at least that's what we felt as we watched over him for many hours).

Finally, one of the doctors said, "He has a very strong heart. Maybe a little extra morphine?" I nodded yes. The end had come. It was August 1980.

No shrinks in August, and indeed there were few therapists in Philadelphia. I called those who were still around and available. About 18 people agreed to attend a small memorial service. I remembered a family therapist friend, who was also a clergyman, and who lived in nearby Princeton. I asked him if he would officiate at the impromptu service, and then located another friend who played the trumpet. He helped send Al off to the sound of taps, because Al loved the Navy. I had a quirky idea about great people needing a death mask. During the last two days of Al's life I contacted an artist who would cast the mask shortly after his death. I had five copies made. At first that seemed too few. Everybody wanted one, but ultimately the interest ebbed. I threw away my own white plaster copy a few years ago.

I took Al's ashes home. He had loved the sea. I waited for an opportunity to sprinkle them on the ocean. Dealing with someone's ashes, or *cremains* as they are now called, was a new experience for me. I was impatient to get them to their ultimate destination. I wasn't able to mobilize Al's children to participate. It is possible that some of them did not approve of cremation. I had not checked with them.

I asked Al's old friend Milton Berger if we could take out his fishing boat so that I could sprinkle Al's ashes in the waters off Montauk. In early September, I took the ashes and met Milton, who had agreed readily and unceremoniously. I don't think he considered himself involved in the ritual. I stuck my hand into the bag and, fistful by fistful, I sprinkled the ashes on the water. I was struck by how many bone fragments there were. I had managed to do it. I said good-bye to Al. When it was over, Milton asked me as a formality, never expecting me to demur, "Kitty, I hope you won't mind if I do a little fishing now."

"No! No! No! We just put Al in the water. I don't want to have him for dinner in some fish's stomach!"

As I turned my attention to help Melanie plan her coming year, we agreed that going to a college in Switzerland might fit the bill nicely. Franklin College in Lugano accepted her. She was familiar with Switzerland, and we had family in Zürich. I thought of Franklin as a safe and felicitous circumstance. The school had an extensive travel program. The first trip was to Yugoslavia and was wonderful and uneventful. The second trip, to Prague, had a series of long-lasting consequences. Melanie was the first person in our family in over 20 years to visit Miroslav. She managed to find people who knew us and took photographs of what was left of our original house.

One day I received an ecstatic call from Melanie: "Mom, I am in love." I asked, "With whom?" She said, "I am in love with Czech-Indian twins. I can't decide which one."

From the complex ball of yarn too long and entangled to unravel, the one important thread that emerged is this one, which took Melanie back to India: Knowing how helpful and generous my Uncle Leo tended to be, I asked him to please not finance any travel to India that Melanie might want to undertake. He told me he was defeated by her intensity. There was no stopping her. He ended up paying for her ticket. Equipped this time with addresses for her, I made arrangements to send small amounts of money every few weeks so that she could sustain herself. But before long, the letters I sent were returned unopened. All contact was lost.

I never discovered everything that took place during her stay. She had made a date with one of the twins to meet in India, which he failed to keep. Later, I received a letter from their mother explaining that due to political reasons, her children were not allowed to re-enter India. At the time she wrote the letter, she was getting ready to get on the train to meet Melanie and explain the situation. I think the entanglement was on the level of the East-West conflict, the details of which I am in no way qualified to pursue.

I decided to turn again to my old acquaintance at the American Embassy in New Delhi, who greeted me like an old friend, "Dr. La Perriere, we've been trying to get in touch with you. We had a communication from the consul general in Calcutta that your daughter is in some trouble. We suggest you come immediately." I heard his message with wildly mixed feelings. There was happiness that her whereabouts were now established, yet there was also serious worry about what trouble may have befallen her. I had a busy work schedule of important commitments, including the first plenary session featuring masters of family therapy, among which I would be one of the three included. This was to be followed by two full days of presentations at universities, which I was to conduct alone. Within half a day, I cancelled everything. Within an hour's time, a doctor friend administered the battery of prophylactic shots required for travel to India. These injections were usually spread over at least a week. I left the next morning. My instantly implemented plans to rush to my daughter with barely a second thought toward how my professional reputation might be affected were congruent with the priorities I held.

By the time I arrived in Calcutta, the worst of the situation was over. An Australian film crew had befriended her. An obliging and compassionate consul had taken a driver in a panel truck and driven from Calcutta to Orissa. There he discovered Melanie, who was living in a shack behind a hotel. The consul who went to collect her quickly won her confidence by suggesting he would buy her a meal. She was pretty hungry by then, having become separated from her possessions, her jewelry, and her watch—anything of value.

Initially, I had hoped to visit a little bit of India, maybe go to Assam. At the consulate, they gently admonished me, "You have no idea how lucky you are. You found your daughter! Many American parents come here and never locate their children. Forget about sightseeing for now. Just get her out of this country."

We were treated with great kindness. The manager of the Oberoi Hotel offered to provide care and nursing services at the hotel, should we need them. One of the doctors we met at the hospital prepared to accompany us to the States, for just the price of a ticket. He had a sister in Kansas City and said he could visit her. With the help of the consulate, KLM gave us priority seating. We were on our way within a couple of days.

This is Melanie's story far more than it is mine. I remain in a quandary about writing any of this. She should not have to re-experience her past struggles on my timetable. On the other hand, her second India trip was the entry point to a most difficult decade for me. It was one in which Melanie's progression toward improvement and recovery impacted my sense of who I was as a parent and as a professional person. I became disenchanted with the psychiatric establishment, whose treatment of Melanie, as well as of me, her family, was often unhelpful, damaging, and incompetent. In bad moments, I felt invalidated as a family therapist.

How can I claim to know how to help families in distress when I was having such a difficult time helping my own daughter and myself? Or worse, dealing with the guilt I should have—and why didn't I? I also became more circumspect about the use of psychotropic drugs. I was ready to help those patients who wanted to go at it without psychotropic medication. Paradoxically, I also became far more helpful to those families who were searching for the relief the medications could provide. I guess what really happened is that I became non-dogmatic on the issue.

Life's Desserts

When Al died, I was 53. I had little doubt I would be in a new relationship in no time. As it turned out, I was alone for almost 20 years.

As a still relatively young woman, with expectations and hopes for my future, I engaged in the searches single women do. Like my contemporaries who had also passed the half-century mark, I ran headlong into the realization that, as far as men were concerned, I was invisible. A few well-meaning friends set me up with blind dates; they were awkward encounters. Usually an accomplished widower waited for me to build up his ego by praising his triumphs and distinctions while also easing his grief. Since none of them ever called me for a second date, I must have failed on both counts.

I made a hopeful phone call to the then newly established match service Godmothers, created for mature and accomplished people. After a friendly conversation, I was advised to save my money. The person I spoke with suggested I look for life satisfaction elsewhere, because women of my description were not desired. For a desperate and adventurous few months, I dated a Highlife musician from Ghana, but the cultural gulf between us was too wide.

In my practice, I worked with many women whose husbands had left them for younger, more exciting women. I helped them to discover that the essence of a childfree postmenopausal life consisted of finding relatedness in friendships with women and life's meaning through an increased concentration on work and other activities. I also worked hard to acquire this attitude for myself. Certainly some of the pressure to be coupled diminished for me, although the old social norms lingered.

My intimate world constricted to the point where there were few heterosexual men in my circle. And with that, my world of heterosexual expectations, experiences, games, and dreams diminished and then vanished. Then, a few months after my 72nd birthday, I received a call that upset my self-sufficient, somewhat resigned, but peaceful existence and made me question how substantial my resolve had been.

"Hello, this is Larry Ellman. Am I speaking to Dr. LaPerriere?"

Larry Ellman. I had made his acquaintance some 25 years earlier, when I invited him to my office in connection with therapeutic work I was doing with his ex-wife and their children. I remembered him as an extremely well-dressed, somewhat portly and self-assured man: Italian custom-tailored suit, perfectly matched tie, French cuffs and cufflinks. This was a rarity at the Ackerman Institute. He assured me he would be responsible for the bills incurred for his children but would not underwrite his ex-wife's therapy sessions. He expressed great love and attachment to his four children.

I saw Larry again some 15 years later when a woman referred to me by her cousin made an appointment for herself and her husband. The couple arrived, and it took me a moment to recognize that Larry Ellman was the husband. He did not recognize me; our prior encounter went unmentioned. That therapeutic work essentially consisted of exit counseling. The marriage was on its last legs. His wife refused to return for further sessions. He came by himself to inform me of her decision. As was my custom, I walked him to the door, and when he left I said, "Take care of yourself, and good luck."

Eight or so years later, here he was on the phone. "Who is he bringing now?" I asked myself.

"What can I do for you today?"

"I'm not calling you professionally. May I take you out to lunch?"

It felt like an invitation from a different world. Part of me remembered that world enough that a spark was ignited almost immediately. I quickly ran over in my mind the amount of time that had passed since my last professional meeting with him. I decided I was on safe ethical grounds.

I said, "I have no time to do lunch, but I will be happy to meet you for dinner," thereby conveying to him both a modicum of interest and the fact that I was most likely unattached.

Our first date was on February 19, 1999. It was a cold evening when Larry called for me; he was attired in a stylish fur jacket and an elegant, if slightly dated, fedora. My memory of him was of a man of means; incongruously, our restaurant destination was a nondescript, if acceptable, diner. Larry's first words were so welcome and unexpected I quickly forgot where we were.

"You know so much about me, and I know hardly anything about you. Tonight will be devoted to making up for that deficit. I want to know all about you."

What an unusual request to hear from a man, to say nothing of the fact that it was a first date. I was so thrilled by his interest I may have dropped the required caution of revealing my past. I told many more details of my intimate life and, I thought, quite entertaining stories than might have been wise.

The structure of our second dinner was equally startling.

"Last time we spoke about the past," he said, taking my hand, and looking at me with a loving focus. "Tonight we'll talk about the future."

It was such a heady concept that I don't recall a thing about the content of our conversation beyond an understanding that neither he nor I were interested in engaging in a prolonged dating process. Larry was going away for a month to visit his sister and his children. He informed me that he would phone at 6 P.M. on the day of his return. Any sense of certainty I harbored about my secure and calm self-sufficiency rapidly melted away. I felt like Cinderella. The pumpkin coach had driven up, transforming into a real coach, with the mice turning into white horses.

Friends with whom I shared the "miracle" of a 72-year-old woman being courted cautioned me: "Don't hold your breath." Or "Be careful! He's just a talker." I realized that might be true. Nevertheless, I gave my imagination full rein, telling myself, "There is nothing wrong with being an old man's sweetheart." Getting married again was not on my mind. Instead I went out and bought several pairs of high heels, a couple of fancy nighties, and other underwear items I imagined would enhance the allure of a love well beyond the first bloom of youth.

At times I have berated myself for the rapid abandonment of critical thought and common sense. My life had become stable and predictable, but when Larry rushed into it, the feelings from my youth returned. I felt once again like a young woman ready for love.

Larry dazzled me. He was persistent and had an ever-upbeat hopefulness. Matrimony was on his mind from the start. That ours would be "a marriage made in heaven" was his firm conviction. I drank in what he gave the way the desert absorbs a flash rain. Larry offered total love. He claimed me, was 100 percent committed. I was intoxicated by his certainty, his arm firmly cupping my shoulder. Even if I had stopped long enough to consider how much personal freedom I would lose, I still would not have resisted. Gradually, my professional involvements diminished, then all but disappeared. My friendships became limited to weekday lunches and then atrophied. I was in the process of becoming a not-available friend and on my way to becoming a former friend.

Larry insisted he would devote his life to making me happy. In doing so, he created an image of me that he cherished and valued. It was not an image that reflected the one I had of myself—an independent, self-directed woman who valued her intellect and owned her sexuality more than she cared about her appearance and social niceties. I had, after all, shaped my own life, had my own friends and ideas. Larry had been successful and lived in affluence for much of his adult life. There had always been enough money around so that he could buy whatever he felt like having. There had never been a toy he wanted that he did not buy, from an Italian sports car to a speedboat. And he was wildly generous with his wives and children.

I was past 70 and had been without a man for almost 20 years. I felt basically content. It was also true that I had not been successful in removing a certain mutedness from my consciousness, which made me aware that I was a solitary soul. I had vanquished the ache of longing and yearning that, with the exception of a few years, had been the emotional tone of my life. I valued my work. I valued my friends. I loved and worried about my daughter. I had achieved what I considered an acceptable balance and no longer needed to prove myself either intellectually or sexually. When Larry appeared in my life, I was swept along by his considerable energy.

It became clear we were both interested in a serious and lasting relationship. Would we be able to achieve one? To bring some reality to our wishes and dreams, we decided to rent a summer house in Little Compton, Rhode Island, near my friend Claudine and her husband. We wanted to discover what living together would be like. In voicing our greatest fears, Larry chose my sharp tongue. I worried about being bored, since he had periods of retiring into himself. By putting our worst fears into words, it seems that we dispelled them. Halfway through our summer rental, we had fallen deeply in love.

Several encounters clearly illuminated our differences. Each time that happened, I could not face the possibility of losing him. The first issue was the form our future relationship would take. I had hoped to go on with my life and to have Larry go on with his. I saw our separate lives enriched by a love that was catching fire. Larry wanted none of this kind of independence. For him it would be marriage or nothing. And it would be marriage on his terms, predicated on the erroneous assumption that I had been a relatively conventional and sexually constrained woman. He was willing to forgive and forget the departures my actual life history represented. In this process, I acquired an original flaw, for which I was to atone.

His growing commitment to a joined life and exquisite form of persuasiveness wormed into my being. There were specific realities of his life, especially the condition of his personal finances, which should have advised more caution. Instead, I found myself sliding into the world as Larry painted it, as if oil had been poured on my path and I had lost my traction.

To marry Larry was to come to a healing home. I sensed he was the man my parents would have been happy to see me marry. Although we were catching the happiness train at the next-to-last station, we would go into old age, the hardest stretch of life, together. As a married couple we would brave its unknown and unforeseeable perils.

We set a wedding date, April Fool's Day of the new millennium. Going over the text for our wedding ceremony gave rise to another small controversy. The judge who would officiate wanted to use a Kahlil Gibran quote: "Stand together, yet not too near together. For the pillars of the temple stand apart. And the oak tree and the cypress grow not in each other's shadow."

Larry raised strong objections. "I don't want any of this standing tall side-by-side stuff. It's two trees leaning into each other, supporting each other. That's what we will be."

Actually, I think he may have said one tree leaning against the other. I understood that meant I was going to lean against him. His habitual way of standing next to me was with his arm around me. I gave in on the crucial relationship-defining points. The sweetness, comfort, and seduction of such a fully committed, ever-present claim on my person invaded my being and silenced any concerns I might have had.

As the daughter of a beautiful mother, I learned early on that I didn't measure up in the beauty department. At one point in my childhood, my mother talked about corrective surgery to thin my chubby wrists and elongate my rather stocky peasant legs. Not surprisingly, I had instead relied on my intellect to help me through life. Now, here was Larry, truly not interested in my brain, looking at me adoringly. "You have the most beautiful smile I have ever seen," he would tell me. Larry's view of me as his beloved and loving wife, who would accompany him on life's path, began to win out over the remnants of the life I had built for myself as a single woman.

Larry babied me. I talked to him endlessly about my health. I had a variety of GI problems, and he was an angel of patience, offering suggestions, commiseration, and comfort. He called me his "Stradivarius." He happily chose my clothes and offered consultation when I was getting dressed. At first, all this seemed quaint, and I didn't take it seriously. I thought he was playing at it, but insidiously it crept up on me and into me. Being with him began to heal part of my aggression and anger, which I carried from my hard and difficult life, particularly from my mostly unhappy relationships with men.

Early on, he decided we should sell my house on 95th Street in order to have some liquidity. I resisted the idea. I had envisioned living in it until I died. Still, there was no question that the house was less satisfying. Its darkness oppressed me. I had neither the imagination nor the resources to reconfigure it and move into the upper two floors, which were light and sun-flooded. And the house was showing its age.

The shoestring renovation Al and I had undertaken was calling for the next round of care. The staircase sagged. Whenever we had a heavy rain, or particularly after a snowfall that froze and then thawed, melting water would seep down the walls, cascading three stories from the second-floor extension down to the basement. The tuck-pointing had become spotty, and the repairman I had paid to repoint had done a less-than-slipshod job. Al and I had intended to bring the house into a livable condition, then sell half of it and move on to the next project. But Al died before that could be accomplished.

The house had been a cornerstone in my finally feeling that I was a real New Yorker, no longer a refugee, but at Larry's continued urging, I sold it. We then rented an apartment in New York and bought a small country house on a small lake in Pennsylvania. It was a pleasant enough retreat, romantic and convenient. We considered using it more extensively. We talked about it as a possible full-time retirement home, but its location in the midst of redneck country made us realize that we had made a large mistake. It was impossible to find congenial friends. When election time rolled around, we observed that every house in the landscape was bedecked with Bush-Cheney lawn signs. The residents of Hemlock Farms belonged to a social club, and that, too, was awash with Republican propaganda.

On Election Day, groups of enthusiastic Republicans marched around encouraging voters to get out and vote. Three elderly ladies, who looked like retired school teachers/librarians, proudly and valiantly sat at a rickety table with a sign reading DEMOCRATS

HERE. Helping us reach a definitive conclusion were our neighbors, from whom we purchased our house. They occasionally hosted brunches at their home, providing samples of their catering skills. They stopped inviting us after a brunch during which we stumbled into a political conversation. I suspect Larry might have been able to acclimate to this, but I could not.

Having lived as a refugee in a hostile society was one thing but choosing to put myself into the middle of a community of reactionary ideologues was unthinkable. Given our failed experiment at country living, I became more inclined to go along with Larry's lifelong dream to purchase a home outside the United States, so we decided to buy a house in Mexico. During a vacation trip there, a friend urged us to visit San Miguel de Allende. She handed us a list of eight or ten friends of hers there and said we should call them. She insisted we would find the place welcoming. Indeed, more than half of the people on her list were hospitable and open-hearted. They welcomed us like long-lost relatives to what might become a life in San Miguel.

I was still working full-time and not ready to abandon my practice, or the source of income it provided, which was essential to our life. Larry and I arrived at a compromise. We decided to spend summers and winters in San Miguel, while retaining our Manhattan presence in autumn and spring. My mostly cooperative patients made it possible for me to maintain most of my practice. Regular or occasional telephone sessions bridged my absence. On the face of it, this arrangement appeared to provide us the best of both worlds. In reality, it provided the dual experiences of getting settled, and then, in a sharp turn, preparing to return to New York.

Almost immediately and impulsively, we had decided we didn't want to spend our vacations searching for the next vacation rental. We thought it best to buy a house. We had a few unsuccessful outings with real estate agents, who showed us affordable but unacceptable homes or beautiful and totally unaffordable homes. We answered an ad in a San Miguel newspaper placed by a builder named Carl Selph. An American expat, he had first ventured into San Miguel in the 1960s. He picked us up and showed us two houses he had built, but they were not what we wanted. On the drive back to our lodgings, he told us he needed to stop by his house.

We were driving along unpaved dusty, unnamed roads defying any reliable orientation when we came to a stop in front of a free-standing house surrounded by a red brick wall. Carl invited us inside. With our first steps into his home, we saw an expansive vista. Three arches extended before us, framing an iconic view of the famous pink-hued Parroquia church surrounded by San Miguel de Allende's old center. There was a mountain range in the background, and in the foreground, tropical greens filled Carl's terrace. Everything was illuminated by afternoon western sunlight. The setting captivated me. In Switzerland, views from one's apartment were everything. Carl's house was beautiful and simply built, reminiscent of a Tuscan farmhouse. I turned to Larry and said, "Now, this is a house I like."

Carl instantly replied, "It is *not* for sale! I built this house for myself and I intend to die here." A few moments later, he said, "Would you really buy it?" Before I could give a reasoned answer, Larry asserted, "Yes, Carl, we would. How much would you want for it?" Carl named a high price. Larry asked if it were negotiable. Carl responded, "No, it is not." Larry replied, "That's ok, we'll take it."

Larry's point of view was "Darling, if you love it, it is worth the price."

Location? Neighborhood? Actual value? Larry could not be bothered with such trivial considerations. I was convinced that

Larry's life of buying and selling homes made him an expert. I reverted to my role as the younger sister whose older brother always knew best. We settled the deal on only a handshake and took up residence within a few weeks. We paid Carl rent until the transfer of the deed was registered. Carl became a good friend. And he built himself a bigger house.

San Miguel de Allende exerted an ever-stronger pull over Larry. His former life as a restaurateur worked well for him in San Miguel, where it was possible to meet endless people with fascinating backgrounds, real or imagined. We met many couples, as well as single women, who all adored Larry and the attention he gave them. Our friend Carry said, "I like you, Kitty, but I would much rather spend time with Larry." I could not partake fully of the bounty and pleasures of this Eden on earth. I simply could not again undertake another cultural transition. And I had no stomach to remain a stranger in what was to become my home. On a more basic level, the talents that helped make life there so pleasant were not ones I had. I am not a creative artist and don't choose to dazzle people with decorative inventiveness in my home. Nor do I delight in displaying impressive culinary feats. What I required to be happy, to feel settled, was a life experience that delved more deeply into the stuff of daily life. The melody my being emitted did not harmonize with the songs being sung. Voluntarily living as an expat was uncomfortable. I did try to own my decision, claim it as my own. In the process I transformed myself into Mrs. Larry Ellman.

My self-sufficiency had made me both proud and resentful. At the beginning of our marriage, Larry's affluent past grated on me. In our travels, we sometimes visited places that both of us had been. Rome was such a place. In my previous life I had good times there at conferences. I usually stayed at a decent, but modest hotel. Larry pointed to The Hassler Roma, a luxury five-star hotel in the center of the city, indicating it was where he stayed with a previous wife. Another time, we were in Marrakesh on a timeshare that lodged us in a pleasant, if modest, inn. We met congenial people and I had my first encounter with the Turkish bath known as a *hammam*.

On the top of a hill, situated amid glorious gardens, was the fabled La Mamounia hotel. As we walked through the hotel's lush grounds, Larry indicated it was another luxury destination where he and a wife had stayed. I appreciated his openness but could not overcome feeling angry and envious. After a few years of marriage, these resentments disappeared. Larry taught me how to enjoy a more relaxed style of living. By nature, I was more frugal than he was, probably exceedingly so, but he never complained or gave any evidence that he noticed or cared about his diminished financial situation. By the time of that diner first date, he was relying on his wits and charm, not on his personal power or fat wallet. He still had the powers of seduction, without the assistance of resources.

Larry forced me to discover my limitations and push against them. On my own, I probably would not have sold the brownstone. I might have continued to live in inevitably financially constrained circumstances, since the house needed significant repairs. I clung to my childhood expectation of a contained, steady, predictable world where people stayed put and relationships were deep but few. Unlike many people who make themselves more viable and functional for a world that is nothing but impermanent, I remained mired in my childhood belief that life is changeable, requiring adaptation and new thinking. I could say Larry pushed me into making more out my reality than I could have imagined possible.

Nevertheless, in some ways I felt I'd sold out to Larry. I had been proud of my independence and active in my friendships. But by the time I met him, I had also begun to run out of steam, tended toward stretches of dispiritedness, if not depression, and carried with me the knowledge of having lived a hard life. My friend Laura said, "Kitty, you became a different woman after you were with Larry. Softer, not so edgy, not so confrontational, not so readily aggressive."

For a few years I felt a legitimate member of a middle-class "in" group, maybe a class my parents had belonged to, a group I could not reach on my own either in Switzerland or pre-Larry in the States. I felt better. I felt happy. Happy? In the past, the concept would have seemed ridiculous. Who has a life that allows them to be happy? What can that possibly mean other than settling on the surface and not seeing or feeling too deeply? But I was happy and felt secure as Larry Ellman's wife. At the same time, I feared I was becoming dumber and more timid.

I told Larry that he saved my life. Before we loved each other, I had given up on strong attachments to life. I carried on, in an acceptable way, without deep joy, without much passion. Then came Larry with such an earnest hunger for life! Such skill in enjoyment! Such eagerness to travel, to experience, to show me places he had visited and loved before. He was elegant, looked good, helped upgrade my appearance by purchasing clothes and jewelry, treating me like a beautiful woman. He admired my hair, my shape: I felt so loved that a long-neglected aspect of self-confidence grew and flourished. At times I was annoyed that Larry didn't appreciate my intellectual talents. These skills had served me so well throughout my life. All the same, the change was refreshing.

I didn't completely abandon the struggle to hold on to my own way of being, with its mix of features I valued—autonomy, competence, and a life of ideas, along with features that constituted the less appealing parts of the packet: a tendency to criticize, pessimism, laziness, and shyness. I was not secure and strong enough to enjoy Larry's gifts while simultaneously protecting my sense of identity when it came into conflict with his idea of who I was. Perhaps he loved a vision of the woman he needed to love.

Perhaps I also selected out and added on to see in Larry those features I most needed. Truth be told, I cannot now name any of those features that constructed my fantasy view of him. I think everything I loved and valued about Larry was truly there. There were some qualities that might have bothered me, had I allowed myself to fully consider them: I am thinking particularly of his great skill in manipulation, in how he planned to win me, weighing the likelihood that I had sufficient financial resources to carry us. By now these seem petty points. He was explicit from the beginning when he expressed his anxieties about being with a woman who might not take care of him should illness and old age require it. I didn't take in the full gravity of this potential state. I figured together we would do whatever needed to be done.

Larry loved our home in Mexico, and we traveled back and forth between New York and Mexico for three years. He wanted to live there year-round, but I could never reconcile myself to a permanent move to yet another country.

In January 2009, Larry injured his back working out with an incompetent and reckless trainer who insisted he lie on his back on a medicine ball. For weeks afterward, he slept in a chair, unable to lie in bed. He could not drive and could barely tolerate riding in a car.

His sister Lyn had visited us in Mexico. The day she was returning to Florida, Larry bent to light the heater and fell. We went to the emergency room and the X-rays indicated there was no fracture, but Larry was in a tremendous amount of pain. An internist and a gerontologist each prescribed pain medications that led to confusion and disorientation. After a while he had some microcurrent treatments that eased his condition sufficiently so we could risk our trip back.

Once back in New York, he healed more. We decided to return to San Miguel de Allende in July. Three months here, three months there. It was our attempt to make our compromise work. That summer in San Miguel was all right, but we kept a gentle and careful pace. It became clear that we were not going to undertake any more excursions, even locally. We went to restaurants with lovely gardens and leisurely service. We saw friends, sat on our terraces, upstairs when it was cold and downstairs when it was hot. That last summer, both of our pets died, Polly of old age, shortly after we got back, following an estrogen injection that was supposed to ease some of her problem. I sat and watched her die during the night in great discomfort. A few weeks later, I noticed Eliza was limping and felt pain when held. The vet found there was a recurrence of her cancer, right at the two-year mark that had been predicted. And so we put her to sleep. It was a sad winding down. Fortunately, as it unraveled, we were unaware how bad it was and what the future held.

Once back in New York, we could not know our next scheduled trip to Mexico that December would never happen. We were packed and ready to go. Larry had been complaining of shortness of breath, carefully choosing the blocks around our apartment he was willing to walk. He had become keenly aware of the degree of incline on each segment of sidewalk. He decided to make an appointment with his new cardiologist; his previous physician had just retired. The new cardiologist noted Larry had severe aortic stenosis. And the malfunction of other parts of his heart had progressed from moderate to severe. Further tests were required. The situation was urgent.

We unpacked, and then discussed which hospital we would choose should surgery become necessary. We made a February appointment with Dr. Valentin Fuster, a world-famous cardiologist, and the physician of my late friend Liliana. It was then December. An angiogram was scheduled for the following Wednesday at Lenox Hill. Following the test, we were told by the doctor, "The procedure went well, but we cannot let you go home. You are at imminent risk. I have made an appointment for you to see the surgeon for 4 pm today." That was the end of any notion that we could carefully choose the best surgeon and hospital. Tests and pre-op preparations were scheduled for Thursday. Open heart surgery was scheduled for 7 am on Friday. As it turned out, a snowstorm delayed the surgery a few days. Larry remained brave and optimistic. He said, "Darling, we don't know how this is going to end. Anything can happen. I want you to know I love you very much. I have been very happy with you. Whatever happens will be alright."

I agreed and told Larry that he had given me the most happiness I had ever known, and I, too, would be alright. At that moment, his decision to go forward with the surgery was like a distant and barely heard dissonance. I remember feeling as if my breathing had stopped. A clammy sense of horror crept up my back toward the nape of my neck. When I was able to gain control of my thoughts, I had a sinking feeling it was folly to do the surgery.

Recovery was only a slight possibility. I suspected the doctor might well advise against going forward. To the contrary, he reassured us that this kind of surgery was now routine and that he had performed it 4,000 times (at least I think that was what he said). He told Larry, "I am happy to operate on you. You have a wonderful attitude, and that will make things go well."

I don't really know when the curtain descended, and at what point I realized our wonderful marriage was essentially over. Following the surgery, I morphed from wife into caregiver. Larry withdrew into himself and did not return emotionally to our marriage until around four months before his death three-and-a-half years later.

I felt enormous tenderness and love for Larry. I was saddened that he could not reach for a bit more of the good life. It was an extremely difficult time for us. He did soldier on, using the same strengths that had served him well in life. He focused on what he needed and demanded it. He did not dwell on things that made him anxious. *Don't strain. Give no evidence of what you cannot do. Better to make it seem a matter of choice.* He pushed and he bullied. This was the only way he could cope with his rapid decline, fatigue, weakness, and complete loss of power.

When people were around, Larry summoned his charms and appeared in a good mood, not wanting anyone to see his spirit diminished. He still proclaimed his love for me, but he was also angry, often withdrawn and refusing to engage. I felt that nothing I did was right. I wanted to reawaken him to some kind of relatedness between us, but there was no way. He was happy to speak to, and especially to see, his children. He was attentive to his aide and articulate and welcoming when his friends came over to see him.

I learned to control my own anger and my frustration. I kept repeating to myself, "He does the best he can." I suspected there was a complicated set of unexpressed feelings, which he probably never could have put into words. He had acted as the leader, the boss, the rule-setter in our relationship. It must have been excruciatingly painful for him to find himself so bereft of power. He controlled and demanded. Nothing pleased him. He refused to eat if a dish weren't prepared precisely to his liking. Other times, he would eat only very specific things, with sudden changes from one day to the next. From his habitual menu of salmon, tuna, broccoli, cauliflower, separate, mixed, alternating, one by one these items were banned from his plate. Toward the end, he would eat only scrambled eggs with copious amounts of onions sliced a particular way, preferably prepared by the diner.

He continued to believe that he would recover, and from time to time even said to me, "If you get sick, I will take care of you." Larry's frailty steadily increased over the final four months of his life, while his mind became keener and his disposition sweeter. He was interacting more, not just exerting his will to keep himself alive. Since the surgery I had wondered which gradient would prevail. Would it be the upward slope toward recovery or the downward slope toward the final good-byes? Five weeks before his death he whispered to me, as if it were a secret, "I'm beginning to lose confidence."

Larry died at 8:45 am on Monday, June 17, 2013, five minutes before I arrived at the hospital. I so wished they had called earlier. How deprived did I feel at not having been with him at the moment of his last breath? How guilty at not having sat next to him and held his hand during the last hours of his life?

I believe Larry died barely in time to avoid the fears that thoughts of death held for him. I felt guilty for having let him die. I wanted him to tell me it wasn't my fault. He had died, but I needed his permission to go on living. Larry's death made my writing more urgent. What follows is my experience of grieving.

Tuesday, June 18
We have done things simply so far: cremation, no services. Planning a memorial. This morning I am wishing for a bit more ritual, but don't know how and am reluctant to try to put it in place. Will people call? Do I have to be home? Will anyone just come?

Larry's older daughter, Nikki, who lives in Berkeley, called yesterday and offered to come and be with me. So did Judy and also Ede, though I am not clear about what I need right now.

It is twenty to six in the evening. Larry died yesterday morning and already that seems weeks ago. I feel at loose ends with an even looser middle. No deep, rending sobs emerge, and no tears even dampen my eyes except when someone talks to me kindly about my loss. Even then, sadness does not force its way into a cataclysm of despair. Instead it leaks around the edges of daily life like a tease.

I ask myself, *"When will you truly be with yourself? When will the reality of catastrophic loss gush forth with its torrent of tears?"* And then those feelings leave, converted into a restless, searching unease, and I think, *"This is the moment I might have gone into the bedroom to check on how Larry was doing."* To give him a smile, a light kiss on the head, to feel a bit of love between us. Or, in a bad moment, I might have flown in there with annoyance.

"What, Judge Judy again? Let me find you something more fun to watch!" I would say with impatience, probably scorn, and, I see this only now, incredible obtuseness. I perceived Larry watching Judge Judy as stultifying, overlooking the fact that it had a clear, simple plot with enough humor and repetitiveness to allow him to follow and enjoy the proceedings. I could not step out of the moment and shake off my frustration long enough to see and to understand the ongoing tension between expecting Larry to be a husband and coming to terms with him as a feeble old man in need of care. I did not know how to combine the two realities: of being a loving wife to an absent husband and of being a caregiver with no relational needs of my own.

It is Wednesday. I spoke to Jo on the phone and noticed tears beginning to push their way up into my eyes. And suddenly, I remembered the weeks and months and years I had spent weeping, my heart broken by this or that man, longing, yearning, hurting, and how all that stopped. All that was healed or at least hidden by the intensity of love and devotion and need that Larry brought me.

When I remember what it was like settling into being Larry's wife, I am warmed by the feeling of security and permanence, of being enveloped and held by his adoration. I am terrified that now that he is gone, I will find myself exposed and unprotected, denuded of the cushioned support he gave me.

It's Friday. Every day brings a flood of new ideas and perspectives and feelings. Today I happened upon the ubiquity of guilt, and the difference between a funeral service and a memorial service.

If only Larry could have given me permission to go on living even though he could not.... If only we could have spoken about death so as to understand and accept it. if only I could have said to him, "I need to keep myself alive so I can be here for you."

But he was averse to such talk, turning his head if the topic should come up. Perhaps he didn't grasp what I was saying or perhaps he could not let himself accept the impending likelihood of not recovering. I needed and wanted something he simply was unable to give, and I must have tried it this way and that, annoying him and making him anxious.

I would try to get close to him, to sit where I could reach his hand and hold it the way we always held hands when walking, in the movies, before going to sleep, after an argument. But it wasn't easy, barricaded as he was in his electric recliner, surrounded by little tables holding his necessities: Kleenex, cough drops, iPad, Kindle, iPhone, TV controls, blood pressure gauge. What free space slivers remained held a floor lamp, his slippers, and a huge wastepaper basket for the hundreds of Kleenex he deposited there.

The very act of my starting to clear a path to his side made him uneasy. When I succeeded in holding his hand, he might leave it there, unresponsive, then, with an almost imperceptible squeeze, withdraw it. In the beginning, I would find books or articles that I thought might present a departure point for a conversation between us. He might manage to read a page and then would become bored; about half a page of my reading to him was more than he had patience for.

It's Sunday. Every day Larry's absence becomes a little more real. Every day I go through different modes of unexpected feelings. I started out wanting to talk to him about his dying. He had never wanted to do that, ever.

He had joked: *I am immortal.*

Or *I just don't want to know it.*

As he got weaker, more frail, I offered music. Poetry. Buddhist meditations on life. He averted his eyes, averted his face, closed his eyes and pushed the offered object away along with my hand and arm, warding it, and me, off.

I never found a way to achieve what seemed so important to me: the shared acknowledgement that we were now in a different stretch of our relationship.

I realized that what I felt was guilt. Although I knew that self-recrimination is almost universal, I still questioned what I had done wrong to let Larry die. My father died during the half-hour rest my mother had taken from a 12-hour vigil. She berated herself for sleeping, thinking her love and energy could have kept him alive. Then her thoughts shifted to the fact that his preferred doctor had been absent, and had he been present, he would have surely prevented my father's death.

I started out on a similar path. When Larry fell the previous Monday, I asked myself if had I been negligent, not sitting right next to him when he got ready for bed. I had retrieved his Kindle and offered to look for his glasses, and he actually said, "See, I didn't take an hour. It's been a half-hour," referring to my efforts to get him to start preparations for bed earlier because they tended to last until midnight. Was Larry trying to please me? Was he hurrying? Was he trying to prove me wrong or to assert what power and autonomy he had to set his own time? I remembered that he wanted me to keep his ashes in the bedroom so that he could haunt me if I misbehaved. I think I will keep his ashes in the bedroom.

In his absence, I felt so bad, so sorry. I felt such tender love for him. I wanted to make his sufferings of the last year go away. I wanted to cry among a group of crying people. I wanted to rend my clothes and cover the mirrors. I wanted to jump onto a funeral pyre and burn with him. I think once a person has died and his actions can no longer impact you in such a way that you need to defend and protect yourself, loving and bereft feelings are finally fully permitted to emerge.

Monday, July 1
All day long I have been going around thinking and saying, "Larry died one week ago today." Then I realized that it has, in fact, been two weeks. Time has a jumbled, discontinuous quality. I reexperience and rethink events. I search for my feelings over and over, and I come up with seemingly different fragments each time. What I perceive about what has been happening is like a kaleidoscope, changing form and color at every turn. I lie in bed berating myself for not having had the wherewithal to bring little pleasures and tenderness to Larry. Why didn't I whisper to him, "I will always love you?" Why didn't I bring a card with a poem for my very best of husbands? Why didn't I say, "You will live in my heart always?"

Larry always insisted on a full serving set: knife, fork, two spoons, napkin, etc. Sometimes I was too tired to even slap a plate on the table and put out food. When I did manage to get dinner, my guilt berated me for not setting it up the way he wanted it. And *tired* was what had come to define me, just as it had insidiously crept into Larry and dominated his last years of life. The Larry I married had prodigious energy. He often worked 12-hour days, and when I mentioned that I was tired, he would say, "Tired? I don't know what that word means. I never feel tired." Yet in his last years, his fatigue was so palpable, so extreme, it emanated from him and seeped into my entire being, too, rendering me depressed, defeated, exhausted.

I would often wake up in the morning rested, turn toward Larry, tentatively touching his arm with what was intended as tenderness. Most mornings, he lay on his back, straight, arms usually down by his sides, encasing himself in sheet and blanket. I would wait for the verdict, whether he would receive the caress by freeing his arm and taking my hand, or whether he would refuse it by pulling away and shaking it off. Sometimes I thought that he was angry about something. He still had short bouts of pouting, which, in the early days of our relationship, had tended to stretch over hours or even days, but when I asked him whether he was feeling angry he would shake his head and I would suddenly feel his lassitude swallow me up. In German, there is a word, *totmuede*, or dead tired, and that's what I felt: Larry was *totmuede*, and sometimes, instantly, I became the same. It got so bad that I could not drag myself to do any tasks. Sometimes, in the morning, I felt as though I had 20 units of activity in me; I might then spend 15 on helping Larry get himself together, especially on those days when our aide was not present, leaving me with only five units. Usually Larry would need a couple of things along the way, and I would feel, despairingly and resentfully, that I did not have any more to give him.

This state of exhaustion intensified as his invalidism lingered. I felt cut off from all sources of personal vitality. I felt like a prisoner in our apartment or a dog tethered on a short chain in a fenced yard. And worse still, I had begun to see the world outside the apartment as beyond my limits. No trip to town, no visit to a new restaurant, no stroll in the park, no fantasy of an impending trip. Larry's condition drew a curtain across the world for me and I began to weaken, sink into myself, and atrophy. I was, in a sense, almost as bad off as he was. I had nothing extra to give him. I wanted him to see me as old and feeble, so that he might feel comforted that we were both sinking together. Yet he never admitted that he was sinking. He could not give me the comfort of knowing that we were on the same page, aware that our relationship was gasping through a challenging stretch.

I need to remind myself of just how debilitated I felt, how angry and exasperated sometimes with his inaccessibility. I wonder now, as I did then, whether there was any volition in his withdrawal, whether he was able but unwilling to understand, or whether he really couldn't. Or whether it was so deeply ingrained in his character to be positive to the end and forbid any thoughts that this might be the end stretch for us.

The recognition of my deathly fatigue was the first change I noticed after Larry died. During his final hospitalization, I could barely keep myself upright and awake at his bedside. The morning after he died, I woke up restless, charged with energy, exhausted, but not tired. All the guilt I have felt, all the thinking about what I might have done for him, fails to take into account what condition I had been in. I have to remember that.

This process of remembering is like panning for gold: You put pounds and pounds of dirt into the sieve until you get a few dust grains of gold.

Tuesday, July 2
Here I am looking at five days that are essentially blank and open, with the exception of a date with Peggy for the fourth of July: movie, meal, watching fireworks on TV. She called a few days ago, eager for a connection. "I hate the holidays," she said.

Today I said good-bye to Maguere, Larry's aide. It was time; she had been ghosting about the apartment as if she was a professional mourner. She seemed to look for Larry and miss him, and I felt her disapproval that I was not collapsed in sobs. She told Santi, who helps me around the house with technology and errands, how sad she was for Larry.

I spent part of the day going through tons of pictures Santi had located in Larry's computer and which we are transferring to mine for the continuous loop show to be displayed during Larry's memorial. I had forgotten everything—the pictures of the Hemlock house, how pretty it was and how well we had furnished it; the lake and the woods in autumn colors and glittering with snow crystals; our dog, Polly, and our cat, Eliza, sharing a bed in a careful standoff. There was the boat trip we took out of the British Virgin Islands; the trip up the California coast to the wine country; Switzerland; France.... I carry it all inside, I recognize what I see and can add the memories, but I don't feel it yet. I feel so little.

Right now I feel very much alone, at a loss for where to put myself internally. This apartment has no spots yet that might comfort me. Everywhere there is the reflection of Larry's presence, or, more accurately, his absence. When Larry was alive, I had often wished to have a few peaceful hours in the apartment without the urgency of his discomfort, the sadness of his bravery, and the demand for this or that little service. I was not able to build a barrier for myself that would have allowed me to rest while still knowing that he was here. Knowing he was here made resting impossible. Yet now that he is gone, I still don't know how to be with myself.

Earlier I even started wondering about where a diagnosis had been missed, where a mistake had been made, what had been neglected in extending his life; I already forget how strongly I felt that he was suffering and that his time had come too soon. The cause of death was given as aortic stenosis. It made me wonder whether the surgery had been incomplete. I recall the surgeon saying that there had been a problem with a frayed aorta, but they had repaired it a little rather than inserting a stent as they had planned pre-op. So I wondered whether the surgeon had been as good as I had thought him to be. I wondered whether the postsurgical care was all it might have been.

What if we had gone to Mount Sinai and worked with Fuster? I wished we had done an autopsy. I thought when I declined it that I would be sorry, just as had happened with my father, whose autopsy was declined by my mother for religious reasons. Orthodox Jews do not permit the body to be tampered with. All those thoughts were present when I declined an autopsy. I think I wanted to affirm the finality of Larry's disappearance, and thought knowing the details would be useless anyway, just prolonging the "what ifs" and the "I should haves" that seem to be the mandatory accompaniers of grief.

In his final four months, I was torn between welcoming Larry's cognitive recovery and the strong sense it would most likely be outpaced by his physical decline. I had tried to find new ways to engage his mind and soul, through readings of poetry and new discoveries, but none of this reached him. At one point, as his clarity of thought improved, he said, "I lost two years of my life," and, turning to me, asked, "Where were you during that time?"

During those two years, I often felt that he didn't relate to me as a husband at all. At first I tried to establish some sort of explicit understanding between us that we had entered a new era of our marriage, but I could not find a way. He treated me like an inadequate health aide, demanding and critical. During that time, he managed to be responsive to other people in a less angry way, and I wondered whether he was, in fact, furious with me, as I eventually became with him. He was demanding, difficult, and often bossy and uncooperative. Sometime during the last few months, his awareness shifted, and he began relating to me, was sweet, and spoke lovingly. My anger dissipated and was forgotten. I became even more captive to wanting to help him live.

It was a futile, frustrating state of being that preempted all my time from morning to bedtime, with the exception of the occasional therapy hours I maintained, which served as islands of rescue for me. In every other moment, my attention and energy were streaming toward Larry, whether I was in the next room or out of the house. When asked how I was, I would respond with, "Today, Larry…." I was incapable of thinking of me. When I shopped for food, it was with the intention of finding something he would eat. When I considered ordering some clothes online, it was his requirements that I tried to decipher.

A few days ago I began to notice that I was not tired at night. I stay up now well past 11, whereas when I sat with Larry I was unbelievably exhausted practically as soon as the aide left around 5 pm. On awakening in the morning, I might have felt ok, but within minutes, Larry's energy level and mood had taken me over. I was never *not* tired. I wake up early now, perhaps too early. I am restless but energized. I may not know what to do, but I want to find my way to doing *something*. But through it all, that is what stands out most: *I am not tired.*

Yesterday Larry's son Kevin called from California. The gist of the call was that with his father gone and the situation changed, he and I should try to start from scratch. I was moved and grateful for his reaching out.

Friday, July 5
I awoke early and was on my way to the park by seven. I forced myself to walk around the reservoir. It was a normal walk, a little slow, and by the end, both my knees hurt, but I was thinking normal

reservoir walk thoughts. There were not many people at this time; the early birds who run before going to the office were done, and the leisurely walkers and tourists were as yet sparse. The grey mugginess of the morning dissolved into a hot day; the sun was out, and two dogs were lined up with their owners by the 78th Street water fountain. On the last stretch, I thought of Larry as a healthy man, of our kayaking in Hemlock Farms and how strong his arms had been, and a thought flitted through my mind that it was lucky that the memorial was scheduled five weeks after his death because by the time it took place, I would be fully able to celebrate Larry's life. I found a website where you could search old newspapers and wondered whether I could find any articles about any of his restaurants. I wanted to have a couple of photographs speaking to the high points of his career. He worked well, and he lived and played hard: most of that was slowing when he came into my life.

I spent the day with fond memories of him. I realized that there were no wonderful times with him in this apartment, just occasional oases of good strength and good feeling so that we could see friends or go to a movie or the Metropolitan Opera simulcasts.

Saturday, July 6
After a good night's sleep I awoke missing Larry. On Saturdays we usually would lay in bed and listen to NPR, holding hands and "snuggling." I would scoot down and put my head next to Larry's chest and he would put his left arm around my shoulder. A faint flicker of past affection.

I walked out of the house to get a haircut. Fifth Avenue was pretty deserted, but shady and peaceful. The heat of the day had not yet fully set in. I felt no sense of appreciation for what I was noticing. I felt that the me who was walking down the avenue was damaged, sliced off, and that I wanted to hide the damage from the world.

Never one to have enjoyed going out by myself, after my haircut, I pushed myself to go to the movies and saw *Museum Hours*. Quite a suitable film for me. I responded most to what had not been mentioned in any review: the greyness of the fall and winter landscape in Vienna. It rained, it snowed, and it was overcast, no sun at all: pretty much the colors of my growing-up years. I fleetingly felt that if I were forced to live in Vienna now, I'd do myself in.

I questioned my continuing to present myself to the world as Mrs. Larry Ellman (even though I was no longer her). Do I misrepresent myself as Mrs. Ellman? Or do I meet the world as Kitty, a single woman? Rationality and custom were nowhere in sight as I teased this conundrum. What is it about? Larry needed the security of owning and being fully in charge of me. As for me, I guess I needed to be owned and claimed.

Thursday, July 11
I've spent the past three weeks noticing and shaping and discovering just how I had fallen under Larry's various thralls and how surprising and freeing it was to lurch free of them. But as of last night, I am now more aware of the Larry that I loved and lost.

The package with his ashes arrived today, plainly labeled on the outside. It annoyed and embarrassed me: everyone at the concierge desk had seen it. It was heavy as I carried it upstairs, and it rattled a little. When they asked about pacemakers, etc., I had forgotten to indicate he had a titanium pin in his femur. Maybe the rattle was not bone pieces but the rod. "Well," I said to the box, "you wanted to be on the mantelpiece in the bedroom. This bedroom has no mantelpiece." So I put the package on Larry's chest of drawers, unopened. Will it spook me?

I wish Larry and I had had more conversations about how it might be if one of us were dead. I wish I could recall such conversations, so that I could have them again now with him, even though he is no longer here. The few times he spoke of surviving me, it was in high anxiety about finances, when he wanted ever-larger segments of the money available to meet his unforeseen expenses. I felt I had been generous in sharing what I had when he no longer had any of his former wealth, but it fell short of what would make him feel safe.

We had bad feelings around these discussions, and it seemed a win/lose situation between Larry and Melanie, so much so that I tended to forget that I, too, had a claim on this, my money. I solved my conflict with the belief that I would most likely survive Larry, and that I was humoring him by agreeing to the rather large share that he insisted be made available to him. Those were rough spots. There were others. But being with Larry was so wonderful in so many other ways. And it is the loss of these that I mourn. The time is upon me to just plain miss him.

Friday, July 12
Today is Larry's birthday. Just a few weeks ago he had talked about making it to 90; he almost did.

Kevin called to tell me he was sending me the papers I had asked for: the will and the revocable trust, with any codicils and addenda. Then he added that he wanted to go over some papers his father had left, and he wanted to do that in person over lunch later in the month. He would not tell me what they were, which made me concerned, and then angry with him. Then I thought that whatever they may be, I did not have to follow anything that might be written in there. Perhaps he has made some designations about what should happen with the cello, etc.

I went to the Met museum with Rachel and Michael today and was measuring my stamina against the total fatigue that had been my habitual state while Larry lay ill. I feel I am beginning to lurch back toward my usual state of not having much energy. The young me that emerged for a few days after my emotional imprisonment had ended and is slowly approaching her chronological age. I ain't no spring chicken. That's for sure.

Sunday, July 21
It's a beautiful day, the kind of day when, in Larry's last days, I would chafe and grumble at the restriction of not being able to go out, not seeing a time in my life when I would ever be able to go out. And today I cannot find the get-out-of-the-house button. My lifelong tendency toward inertia is in full force: I feel depressed; without energy; without any élan or joie de vivre; without a plan. This is the kind of state that would often visit me before Larry was in my life. This is what I was referring to when I told Larry, "You saved my life."

I had said good-bye to Larry at the time of the surgery, and then with finality a few weeks into the lagging recovery process. It might have been helpful if I could have detached myself before I became exhausted and welded to Larry in my inner mandate not to leave him and to see him through. No detachment occurred, but my anger subsided as I got more help from a home health aide. I reinvested myself in hoping for, plotting, and urging his recovery. In the last three or four months before his death, his personhood began to re-emerge; he became sweet and related, and also had better cognitive abilities. A year or two of better-quality survival seemed almost possible, especially if I ignored his visibly weakening physical state and frightening frailty.

Now when I think of Larry, I mostly feel the years of happiness; I hardly feel the years of illness. When I mourn him, I feel heartbreaking compassion for the man who met calamity with equanimity and bravery that consisted of patience, acceptance, and massive denial of the severity of his condition. If I could I would hug and stroke and kiss him, but I also think that he was no longer open to much contact with me. He drew inward and used his strength to hang on.

How am I going to remember all the wonderful things about him and speak about some of them at the memorial tomorrow? Perhaps the energy of the occasion will carry me. It seems to have acquired some sort of watershed importance; the closer it gets, the more the reality of Larry's absence intrudes. I had my nails done today by a friendly, chatty Nepalese operator who asked me why I was living in the States and who my husband was. I said he was American, from Brooklyn, and at that moment I felt a warm expectation of going home and finding him there, still waiting for me. Not the way he was during his illness, but cheerful and welcoming and full of plans for the evening. It was as jarring as the insertion of an out-of-sequence page in a novel.

Tuesday, July 23
Today is the memorial. I slept alright but woke up anxious and uncertain.

I called Melanie a few minutes ago to touch base with someone, but I realize she is not a good person for me to steady myself against. Her own needs are unpredictable and always seem to take precedence. I made myself what was to be a nice breakfast, but it turned rotten because I half-burned the peach and apple that I stewed and had to throw it all out. I am getting better at throwing food out that I don't feel like eating.

I woke up with surprising low-key angry feelings at Larry. It's as though I had been waiting for him since the surgery to come back, to get well. Even though I suspected from the beginning that he wouldn't, couldn't, I went along with his unfailing belief that he would and could. I preferred his view to mine. I scaled down my expectations of what "coming back" would mean. Ultimately I just wanted him to be present enough to be able to acknowledge the reality of our marriage now. He had always said it was important to marry a woman who would take care of him were he to fall ill. So why couldn't he let himself know that the time was upon us? I do believe that, had the situation been reversed, Larry would have taken care of me and found fulfillment in the process; a validation of what he felt marriage was about

The memorial unfolded very well. Almost everybody came. Melanie got there just in time. She spoke, and I am glad she did.

The three Ellmans did great: the stories of their experiences with their dad reflected such an enormous affirming love, vitality, and fun, and touched on the characteristics Larry kept, in a muted way, into his later years.

Saturday, July 27

My urgency to write appears strongly and then abruptly disappears and is difficult to reawaken. I have to wait for the next surge.

I tried to take some notes in the middle of the night when my insides were a-roil, just code words to remind myself, and you know what? I can't find the little yellow pad! Perhaps I will come upon it. What made me want to write is that, in the middle of the night, I felt that I had walked away from an argument with Larry. In its cessation, I understood that this argument had been going on, probably on a number of levels that I do not as yet understand.

The most accessible level was that I was trying to keep Larry alive using my knowledge while he fought me, perhaps wanting to rely on his sense of what was helping him. Closely linked to that push-pull was my deeper need of connecting with him on a level of recognized reality that included, in the very beginning, the fact that we were both deprived of our individual lives and of our life together, and that we were going to carry on under altered circumstances. Larry may not have recognized any of that. Indeed, he often felt as though he had just gone through surgery and was recovering from it; he could not hold the passage of time in any stable manner. I felt that he had cut off his relationship with me, and part of the struggle consisted of my trying to reinsert myself into his awareness. I did not want to write him out of mine, although there was a definite danger of my just wanting to be gone during the months when he was essentially just bossy, critical, nasty, and absent. He must have marshaled all his energy trying to save his life and he did that with the resources that had always served him: taking control, pushing, commanding, and demanding.

As I played back the times I had been unkind to Larry, less obliging, less loving, less resourceful in finding ways to please him, when I did not just sit with him quietly watching Judge Judy, I noticed several old themes.

Larry had always liked to be waited on. He never wanted to participate in any housework, with his solution being to get paid help. While he did certain iconic things, like make the coffee in the morning, it took a lot of editing to maintain the feeling of a balance. From our earliest days I had declared my non-interest in being in charge of the food department; he had been a restaurateur, let him take over our provisioning with whatever means he would do that. It was a sustained tug of war, and as he became more ill, I had to concede defeat. On this issue, he had won totally. Nothing further could ever be expected of him. And so, when I encouraged him to put on his socks and his shoes, to close the packages of cereal after breakfast, to screw the cap back on the jelly jar, the maple syrup bottle, the catsup, it was, I admit, a combination of wanting him to remain actively engaged in manual dexterity and wanting to give him an opportunity for a symbolic carrying out of his now totally lapsed obligations of reciprocity.

I remember the first battle we had that had ended in my total capitulation. I saw no other way to build our relationship, but the defeat lived on under the surface, fueling a certain contrariness and challenge to Larry's authority. After the surgery, when he was so helpless, that source of my resentment dried up.

The original battle? Larry held an almost religious belief in marital monogamy, and adultery to him was the equivalent of a mortal sin. Perhaps this strongly held belief was strengthened by his jealousy that verged on the pathological and encompassed every past relationship. I hold a much more relaxed view on sex, and while extramarital relationships often are sources of pain and misery, for me, they always constituted an expected part of the emotional and sexual landscape. Even proud that my sexuality was a freely felt and experienced aspect of being alive that I had not attached to economic or societal requirements or benefits. I was glad to be a free spirit.

Unfortunately I also believed in transparency in relationships, especially in one in which we were going to be soulmates, as Larry had dreamed of. In my mind, a soulmate is someone whose inner life you try to understand, not judge. And equally unfortunate was the fact that I had started to live according to my precept, telling Larry about some of my past. He became very upset, but he was not ready to break up with me. So he decided, very magnanimously, that he would forgive me. Implied in this positioning was the fact that he was morally righteous and superior, and I had erred, sinned, and fallen. He would forgive me as long as I understood the error of my ways and promised to accept the true faith.

The posture that Larry's way was the right way, that his preference was the norm and any difference was a flaw became the underlying law of our land. I probably conducted a guerilla war against that assumption even as I bowed to it in our daily life.

Friday, August 9
The memorial, I discovered, fulfilled the role a good ritual does: It ends one segment of life and opens the door to the next. My urgency

to go over and over events that took place during these two-and-a-half months is decreasing, vanishing as a state of being and only occasionally reappearing. At this point on the path to rediscovering who I have become, I notice unexpected occurrences that help me along.

I am on the bus, returning from a visit with Jo in Warwick. I looked out and saw Greenwood Lake. My usual mindset compares every landscape to Swiss landscapes and usually finds it wanting. "A nice lake," I thought to myself, "large enough, unexciting, undramatic, ok." And then suddenly another voice insinuates itself from the edges of my awareness. "Pretty good sailing here," says Larry. "We could kayak. Let's see what houses are available." And, I recall, we had indeed looked at some property at the shore of this lake, and Larry had particularly enjoyed a big slightly decrepit house that had an opening for a large boat slip. And for the next moments, a welter of memories tumbled in on me, of Larry wanting to travel, to experience where he had not been, to enjoy what life and money could offer. He was an active doer, a mover, hungry for life, eager for experience, pushing to engage with his surroundings, while I was happy to contemplate, to see, to feel, to dream.

His energy invaded me and sharpened my appetite for life. I worried what would happen to me now that I no longer had access to his impulsive energy. Would I resettle into what had been a quiet state, perhaps a low depression that made me feel life was pretty much over? It was too soon to tell. I went to bed at night struggling to banish the longing that the empty space in the bed and in the room intensified in me. I talked to him when I woke in the middle of the night. I was reluctant to awaken into a day where he was absent.

And then, this morning, after a night of deep sleep that followed three days of deathly fatigue, I woke up feeling good. I hadn't awakened feeling good in close to three years. And I only discovered this today, when my waking up was different. *Am I healed*, I asked myself, *now that I can feel good just in myself?*

An hour later, a patient was telling me about a place in Mexico, encouraging me to visit the beautiful coast, where there was an elegant dreamy hotel, swarms of butterflies, and surrounding small fishing villages. The longer she spoke, the sadder I got. I knew I needed Larry to go with me to a place like this in order to feel the fullness of its beauty.

Sadness lingers.

Late August/Early September: San Miguel de Allende
I had given myself the task of sorting through our many photographs in an effort to decide what to do with them. Almost immediately I came across large portraits of Larry's parents, and a couple of him. The visual reminders loosened a repressive barrier I had built. By the time I was faced with four packs of pictures Larry took on our Moroccan trip, I could not continue with the task. I quickly put all the photographs away, but I could not release the painful grip radiating below my ribs. There was a tension to my breath and my stomach flooded with acid.

These photographs opened a crag, one that reached deep into a pool of inchoate sadness. Suddenly, losing Larry had become a direct gateway to the subterranean ocean of loss that first filled me when my childhood home vanished. This resurgent grief brought forth familiar feelings of being without either home or direction. I had barely tamed these demons in the 20 or so years I lived alone before I married Larry. I had worried they would reappear when he died. Now I found myself recalling how hard won that equilibrium was, how readily it would tilt and settle back into a default mode of sadness. A sadness that originated in the expulsion from my childhood paradise and had aggregated onto it the numerous disappointments and humiliations life washed over me.

Larry had insisted on returning to San Miguel de Allende after his surgery. The cardiologist said, "You might as well go." We did return; it was nothing short of a three-week nightmare. Larry was in agony. It was an angry suffering, fighting for breath and for consciousness.

On our very first evening back, we had dinner with his physical therapist, who immediately noticed that Larry was struggling. "You can't breathe. We need to get you oxygen." As he spoke, he activated his cell phone, and within minutes ordered the delivery of an oxygen unit, which came the next morning.

Our trip was the good-bye to our life in San Miguel de Allende. It was clear Larry would never come back. The previous year I had spent a harried week preparing the house for Larry's arrival, whenever that became possible. There was so much to organize: installing the necessary grab bars and railings and creating a ground-floor bedroom and a refurbished bathroom, should he be unable to manage the 21 steps to our upstairs bedroom. It was a manic week that included rushed meals and meetings with a few friends. There alone I took notice that Larry and I had made a happy and good life.

Returning as a widow, the tranquility, spaciousness, and beauty took me by surprise. We had chosen every piece of furniture and each decorative pillow, every piece of folk art. We had worked hard to create a beautiful and comfortable home. We had our books brought down, our papers, our photographs, and other objects that really mattered to us. The house, with its little walled garden, was heavenly. But this time, I could barely stand looking at it, knowing that Larry would never be here again. I became totally undone, and for several days was unable to pull myself together.

I thought perhaps I should get rid of the whole thing: the house, furniture, and, with it, the memories. After about a half-hour with a real estate agent, I became convinced that selling was not the right thing to do. One piece fell into place, and then another, and so forth. I spoke with Lidia and extended her employment for a year. I decided to make some needed repairs: the doorbell, the front fountain, and a bird infestation in the loggia. These tasks grounded me. I might have felt miserable, but there was work that had to be accomplished.

On the third evening of my return, I went to an exquisite chamber music concert. I was there with Larry: that is I had an acute sense of his absence. Friends came up to me and commented on his death. They said what a swath he had cut, what a lovely man he was, how much he was missed. I would have felt terrible if they had said nothing, but what they said did not provide any comfort.

After that I experienced a brief respite and barely thought of him. Roaming somewhere inside me was a vague feeling he was still at home in New York, waiting for my return. A few times, I told myself I would postpone calling him by a few hours. Then with a start I would awake to the reality of his utter and eternal disappearance.

More of our friends emerged in the last days, surrounding me with warm affection. What am I saying? Life became a little busy, and that has helped me look outward, and to some extent, to look forward as well. A bit of healing occurred. I no longer felt the burden of anger and confinement I experienced so strongly during the last three years of Larry's life. I was able to recall pleasant times in what was a happy marriage. Yet it all feels so very long ago.

One night I watched *The Artist* with my friend Ede. Larry and I saw it many years ago at the Paris theater in Manhattan. As I watched it again, I was filled with anxiety: my unglamorous, unnoticeable self was looking wide-eyed at the movie's glamour.

Larry had opened the door to that world for me. He was elegant and self-confident, at home anywhere. Through Larry I found myself at home there too. What will I fall back into now that I no longer have him at my side? I don't think it will be that sort of nostalgia for a phantom lover that never was, because Larry was that lover, very much in the flesh. The question is what will I find missing now that I am not propped up by his unconditional love?

Thinking about leaving has caused departure malaise to set in. I don't want to go. Yet, at the same time I can't wait to be gone. In the last week or so, I detached from most of my feelings for this house, the town, the people. I've come full circle.

I went back and forth. I thought I should (and wanted to) keep the house. The setting lent itself to making a new life; I could develop a few more compatible friendships. Then, almost in the same breath, fear overtook me. I knew I didn't have the energy to invest in two places. My hands were full trying to shape some kind of a life in New York. "Just get rid of the house!" I commanded myself. I no longer made sense to myself. I couldn't think it through, because I didn't know what I was going to feel from one minute to the next.

On Sunday, I prepared to return to New York. Surprisingly, I am more focused and grounded than I have been in a long time. I finished going through more papers and the photographs. The realtor came by to give the house a once-over. Her summary statement relieved me. She said it was a desirable house and had many good features. If I put it on the market at a realistic price, it would likely sell within eight months or so. Canadians, Americans, and Mexicans were buying, she said. Her conclusions took a large burden from me. I would not end up stuck with a house I couldn't sell (if, and when, I decided I would be better off without it than with it). In the meantime, the market was not likely to go down, so holding off the decision for a year or so should not present a problem. Somehow I anticipated that New York would be easier, but I always do when the time comes to leave San Miguel.

It's true that getting around Manhattan is less challenging: no narrow sidewalks with treacherous holes, protrusions, slopes and bumps, further narrowed by jutting window guards and water release spouts. There's the crosstown bus, which stops right across the street from the apartment. I think about movies and restaurants and food stores, all in such close proximity. I think of these things in terms of how they might fit into my life. Will I find a new rhythm? Take care of my health? Resume my writing? Can I rearrange the apartment to suit me, make it comfortable and visually pleasing? The New York apartment is not just the embodied shadow of Larry's life there, but also the result of the suddenness and speed of its acquisition.

The living room sofa is the wrong size. I bought it cheaply at Housing Works, because it could be delivered that evening. I thought then that the mossy teal color was acceptable. The Chinese étagère displaying Larry's collection of small antiquities takes up too much space for the amount of aesthetic pleasure it delivers. The china closet, inoffensive in itself, is massive and impractical. None of the chairs in the living room affords me comfortable seating. The carpet (an error by the auction house delivery service from the get-go) ties it all together into a somewhat dispirited and dull formality. The dining area is lacking; the table is too large as are the dining chairs, but they are comfortable. Fortunately, my office is fine.

The bedroom is one step away from where Larry's constricted homebound life was orchestrated. The bed we shared is the same. I still can't break the habit of walking the long way around to climb into my side, further away from the door that leads to the bathroom. I still lie there, contracted and bundled up close to the edge of my side of the bed. Now I am acutely aware of the empty space where Larry lay for so long, tidily wrapping himself up in his sheets like a mummy to contain his body, to steady it, and perhaps to protect himself from incursions of my hands or feet. As I lay next to him, I was aware of his presence and simultaneously of his absence. I was cemented into an ambiguous position, being in bed with my husband, wanting to touch, to caress, to hug, at odd moments even to seduce this form whose self-containment I often experienced as rejection. At times I resented feeling pinned there, condemned like Tantalus to want and see but never get what I needed.

Sometimes I thought how much easier it would be if the bed were empty. Then I could truly feel what I was experiencing, be it the loneliness or the sexual tension or the longing, without the feelings being stopped by the almost inert presence of Larry's body. Now I am alone, and I do miss that inert body. He was a huge presence, which sated some of the hunger, even while it thwarted its satiation.

Here in San Miguel, I adhere to my side of the bed too. But I have a much-diminished sense of Larry on his side of the bed. Two nights after I returned here, Larry's side became empty, unoccupied.

Friends ask if I enjoyed this time in San Miguel. It is true that I was able to spend hours barely aware of Larry, but that part of me that was so joined to him is also absent. From time to time I could think of Larry just as a person who has died. I went through his clothes and chose which to give away and which to keep for a while. I have dismantled his desk. His papers no longer matter. Whatever he had begun will not be finished. Whatever he finished and documented is no longer needed. Now he lives only in the memories of people who knew him.

My own memory of him is undergoing a considerable upheaval. How I want to remember this man is not yet shaped, not yet defined, not yet finished. Every day new elements come to mind and need to be added, woven into the memory of our life together. Going through his papers, I read notes to his wife Harriet, which close with *I love you,* long after they were divorced. Reading their wills, I see how thoughtful and generous he had been, leaving her practically everything he then owned. As I observed these silent witnesses of his past lives, I felt small pangs of jealousy, and a little anger. Mainly, though, I understood him better and loved him more.

Back in New York for a time, I decided to sell the San Miguel house. I faced that it never was my favorite landscape, semi-arid desert that it is. It was not a culture I wanted to explore, to enter, on my own. San Miguel is an intensely vibrant mix of Catholicism with remnants of Indian rites and imagery, colors, dance, music, processions, and celebrations of profuse beauty. I appreciated all of it, but I am not of it, nor could I imagine even the smallest part of me overlapping with it.

I do not want to live again in a place where I am the stranger. Too much of my life has been spent looking and longing for that patch of land, with its history and language to which I do belong, and to which I might have a claim of provenance and ownership.

Not since I was a child in Czechoslovakia have I felt unequivocally that I was entitled to belong where I was. There it was different, likely by virtue of my birth and the ardent love I brought to the sense of place. This feeling did not die because we were no longer wanted there and had to flee for our lives. Eventually, that intense longing diminished as I grew tentative rootlets in New York. But these rootlets never brought forth a strong trunk that made me feel, without a doubt, that I belonged, and was entitled to a voice, that I was "of here."

The search for rootedness and home and heart has defined most of the choices of my life, sometimes occurring quite out of my awareness. Only now, as I have gone back and forth about living in Mexico, has it become explicitly clear that I am incapable of taking on another acculturation process. On my own, my energy level is barely sufficient to reconstruct the New York life to which I return.

In the Land of the Old

Mother remained energetic until well into her 80s. She was active and enterprising. Still a beautiful woman, she was flirtatious and appealing to men. Around her 84th birthday, she visited me in New York. One of my colleagues confessed the impact she had on him: "I know how old your mother is, but I get a hard-on when I speak to her on the phone. She said to me, 'Doctor, please tell me why I forget all other names, but I always remember yours.'"

Mother had returned to Switzerland in flight from Hitler and remained there for the rest of her life. Being in Switzerland fundamentally settled and pleased her. She was at home. And as she became older, I was able to forgive her for having been an amateur mother to me. She had been an admiring mother to my brother and a life saving and devoted wife to my father. For a long time, Mother's aging didn't feel at all relevant to me.

When she was in her 70s, she, her brother (my Uncle Leo) and I were sitting on a bench, next to one of the green hills in the Zürich environs. She turned and said to me in a matter-of-fact tone, "Here is where I used to take my children skiing." It was clear she did not know to whom she was speaking. I replied tactlessly, as was my wont, "Mom, I am one of those children, and we never came here." Leo, who was some 15 years younger than my mother, turned to her, his face inflamed in anger and embarrassment. "Anna, don't talk such nonsense!" I wrote it off as an aberrant one-time slip. Even with that stunning lapse, the idea of her becoming truly old and impaired remained dormant to me for another decade.

Once she told me, "My darling, you live far away. If anything happens to me, you might not be able to arrive in time. Let that be all right. I have had a good life. I'm ready to go whenever my time comes." This comforting and reassuring comment would prove prophetic in its untruth. About a year later, Mother began to make semi-weekly visits to my father's grave. It was the place where they would ultimately be united. These habitual trips were driven by anxiety and worry about the permanence of the cemetery. She wanted to reassure herself that the cemetery and graves were really there.

About that time, Mother began to hear music. After checking both television and radio only to find they were not turned on, she decided that a small band was outside the window and that they were serenading her. At first she reported that the band was playing Swiss tunes, a popular love song or two. Rather quickly, they shifted to songs of the National Socialist Storm troopers, and that is what found its way into her mental playbill. I flew from New York for a visit with what I thought was a way to ease her sensory deprivation. The hallucinations were triggered by greatly diminished eyesight and almost-absent hearing. I bought her a pair of super earphones, reasoning that they would permit her to listen to actual radio programs. My well-meaning effort rushed toward a dismal and dramatic failure.

Upon seeing the earphones, an unstoppable terror flooded her. She fought me physically, ripped the earphones from my hands, and screamed, "I won't let *you* kill me!" The noisy outburst and ensuing commotion alerted a neighbor, who rushed into the apartment. Upon seeing me, a total stranger, she commanded, "Get out! Whoever you are, leave this poor old woman in peace." It was a singular and undeniable event, and it was clear then that

Mother had crossed a threshold. Finally, I was forced to recognize that she had slipped forever from my grasp.

My brother had made arrangements for Mother to take her meals in a Jewish old age home, just three houses away from hers. She went each day, noon and night, for lunch and dinner, fair or foul weather. She didn't like its overly religious atmosphere, but she went in order to eat, and to hold to a personal routine. On a February night, at about 2 am, "her" band awakened her. She was sure the German army was approaching. She put on her clothes and hurried to the home. She was accurately reliving what had happened many years before in Miroslav, when she had run from house to house, alerting other Jews to leave their homes quickly and flee toward the Protectorate. In this same way, she banged on the door of the Jewish home, screaming, "Save yourselves! Save yourselves! The Germans are coming!"

This presumed refuge of Jewish kindness and understanding called the local police to report a disturbance. The police arrived, identified my mother, and then called my brother and told him to come and get her immediately. My brother and his wife, who were leaving the next day for a skiing vacation in Davos, decided to temporarily lodge Mother in another Jewish old age home two hours away, which was along their route. They dropped her off and continued on.

The phone number they had left at the new home did not go unused. There was a message waiting for them at their hotel: "Your mother believes she is being delivered to a concentration camp. She fought us tooth and nail. It took six people to subdue her, and just barely. You must come and pick her up at once. If you don't, we will sedate her, put her in a cab, and send her to you in Davos."

Still unwilling to give up their vacation, they picked her up and brought her back to their hotel in Davos, where they got a room for her. Mother was extremely tired from the journey and the trauma, and she went right to sleep. During the middle of the night, our stark-naked mother wandered the halls until she found their room, opened the door, and climbed into their bed. "It's much nicer here. It's warm and cozy," she told them.

Sometimes it's hard to recognize when a situation has truly changed. In fairness, my brother had not experienced our mother accusing him of trying to murder her, as she had me. By morning, though, my brother was convinced of the severity of her condition. Admitting defeat, they returned to Zürich, where he took Mother for a full psychiatric evaluation. Years later I read the report:

"This charming life-affirming older lady suffered a temporary psychotic episode (she was then 88). It is expected she will be well enough to go home in two to three weeks."

Mother was then transferred to a state clinic for the aged. It was situated on the shores of Lake Zürich, with a splendid view of both the Alps and the lake. The expansive grounds were beautifully landscaped. There was a coffee shop that served exquisite pastries. My mother never left. Nor did she ever ask what had happened to her or express wonder about her apartment or any part of her previous life. It was as if she immediately transitioned back to childhood, when her parents lived downstairs, and her son occasionally visited. Sometimes she would approach a young nurse in training with an angry admonition. A scolding might include a slap in the face, with the comment, "Kitty! Behave yourself!"

I brought Melanie, who was by then in her early 20s, with me for a visit. Mother could no longer place me. But she quickly formed a strong bond with Melanie, as if they were girlfriends, not recognizing their age difference. At no time did Mother understand she was the grandmother. They joked about bumming cigarettes and about not having any money in their wallets. They were at ease and loving with each other.

After living in the clinic for about two years, Mother had a small stroke, which left her slightly paralyzed on the left side and without the ability to speak. Shortly thereafter she developed pneumonia. The decision was made to let the illness proceed, rather than hold her captive to a life of dubious quality. By the time I was informed of her condition, she lay dying. I arrived just in time to help with the ritual washing of her body in preparation for burial. She was 89½ years old.

During my childhood in rural Mirsolav, my grandparents lived next door to us. Amalia, my paternal grandmother, stood barely 4'10". She had a round head with sparse hair parted in the middle and pulled back into a bun, more for function than attractiveness. She spent her days moving between bedroom, kitchen, and garden, and was kept busy looking after my grandfather. She supervised a maid, and efficiently ran her household. I would watch Grandmother artfully pull endlessly elastic dough into near-transparent expanses to make a delicious apple strudel. Farmers' wives brought edibles to the house: eggs, vegetables, live chickens, and geese. I don't recall ever seeing her go out into the public streets.

I was just 10 years old the last time I saw her, and she must have been in her 70s. She looked so old to me I thought she was a creature transformed into another class of human being, of another world, like a little old lady in a fairy tale. I didn't see her as someone who began life as a regular person and then became an old woman. Grandmother Amalia was not granted the opportunity to finish life in the tranquility of the family embrace. The hurricane of World War II splintered, and then obliterated, her world.

As a fortunate escapee from the German occupation, I spent my second decade in Switzerland, living with the family of my maternal grandmother, Rachel. She, too, lived a circumscribed life, a domestic woman's life. She shared her space with two grown children, and then, unexpectedly and without choice, two grandchildren. Grandmother Rachel spent her days looking after the apartment and preparing meals. This was a ritually demanding and labor-intensive job, as the food was Eastern European kosher cuisine. In spite of her very hard work, the food wasn't pleasing to everyone's palate. Like my paternal grandmother, she hardly left the house, and scarce effort was spent on her appearance. She semi-tamed her unruly grey hair with a few hairpins, and stray ones were strewn around the apartment. She spent many hours in a chair, rocking as she read from the Chumash (the Yiddish version of the Old Testament in book form). She spoke and read Yiddish, as well as Polish and Russian, but did not attempt to master written or spoken Swiss German, although she could read and understand quite a bit. When she needed to do so, she made herself understood.

Rachel also remained within a closed circle, although it included more than just family. Originally she was part of a group of observant Jewish families who founded a prayer house with a minyan. This small closed religious community constituted her world beyond the family. Within our family, she was the matriarch as well as a center for cousins and their children. By the time I was living in Miroslav, many people had left. Jews with the means and resources to do so relocated to England, Palestine, and North or South America.

In those increasingly depeopled times, my grandmother forged a close (perhaps unacknowledged friendship) with her cleaning lady, who also was close to 80. She had been in service to the Astor family for some years and returned to Switzerland with a large stash of savings. As a farmer's daughter, she was better placed financially than my grandmother. I suspect she also felt disconnected from her family and partially took the job to have (and be) a companion. She helped our family out with food, an extremely scarce commodity during the war.

My grandmothers comprised my first layer of emotional knowledge about old age. I assumed that when I reached that stage, I, too, would live in something akin to their contracted worlds. It was a picture of both temptation and terror. Throughout their lives, and in their old age, my grandmothers were the image and essence of family embeddedness.

I have reached 90 years of age in a fairly intact state. Sometimes I forget that horrors might be awaiting me. When I do think of myself as old, it is the images of my grandmothers that provide much more guidance than any images of my own mother's aged self. My grandmothers lived quiet, peaceful lives, within their families. I think that is what I would like also. Yet both of them had horrific ends. Grandmother Rachel died of acute bowel obstruction, from which she suffered severe pain in the last three weeks of her life. Grandmother Amalia's life ended in the camp of Terezin. As I consider questions of old age, I realize how unformed and insubstantial my ideas are. I am walking in the land of the very old as a traveler equipped with only the most cursory guides and maps.

In my later years, I've become rather averse to choosing clothing. Ease and comfort, more than style, inform my selections. I would rather continue on with the same outfits, as long as the fabric is pleasurable to the touch, agreeable on the skin, not too hot but warm enough, and not at all scratchy! An interest in self-adornment, while never particularly dominant, has all but disappeared. At one point I observed that I was wearing the same earrings and pearl necklace every single day. After Larry first died, I thought it appropriate to put on jewelry to see patients, and the pearls were a gift from Larry. I reminded myself that pearls are formal, too dressy to go with a T-shirt and pull-on pants. Now I pay less and less attention to such passing thoughts, which occur infrequently.

I am on the verge of reaching the inevitable stage of emptying closets too full of stuff, much of it old. Although once beloved, these clothes are now retained out of a sense of loyalty or sentimentality. Maybe a small anxious voice inside insists, "But what if I need it?" Occasionally I choose a vintage piece out of an anthropomorphic feeling that I owe the outfit a wearing, as a kind of renewed validation of both it and me. Any day, these *costumes* will dwindle, as I convince myself that someone somewhere needs them and would wear them regularly.

Make-up has become part of my past as well, beyond lipstick and an eyebrow brush. Recalling the fun I used to have experimenting with skin-care products, I recently ordered some promotional sets. When they arrived, I discovered that practical obstacles have blocked even such a harmless amusement. The tiny containers were so difficult to open and use. The text of instructions was so minuscule, my immediate memory somewhat unreliable, that each foray required preparation with magnifiers and lights. Not worth it! This experience brought to mind my mother, who had been so meticulous in caring for her face, but by old age was down to two pots of cream, one for day and for night. Her once elegant wardrobe similarly reduced to easy and relaxed pieces, some discreetly stained. Whatever our discords and disharmonies were in life, these similar behaviors of my older mother and my aging self join us.

The other day I wondered what bothered me more: not seeing or becoming older and slower? My visual competence is greatly reduced; there was a time when I carried a pair of reading glasses and a pair of distance glasses. Neither did the purported job at all well. I fumbled, replacing one pair with the other as I searched out an item and then donned reading glasses in an attempt to decipher details. Occasionally people couldn't help but say, "Have you ever heard of progressive lenses?" Although the opinion wasn't often put into such precise language, I sensed a question lurking, unspoken. Even unasked, I wanted to state, "Progressive lenses do not work for me. My eyes are not organized like other eyes."

Failing eyesight does not upset me as a sign of old age, but it is surely upsetting. Difficulties reading clearly, eye fatigue, and street signs consisting of mysterious blurs all lead to increased timidity about moving around. Of course, old age and failing eyesight play together. They walk hand in hand, as one negatively enhances the other.

A combination of visual uncertainty and the uncertainty of very old age has slowed me down, made me fearful to navigate unfamiliar locations. I have become more confined to known spaces, but also realistically incompetent beyond a couple of blocks. I no longer accurately judge distances. I have trouble seeing things in the upper quadrant of my vision. I can't reliably hail a cab at night because I can't tell if the light on top of the taxicab is illuminated or whether the light I can see is from various reflections that dance around streets and cars. Even during the daytime, a cab's light is hard to discern from more than a few feet away.

When the stacks of newspapers on the coffee table get too high, I question why I continue to subscribe. I can access *The New York Times* on my computer as well as on my iPad, as I occasionally do in the audio form. Yet I am unwilling to give up the hard copy. I have reduced the subscription to the weekend papers. I still like to see and feel the actual newspapers, the headlines, the photographs, and the advertisements, especially those relating to theater and movies.

I once loved conquering the Sunday crossword, but I can no longer see it, and doing it with my desk magnifier is increasingly effortful. The previously clear print blurs, or if sharpened by magnification, becomes too glaring. Reluctantly I have admitted my puzzle-solving skill is also in decline. No more Sunday puzzle done in ink before noon! My alienation from contemporary popular culture becomes all too clear when I no longer understand or know the clues related to games, television series, movie stars, and celebrities.

As for the actual text of the newspaper? I barely make out headlines and can take in only the mostly audaciously advertised movies. Despite this, every week or two, I sit down and sort through the newspapers that have stacked up, as if I were just about to get around to reading them. I save the Book Review, the Magazine, and the Week in Review. Sometimes I hang on to the Style section. I only recently abandoned the Real Estate section. There are no longer fantasies about moving to an apartment with a fine view or a fireplace or terrace space.

I finally gave up on the Travel section. Just taking a trip downtown requires fortitude and decisiveness. Forget about Bali and Japan, or even revisiting my favorite European spots. Perhaps I'm not quite ready to say never again to Europe, but I'm surely not going via a *New York Times* article. My reality, not unlike many in my age group, would require helpful people, friends, and/or intermediaries and facilitators to organize and assist in any travels I might now brave.

When my mother was getting older, but long before she had dementia, I watched her sitting in a chair, holding up the newspaper. I don't think she actually read the pages. From time to time she would refold the double spreads into a smaller, handier format. She frequently fell asleep with the paper covering her face, providing shade, privacy, and perhaps a bit of the familiar smell of newsprint. On other occasions I observed her at the dining room table playing solitaire. I knew she could no longer see the cards clearly. And like a cruel, or at best, rather ignorant person, I asked, "Why do you lay out these cards when you can't see their values?"

She would wave me off casually, as one would a bothersome fly, and continue using a pattern of face cards that may have existed only in her mind's eye, as she needed. She was doing an accustomed movement, starting and carrying out a familiar task in whatever partiality was still available. And this might be the principle I, too, employ when I sort my newspapers. I decide what to discard, what to keep to read in the short term, what to keep for later perusal, although none of the actual reading takes place. Still, I find that there are bits of information that accrue to me during this ritual and know that I would lose even those if I canceled the delivery of the newspaper.

There's still a sense of amplified curiosity with which I await the newspaper, especially the Sunday Arts section, only to realize with an angry-sad impatience commingled with self-pity that it would be a huge effort to find a movie, or be able to see well enough to properly read the review of a play. At some near point, the ancillary benefits that consist of gathering bits and pieces of information, whether perceived or imagined, will fade enough so that I will stop the *Times*. There will be the enormous absence of that small but deeply satisfying act of collecting the newspaper from the front door in the early morning.

Along with that begins the recital of the *No More Chorus*. No more scanning an article, no more leafing through *The New Yorker*. At the same time, there's the defeating admission that I've not achieved (or am still not able to comprehend) the level of technological and computer skills that would make these activities easier. I sometimes judge myself harshly for not mastering or finding the right instructor to assist me in the use and installation of improved technologies: downloading a variety of apps, finding the right reading aid or voice converter.

My declining eyesight is not remediable by glasses, nor can the progressive deterioration be significantly slowed. The macula of each eye is in bad shape. My retinologist, one of five ophthalmologists who have brought kind and caring professional skills to bear on my badly-behaved eyes, explained that the macula is a part of the brain: it is not eye tissue, but brain tissue. Once this was explained, I began to worry about the relationship between a poor quality of brain, which happens to be located in the eye, and a poor quality of the brain, which happens to be located in one's head!

My lowered hearing acuity also acquired a different significance. I am not upset about it as an obvious sign of aging, unless my reluctance to go for a hearing test, with a possible resulting recommendation to get a hearing aid, could be construed as vanity. But I surely am annoyed by my difficulty understanding many forms of speech. Never mind not being able to make out rap lyrics, I often can't understand the lines in old Agatha Christie murder mysteries. I ran into trouble at the Irish Repertory Theatre when I was unable to understand a word of what was being said, after years without a problem. That same difficulty soon arose with ordinary English, and even German, which always had been my easiest language. I had wondered what was interfering with my hearing and comprehension, since I do hear sound pretty well. Then I read that what decreases as we age is the speed with which neuronal connections happen, so hearing becomes like a film at slow speed. Information bits don't make it to the brain, and while vision tends to fill in for omitted images, hearing evidently does not. Our hearing apparatus receives fewer units of sound, and so guessing at meanings becomes harder.

My processing time has also slowed. I play Lumosity games on the computer with regularity and devotion, hoping I might mitigate whatever calamitous decline I feel happening more or less insidiously to my mental acuity. Seeing something and converting it into hand action now requires a conscious decision, and hence I take more time than obtaining an optimal score requires. A similar process of attrition diminishes the other senses. Flowers that used to smell so intoxicating now emit a barely perceptible scent. The futile search for a piece of fruit with a flavor that might even distantly rival the taste I remember is not totally due to the dismal practices of corporate agriculture. There is also a lessening of physical stamina, the walk that requires frequent rest stops, the lists of tasks I need to reconfigure to allow for the fact that an ever-decreasing number can be accommodated per day.

I no longer pay much notice to my thickened finger joints. A number of years ago, the combination of osteoarthritis and inflammatory arthritis that befalls many postmenopausal women made its way from finger to finger, from joint to joint, until all 20 relevant locations had undergone the cycle of painful inflamed swelling that eventually moved on, leaving behind a residue of thickening and bumps. How disfiguring it seemed at the time! That cycle has been over some 15 years. One day the outermost joint of my right index finger sported a red-hot swelling that looked something like Rudolph's nose. I experienced a feeling of welcoming tenderness toward it: "Oh my, hello. Aren't you out of phase? What are you bringing me now?" It must have realized it was misplaced in time, because it disappeared within a couple of days, leaving behind an increasingly skewed fingertip.

My fears and worries both recede and intensify. I have accepted quite matter-of-factly, perhaps even with some amount of grace, the reality that someday I won't be here anymore. We do not become older because we admit we are older. It is unnecessary to deny all the experiences of aging, pretending we are unchanged from the way we were 20 or more years ago. Sometimes ignoring how we feel as an old person works fine. If it isn't a problem, there's no need to dwell on it. In the land of old age, a general rule of social behavior is the expectation that we will ignore what is happening and not speak of what's bothering us. I consciously choose to defy the rule that binds us to silence about infirmities and to the pretense that life is unchanging. I am increasingly curious about my aging body and its failings, and find I am equally interested in the experiences of my few friends who are still around.

The first time I remember being terrified of growing older was not long after my 50th birthday. A friend sent me a red T-shirt with IT'S NIFTY TO BE FIFTY inscribed on it in black velvet letters. Upon unpacking the parcel, I thought, "What a sick joke." Did anybody really feel so accepting of getting older? I hid the shirt in a drawer. I thought it was a dirty trick of a gift, or at the very least an ironic wink.

I felt revolted that I had passed the *halfway* mark. I was well aware of the contradiction between what I felt and what I was working on with patients. As a psychotherapist I frequently worked with women whose husbands had opted out of long marriages, often to marry much younger women. With these patients I explored the opportunities domestic ruptures provided for an exploration of a new life, for a recovery of the self that had been submerged in helping their husbands' careers. Children were grown and gone. These sorts of therapeutic explorations were new at the time. Even so, my thoughts as a therapist were way ahead of my personal emotions.

Regardless of chronological or biological age, old age isn't a steady state of decline. When busy with a routine task, I often perceive myself to be of no particular age. If it's a day when I'm feeling reasonably well, I may think of myself as rather young. Naturally, I want to reassure myself and turn what is an inevitable process into a tool to help achieve quietude. Perhaps this is the ultimate goal as we age—to develop and maintain a level of serenity inside ourselves—as we travel a road full of bumps, nasty surprises, narrow bridges over terrifying precipices, and sometimes enchanting vistas where one can glimpse moments of transcendence, or even ecstasy.

Within a 24-hour period, I can feel like an enterprising young professional woman, dreaming of new challenges and taking great trips, of shifting directions, only to be shocked by an accidental look in the mirror, where I confront an old face. By now, the woman in the mirror gives me a forgiving and forgiveness-asking shrug. A few hours later, an assortment of physical indignities and diminishing energy level make me feel like I have arrived at death's door. Is it time to review my final documents to avoid complications after my exit from the planet? The victory of good feelings over pain and fear is so sweet, so affirming. It is something we want to hold on to so we can retrieve it in the darkest moments, when life seems to have raced by too fast or is dragging along too slowly, leaving us in distress and discomfort.

When I'm feeling good, I'm inclined to extol the freedoms of being an old woman. No longer bound by society's many expectations to play this role or that, no longer conscripted by children or husband or by long-lived parents into caretaking and self-denial, the mature woman can strive to be her authentic self. That sounds promising and enticing, but often it's accompanied by the puzzle of who the authentic self is, or who did she become? Often people reach back into childhood or adolescence as the last period when they were mostly focused on themselves. While some nuggets of selfhood can be gleaned from such historic excursions, we are, in fact, no longer young. We do not have the future as capital to spend or to risk. Our personal resources are limited. And we, as well as the times, have changed and demand different forms of participation.

When I was just past 60, which from my present vantage point I consider middle-aged, the events that precipitated my experience with identity and age had to do with the Velvet Revolution, a notable uprising in Prague that took place from November 17 to December 29, 1989. Under the leadership of artists and intellectuals, with Vaclav Havel at the helm, the repressive Soviet-inspired Communist regime was brought down. It was a regime that had had a chokehold on Czechoslovakia since the invasion by Russian tanks in 1968, when a burgeoning humanizing of that regime, under Dubcek, was squashed by military and political power. At that time I had wept with the realization that the desire for a return visit to my home country had been living inside me all these years, and that the Soviet invasion of Prague had burned it out of my being.

Almost 30 years later, those dreams coalesced once more. When the liberation occurred, I walked around in a state of elation. What had lain behind an Iron Curtain, unknown and unacknowledged by the world, suddenly became part of everybody's reality. The meteorological maps no longer blurred Eastern Europe behind a caesura that ran down the middle of Germany, graying out everything that lay east. There were weather reports for Prague and Warsaw. The radio started playing Dvorak and Janacek, and pronouncing them correctly.

I was propelled into the fervent patriotic feeling that had pervaded my childhood years. I had lost my place in time so completely that, for a week, I walked around with the memory of my long-forgotten ambition of becoming Minister of Public Health of Czechoslovakia. One night I went to sleep with blissful dreams on my mind. When I awoke, I was in a deep depression. I wept, just as I had 30 years earlier. This time my tears were accompanied by the very obvious realization that I was not ever going to be anything in Czechoslovakia. I had aged and lived my entire adult life in another country. For a brief time I felt cheated out of my life, like Sleeping Beauty, except that I awoke old. It took some time to reemerge into, and reconnect with, my actual life, and to find once again the happiness and satisfaction it had provided me for decades.

Many years have passed since I parried, with varying degrees of proficiency, but always with eventual success, the small indignities that getting older visits on us. I have made peace with my place in the professional world. Once I had been important and well-known, but later on, not so much. People who ran into me at meetings were astonished to see me: presumably they assumed I was dead. I also made peace with being a woman alone, albeit somewhat reserved and hiding whatever interest in men I might have had. In my 60s, while sitting at a dance watching the action, I blew off an invitation to get on to the dance floor. I thought a woman my age showing movement and rhythm was pathetic. I stopped wearing high heels, which was a good thing for the health of my back. I also stopped wearing dangling earrings, a practice which benefited not one of my ailments. And then, of course, I experienced a renaissance when I was 72, fell in love, and married Larry. High heels stayed away, but earrings reappeared in profusion, as did lively colors and tours on the dance floor. Larry's across-the-board validation made me believe my looks had improved in old age. He looked at me with love and saw me as beautiful. In my spongelike ingestion of the experiences of those around me, I gloried in a new sense of attractiveness.

Sometimes I wonder if I'm allowing my world to get smaller and find comfort in it? Voices within me argue: Don't let it happen; don't neglect stirring life and maximizing experience to the extent that you can. Don't you want to live fully to the very last moment? On the other hand, they say, how about some comfortable coasting, with all the *shoulds* and *oughts* put well behind? It occurred to me that what I worried about when I thought of getting old was that the time and the experience would be unbearable: so much pain (physical and psychic), discomfort, loneliness, hardship, and the challenge of getting from one day to the next. Perhaps that is yet to come. For now, I live through the days comfortably enough, in a peaceful manner, daydreaming at times but not of stories or content, just a pleasant, vaporous state of simply *being* without much movement, direction, or intensity of experience.

A journalist interviewed on NPR once described how he had succumbed to crack addiction and how, even though he had been clean for more than 20 years, he remained an addict. The longing for the immense experience of bliss and ecstasy grew all these years, with his addiction becoming stronger, even as he continually abstained. I confess my addiction to the ecstatic or even intensely pleasurable experience of life is fading. I don't seek it. I don't dream of it. I don't wish it. It is possible that the body, in its wisdom of knowing itself, realizes that it is no longer capable of such intensity. I have always known I am not an addict; I do not have an addictive personality.

I can no longer run fast, last long, or get drunk, nor do I feel gravely deprived by this state of affairs. It may be that, in a strangely harmonious and even manner, I slip, in lurches it is true, toward an increasingly diminished state of being. Along with that goes an unreliable interest in taking in new information, making new contacts. This is not radically different from the way I have always been. I have always had stretches that could be described as a form of depression, when the need to attach to life significantly lessens. It used to scare me, or at least I used to berate myself for what I deemed to be a real flaw, a handicap in maximizing my potential, not that I have ever felt I wanted to or needed to do that. Often I felt that I was right up against it, that far from using only the five or ten percent of the brain power available to us, as brain research indicates, I had engaged my available brain power right up to the limit, and if I pushed much more information in, it would overflow and jam things up.

I may look well enough for my age and have been spared any of the crippling infirmities that have befallen so many of my friends, but I am nevertheless brought up short by limitations I cannot ignore. They may be brought on by my age, a less-than-sturdy condition, or underlying failings in the many bodily systems that keep us going. I have noticed in the 20 years or so since I have occasionally begun to think of myself as succumbing to elderliness that any signs of it at first surprise, then shock, and, sometimes, very briefly, terrify.

For most of my life I have observed myself to be on the whole cheerful and friendly, though from time to time, I have fallen into a deep lassitude and discouragement. In my teen years, the family physician attributed these swings to a thyroid problem. In medical school, one of the American students, on whom I had an enormous crush, said, "You are an incredibly moody person." That concept was new to me at the time, but I've come to understand it fits me quite well. It doesn't only describe the connectors that my soul sends into the world, which can one moment vibrate with pleasure just at the sheer reality of being alive and the next be so withered I feel alone and lifeless in a world without any connectivity.

The picture of my existence that emerges from my disconnected state is one of a woman of modest achievements, with unfinished projects left by the wayside and relationships poorly chosen and foreshortened. I see myself as willful and having an oppositional character structure that made it difficult for me to go along with others, while keeping me from becoming a consistent and reliable leader.

It isn't difficult to understand that the thoughts emanating from the connected state make me feel good about my life and wonder at the many things I have seen and achieved, considering the obstacle-fraught beginnings that defined much of my early life.

In these aging years, I hope to reach a serene and contented state of being. I want to grab this opportunity (while passable health permits) to experience this last segment of life as a sentient human being, one aware of the past that has taken me this far, as well as having a deeper involvement and growing entwinement with the universe. When my soul is responsive rather than depleted, I can be enthralled by the contemplation of nature. I am but a speck of consciousness in a speck of time, but I can witness miracles that have, over human eternities, created an intricately complex living beauty that envelops us. From this perspective, the destruction that we as the human race have visited upon our earth represents an experiment of mixed success. We are a highly generative creative species, but one that ultimately may destroy itself, and a good part of what now exists.

I want to live with these thoughts, and consciously accept their *fragmented* and fleeting quality as I affirm my place in this world. I want to do this before this or that frailty descends, or worse yet, attention- and consciousness-devouring illness transforms me into an organism whose sole focus of being is but to make each day somewhat bearable. I do have moments when such a peaceful serenity is almost within my grasp, but the inner voices still carry on their evaluative explorations and leave me with an awareness of the ever-new shortcomings that then have to be received and examined and ultimately given their place in a life that must be accepted *as is*. Increasingly, I am distressed when I find myself empty, when neither joy nor love nor compassion nor outrage can stir even a trickle.

At such times I try to remember myself as that young woman I was an impetuous, passionate, justice-obsessed, intensity-embodying human being, with qualities ungoverned by thought or much common sense. In those years, I believed with Schiller, *"Gefuehl ist alles, Name nur Schall und Rauch"* (Feeling is all, name but sound and smoke). I have spent my resources in a life lived with a certain haphazard recklessness, without much minding of the emotional store. I experienced things as a profusion of intensity but learned to present to the world a far more measured persona. There was a time in my professional life when I had the reputation as the person required when a steady hand and cool head were needed in a touchy situation.

But inside, as long as there was life and blood and energy, I did not know how to spare myself. Every unhappy love affair became a tragedy, and it took quite a number of years for me to question that whole process. The classic tragic love affair, of course, is one where you lose the only person under the sun who was meant for you, and who was to make you complete. But how many times can that really happen? At some point, I realized that I was programmed to cope in that way with certain transitions. Eventually I decided to abdicate the drama surrounding men. I retired the role of the spurned lover.

Against all likelihood, life bestowed on me a wonderful late-life dessert course in my marriage to Larry. He sometimes experienced my emotional ardor as not quite hot enough! I shocked myself that I shed no tears during three years of taking care of him after his debilitating decline following open-heart surgery. And I shed no tears even at his death, not even to this day; I do not recognize this tearless state. Not even extremely sad movies make me cry much any longer. Perhaps I am wept out.

What is there to say about being alone when you are very old that hasn't been said so many times, and in so many different ways? When I am able to accept my fundamental aloneness, I think of the way Mimi, the lab mouse Art and I had adopted as a pet, conducted life in full view, deeply alone, busy from morning until night and sometimes from night until morning. Mimi had spent an exceptionally long life (for a lab mouse) in a cage on the dresser of our corner study in our St. Louis home. A superfluous survivor of some experiment or another, Mimi had been dyed pink. This had misidentified his gender to all of us, the conventional observers. Eventually the appearance of a prostatic tumor informed us that Mimi was, in fact, a male.

He was tame and friendly and walked up and down our arms, explored our pockets, and collected small nibbles from the table. But he was happiest in his own cage, to which he would eagerly return. Art and I quickly learned to leave the gate to his cage open so that he could come and go as he pleased. There was a brief experiment to assuage what we assumed was his loneliness. We introduced a wild mouse as a potential companion. It misfired most dramatically, as Mimi killed him. Was the other mouse simply the wrong companion? Or was it that Mimi preferred no companion?

Most of the time he was happily busy in his own cage, sustained of course, by the wide variety of snacks and grains we provided. He cleaned and swept his cage, fluffed his nest, spent hours grooming himself. He held his long tail in his paws and ran it through his snout. Ear cleaning was a long process, both inside and out, and then over again. I remember thinking then, and I still do, what a contented little fellow he was. Despite feelings of companionship, my thoughts of Mimi afford me the incontrovertible truth that a man or a woman is not a mouse. To be old-old without support from others is an unhealthy isolation. Spiritual serenity and the contemplation of a limitless universe do not replace the hands-on ministrations of helpful human beings that old age mandates in varying degrees.

When we are young and in possession of both health and resources, there is a sense that if you're alone it is a choice, and that there's still the opportunity to compose a life you desire. You can go out, make new friends, and involve yourself in a variety of social groups. In many cases, work life provides a context for making connections and friendships. When we are young we can go shopping, take care of our homes, pay bills, and meet normal obligations. When we reach the place of being old and alone, many of these givens are gone.

I have been a reasonably sociable person. As one of European origin, I reserve the word *friend* for those with whom I share a special connection and harmony, one that often goes back many years and implies trust and the ability to turn to each other when in need. Yet even by this more restricted definition, I have had enough friends.

By now, my friends live at distances apart from me, and those youthful visits that had not presented a problem are now difficult, if not impossible, given the stamina and resources required for today's travel. Other friends are unavailable except for occasional phone calls. And, of course, so many good friends have died. Until recently, the absence of these friends made room to develop new acquaintances and connections. New friends replaced those who had left, perhaps not with the same depth of feeling, but sometimes with equal or even greater compatibility and common interests.

A help, if not ultimate remedy, for the aging person, is to have resources enough for actual assistance as might be needed, and to separate that from the pleasures of true friendship. What to say about the daily loneliness? Waking up to the voice of NPR? Falling asleep to the sounds of QXR? There are far worse things. I do find I am more inclined to agree with my friends who have strongly recommended I get a dog. If I become excessively lazy, maybe I'll get a cat. Or perhaps a mouse?

Mostly I have reconsolidated myself. Sometimes I forget to light the little lamp that stands next to Larry's ashes. It may be time to acknowledge that his spirit has wandered far from this house to wherever in the universe it might disperse itself. By now I remember only our happy times: how well we traveled together, what a beautiful dancer he was, and how totally available he was sexually, combining an intense competent activity with open and generous access to his body. During the few interludes when I feel alive enough to wish again for a man in my life, it is only ever Larry that I wish for.

This is not only the summing up of a memoir, but also the record of a life well- and long-lived in real time. I have reached the place I once considered extreme old age, a time when I would understand where I was, when all the old questions would be answered, or at least put to rest. That's not the case. Perhaps because of my relatively good health and absence of physical pain, and in spite of the slowing down of cognitive processes and depleted energy, it seems to me old age still awaits me.

I do wonder if there will be a period when the true horrors of old age will befall me, the ones we think about in the small hours of the night. Will these descend on me suddenly, in full force, and extract their exit toll before I am ready? That short piece of the untraveled road defies closure or predictability. I will have to make do with the review of my life up until this point, and leave unspoken what may yet happen.

www.ingramcontent.com/pod-product-compliance
Lightning Source LLC
Chambersburg PA
CBHW071301110526
44591CB00010B/732